CHILDREN of Abraham

UNITED WE PREVAIL

DIVIDED WE FAIL

Tallal Alie Turfe

Tallal Alie Turfe

with Love

Necmat

iUniverse LLC
Bloomington

CHILDREN OF ABRAHAM
UNITED WE PREVAIL, DIVIDED WE FAIL

iUniverse books may be ordered through booksellers or by contacting:

iUniverse
1663 Liberty Drive
Bloomington, IN 47403
www.iuniverse.com
1-800-Authors (1-800-288-4677)

ISBN: 978-1-4759-9045-4 (sc)
ISBN: 978-1-4759-9046-1 (hc)
ISBN: 978-1-4759-9047-8 (e)

Library of Congress Control Number: 2013908548

Printed in the United States of America

iUniverse rev. date: 7/16/2013

A gift to Wanda, my loving sister and inspiration who symbolizes the essence of empathy, good deeds, and love for her family and community.

Fig Tree

The fig tree forms its early fruit;
The blossoming vines spread their fragrance ...
—Song of Solomon 2:13

The one who guards a fig tree will eat its fruit,
And whoever protects their master will be honored.
—Proverbs 27:18

Now learn this lesson from the fig tree:
As soon as its twigs get tender and its leaves come out,
You know that summer is near.
Even so, when you see all these things,
You know that it is near, right at the door ...
—Matthew 24:32–33

By the Fig and the Olive,
And the Mount of Sinai,
And the City of Security (Mecca),
We have indeed created man in the best of molds ...
—Qur'an 95:1–4

Contents

Tables and Figures

Preface

I am American born, and I had no formal training in Islamic studies. I taught myself the Arabic alphabet so I could read the Qur'an in its original language. English translations of the Qur'an aided my understanding of the Arabic verses. Each Sunday, for sixteen years, I taught young people about the Islamic faith, which further strengthened my knowledge and understanding of the religion. I also spoke to adult groups and at interfaith institutions.

As the growing Muslim community needed more centers and teachers, I became more involved in studying, writing, and lecturing about Islamic topics. Religious scholars recognized my knowledge of Islam, and they frequently invited me to give presentations on the topic. In addition, I made presentations to the broader interfaith community.

For a half century, I have worked in various management and executive positions in the automotive industry and as a consultant. I also taught graduate and undergraduate courses in business administration at several colleges and universities. I have published three books in several languages: *Patience in Islam: Sabr, Unity in Islam: Reflections and Insights*, and *Energy in Islam: A Scientific Approach to Preserving Our Health and the Environment*.

I have served on a number of boards and was chairman of the National Conference for Community and Justice, formerly the Greater Detroit Interfaith Round Table of Christians, Jews, and Muslims. I was a member of former president Bill Clinton's Call to Action: One America race relations group. Dubai Television has identified me as a prominent and influential Arab American.

In October 1995, I was the first Muslim to be presented with the Knight of Charity Award by the Vatican-based Pontifical Institute for Foreign Missions. I was inducted into the International Institute Foundation Heritage Hall of Fame for my global humanitarian efforts.

In August 2000, I was one of two hundred political and religious leaders from around the world who participated in the Millennium World Peace Summit at the United Nations in New York. I have given other presentations on Islam, education and parenting for peace, global ethics, and public diplomacy at the United Nations.

My wife, Neemat, and I have been married for almost a half century, and we have five children and twelve grandchildren.

Tallal Alie Turfe

Acknowledgments

This book is dedicated to the theologians, scholars, teachers, parents, students, interfaith organizations, and all others who have worked so hard to foster constructive dialogue among the three Abrahamic faiths. The success of their efforts is based on the spirit of intention to preach, write, teach, and study the common principles and practices of each tradition and to collaborate with and complement one another.

This book is also dedicated to my parents, Haj Alie Turfe and Hajjah Hassaney Turfe, who were staunch supporters of interfaith dialogue and constant and steadfast in their faith and good deeds. They inspired me to learn about the true meaning of monotheism and its message to mankind.

The eminent and renowned scholar Imam Abdul Latif Berry, founder of the Islamic Institute of Knowledge, spurred me to enhance my knowledge of Islam and write books on the subject. I am very grateful to him for opening my mind to the many facets of the religion and for nurturing me to explore the depths of its philosophy. He always urged me to undertake a study of the contemporary facets of Islam, thereby enlightening Muslims and non-Muslims in America and abroad. A strong advocate of interfaith dialogue, he encouraged me to write about how the followers of Islam, Christianity, and Judaism can cooperate and complement one another.

Children of Abraham: A Poem
By Tallal Alie Turfe

Sun sets on an ancient fig tree
Stout as the sire inside will be.
Three woven by the Divine thread
Moses, Jesus, and Muhammad.
Purified by the Grace of He
Leading mankind in unity.
Faith and good deeds with piety
Truth and patience our destiny.

Introduction

This book explores the commonalities between the Abrahamic faiths—Judaism, Christianity, and Islam. Each of us goes through life wanting to understand more about God's Creation and how we live and function within it. As children of Abraham, we seek knowledge in order to appreciate the three traditions that bind us.

Knowledge affords us the opportunity to have a deeper sense of appreciation for the marvels of existence and how we can become better people. As we strive toward self-actualization, we find ourselves thirsty and eager to learn even more about Creation and the three Abrahamic faiths that the one God gifted to mankind. This book will enlighten those who wish to collaborate with brothers and sisters of each faith to work for the common cause of peace, tolerance, security, and solidarity.

We take life for granted. We function from day to day, not reflecting on our purpose in life. How many of us have tested ourselves to see whether we are in conformity with God's commands? After all, our lives are but tests that will end in higher reward or eternal damnation. Our faith and good deeds, flanked by the search for truth and demonstration of patience, will enable us to successfully pass the test. But what is the test? It is God's decree to mankind to overcome evil with good and triumph over Satan's temptations to lure us to the wrong path.

Part of this test is understanding the nature of our existence. It is from that vantage point that I searched out the many facets of monotheism, its impact on life, and the vital role it plays in connecting our spiritual entities to the Creator. By writing this book, I have become more aware of my own existence and purpose in life, and the knowledge I have acquired has made me a more unified Muslim.

While Judaism, Christianity, and Islam have similar traditions, there often is more discussion about their differences, which have caused a great deal of hatred and distrust, leading to arguments, violence, and even wars. While religion is a system of beliefs, it also can be a reason for feelings of superiority and conflict.

Notwithstanding these differences, each Abrahamic religion is significantly linked to the others, as all of them arose in the Middle East and have common vestiges in their pasts and in the traditions they follow today. Each one received a miracle from God (e.g., the Ten Commandments given to Moses; the Virgin Mary giving birth to Jesus; and the revelation of the Qur'an to Muhammad). They also share incidents of prejudice, violence, pornography, drug abuse, teen pregnancy, and many other problems that have blended into mainstream American society.

It is because of the common histories, traditions, and similarities of Judaism, Christianity, and Islam that interfaith dialogue will result in better understanding, collaboration, and partnership toward a safer and peaceful environment. Prophet Abraham is the thread that binds the three faith traditions together and the thread that runs through this book. The potential for intolerance comes about wherever there are passionately held beliefs. Any advances in religious tolerance have been matched by prejudicial attitudes in all three faith communities. Some followers, be they fundamentalists or others, have closed their minds to the interfaith cause. To them, tolerance is betrayal. Therefore, to overcome religious intolerance, we must deal with religious ignorance.

In our democratic American society, we have the freedom to celebrate our beliefs while vigorously engaging others who believe differently. Interfaith alone will not end conflict, create universal justice, or resolve all of our societal problems. However, interfaith dialogue can be a powerful tool for advocacy, relationship building, and nurturing cultural diversity and pluralism.

History is replete with details regarding the cultural interchange of the Abrahamic faiths. This study delves into the common principles and practices among the three faiths in the hope that their followers will realize that they are very much alike in their outlooks on virtues, family values, and the mutual good of mankind.

Monotheism

Monotheism—the belief in the existence of one god or in the oneness of God—is characteristic of Atenism, Baha'i faith, Christianity, Islam, Judaism, Ravidassia, Sabianism, Sikhism, and Zoroastrianism. Hinduism is sometimes referred to as henotheistic (i.e., involving devotion to a single god while accepting the existence of other gods). It is a diverse system of thought with beliefs that span monotheism, polytheism, and atheism among others. The Hindu concept of God is complex and depends upon the tradition and philosophy followed by each individual.

For the purposes of this study, monotheism will refer only to Judaism, Christianity, and Islam. All of their followers believe in the same Creator, although He is known by different names in each religion. In Judaism, the Creator is referred to as YHWH (Yahweh). In Christianity, the Creator is referred to as God. In Islam, the Creator is referred to as Allah. In addition, the followers of these religions all share a fervent desire to become spiritually elevated in order to attain everlasting bliss and happiness.

While the perception is that Judaism, Christianity, and Islam are each significantly different, they are in fact deeply connected. The prevailing belief and practice of each is faith in God, which transcends all of their predominant differences. It is similar to automobile engines, which all require fuel to operate and run, whatever the brand of the car. In the same way, religion needs faith to stimulate its worshippers to pray.

Although the manner by which each religion worships and submits to God is practiced differently, each one recognizes a supreme power and authority and has a desire to reach paradise. The followers of the Abrahamic religions have the deepest respect for modesty and morality when entering a house of worship. Jews have a synagogue, Christians a church, and Muslims a mosque. The purpose of all three faiths is to congregate at these houses of worship and spend time in prayer and reflection.

Their mutual bond is their common origin in Abraham. However, there are internal differences based on biblical scriptures and practices. Judaism is divided into Orthodox, Conservative, and Reform. Christianity is divided into Catholic, Orthodox, and Protestant. Islam is divided into

Sunni and Shi'a. Each denomination has its own distinctive ideology and interpretation of how the faith should be taught and practiced. However, there is evidence of similar concepts, practices, and laws among the children of Abraham.

The Children of Abraham

Judaism, Christianity, and Islam all believe that God revealed himself to Abraham. The Torah, which comprises the Jewish law and traditions, states that Abraham is the ancestor of the Israelites, and that his son, Isaac, is the first of a line of prophets:

> ... I will make you [Abraham] a great nation and I will bless you; I will make your name great, and you will be a blessing. I will bless those who bless you, and whoever curses you I will curse; and all the peoples of the Earth will be blessed through you. (Genesis 12:1–3)

The oral section of the Torah is known as the Talmud, which describes the primary systematization of Jewish decrees. It comprises the legal and interpretative traditions that were transmitted orally from Mount Sinai and were not written in the Torah.

In Christianity, Abraham is considered a highly revered and spiritual leader as well as an ancestor of Jesus. "If you were Abraham's children, you would do the works of Abraham" (John 8:39). Christianity is based on the life and teachings of Jesus as presented in canonical gospels and other New Testament writings. It also considers the Hebrew Bible, known as the Old Testament, to be canonical. The Old Testament used by Protestants has the same ancestry claim as Judaism. However, Jews either do not widely use or are unfamiliar with the Old Testament. The Old Testament followed by the Catholics includes additional books that neither Protestants nor Orthodox Jews ascribe to.

The Qur'an is the central book of Islam, as it was revealed to Muhammad through the archangel Gabriel. Muhammad is a descendant of Abraham's other son, Ishmael: "... Follow the ways of Abraham, the true in faith, and he joined not gods with God" (Qur'an 16:123). Muslims are also guided by the Hadiths (traditions) of Muhammad.

Still, as mentioned previously, there are fundamental and crucial differences. Judaism and Islam do not accept the Christian notion of the Trinity. Judaism does not accept Jesus as a prophet or the Messiah. Christianity does not share the strict monotheism and devotion to Jewish law or the Sharia law followed by Judaism and Islam, respectively. However, there is a window of opportunity for theological engagement, a call for the acknowledgment of a Judeo-Christian-Islamic tradition.

Theological Engagement

A forum of ethics and trust is the foundation of deferential and effective dialogue and camaraderie.

The challenge we face is to unify and mobilize our resources with the understanding that a sense of open-mindedness and love for one another must prevail. To this end, discussions should center on the similarities between the three Abrahamic religions. Common ground and principles are the basis of successful interfaith dialogue: "Media images of Islam have often obscured the fact that Muslims, Jews, and Christians share much in common" (Esposito 1992). Changing the name of the "Judeo-Christian" tradition to the "Judeo-Christian-Islamic" tradition may usher in a new era of theological engagement. The unifying characteristic would be that all accept that God revealed himself to Abraham.

Rather than spending enormous amounts of time, resources, and energy on dissimilarities and disagreements, Jews, Christians, and Muslims need to concentrate on the religious beliefs that can unite them in peace, including worshipping God, prayer, fasting, charity, and the sanctity of Jerusalem. Of course, there can also be dialogue on dissimilarities but only to obtain a clearer understanding of the following issues: homogeneity, cohesiveness, consistency, and adhering to the highest ethics.

There are Jews, Christians, and Muslims who are opposed or reluctant to engage in genuine dialogue, because their relationship with each other has been weakened due to conflict, distress, and vengeance. However, others have the empathy, compassion, and trust that empower them to look beyond the past and exercise a mutual obligation to foster a better and safer world for our children and future generations.

Believers in the three faiths can help create a just and peaceful world by seeking a genuine understanding of each other's religions. Mutual respect and tolerance will be achieved through interfaith (people of different religious traditions) and intrafaith (people of similar religious traditions) dialogue at all levels. The goal is to focus on the uniformity among practices, doctrines, beliefs, and views. One common factor among the three traditions is the holy city of Jerusalem.

Jerusalem

Jerusalem is the sacred place of the Abrahamic faiths, whose roots all originate in the city. It symbolizes the hallowed ground embraced by the children of Abraham; thus, its significance cannot be ignored nor diminished. All three religious groups originated from one family, the family of Abraham. Jerusalem is the holy land where God's messengers walked, preached, and sanctified the shrines that today draw millions of visitors annually to worship and pray. In essence, Jerusalem is a symbol of holiness, and its aura of sanctity transcends cultural and religious boundaries.

The shrines of the three faiths are embedded on the ground on which they were consecrated. Jews consider Jerusalem to be their holiest city, and the Wailing Wall is where the Temple of Solomon once stood. The Church of the Holy Sepulcher, a Christian shrine, is in Jerusalem. Islam has three holy sites: Mecca, Medina, and Jerusalem. With the aid of a steed named al-Buraq, the archangel Gabriel took Muhammad on a Night Journey of the Ascent (*Isra'* and *Mi'raj*). The journey went from the Sacred Mosque in Mecca to al-Aqsa Mosque in Jerusalem and finally to Heaven, after which Muhammad descended and returned home (Turfe 2010). The Dome of the Rock is located in Jerusalem and is a very important Islamic shrine.

Adherents of the three Abrahamic faiths put so much emphasis on Jerusalem because they believe the city is the spiritual connection between the Earth and Heaven. God made a covenant with Abraham, and later Moses, that Jewish people would settle in Canaan, a region between the Jordan River and the Mediterranean Sea that was roughly equivalent to the modern states of Israel, Lebanon, and the coastal and southern inland of Syria (Cline 2004). The Temple of Solomon and Noah's Ark were built inside Jerusalem. Abraham offered to sacrifice his son at the rock on which the temple would later stand. In Christianity, Jerusalem is the site associated with the Passion and the Resurrection of Jesus. In 1099, Pope Urban II launched the Crusades, a series of holy wars between Christians and Muslims for control of the city. For thirteen centuries, preceding the British taking Jerusalem in 1917 and the creation of the state of Israel in 1948, Jerusalem was under Muslim rule. For Muslims, Jerusalem is *al-Qudz* (the Holy) and constitutes the first *qibla* (direction of prayer) and holy city for Islam (Sainz de Aja 2011).

In the quest for peace in Jerusalem, we face a problem of extraordinary proportions. All three Abrahamic faiths face the challenge of engaging in interfaith dialogue. Jews, Christians, and Muslims need to move away from a platform of alternatives to one of synthesis, from structures to processes, and from building blocks to networks. They need to intensify their understanding of the opportunities and challenges God has given them.

In 2006, I was part of a steering committee asked to find ways to protect holy and historical sites and tourists in Jerusalem. We obtained endorsements from ambassadors at the United Nations (UN), religious groups, nongovernmental organizations, and heads of state, including the Vatican, to move toward a culture of peace in Jerusalem.

Our team also had the endorsement of the UN Alliance of Civilizations, which coordinated a model agreement for the protection of these religious sites. We contacted clerics from Jerusalem who represented each of the three Abrahamic faiths. We asked them to sign a declaration of peace that would be presented at an international conference to be held at UN headquarters in New York. The signed agreement was to serve as a global model for initiatives on tolerance, mutual respect, peace, and global ethics. Each cleric responded in the affirmative and with enthusiasm. However, some of them insisted on a strategy of alternatives rather than one of synthesis. That is, they wanted to address the UN General Assembly before signing the declaration of peace. This was beyond the scope of our project, and it was beyond our ability to approve such a request.

PART ONE
Children of Abraham:
United We Prevail

"I never will, by any word or act, bow to the shrine of intolerance, or admit a right of inquiry into the religious opinions of others."—Thomas Jefferson

Source: Thomas Jefferson, Letter to Edward Dowse, April 19, 1803. From Gorton Carruth and Eugene Ehrlich, eds. *The Harper Book of American Quotations*, New York: Harper & Row, 1988, 499 pages.

Champions of Interfaith Trialogue

In the course of history, champions of peace and solidarity have risen to the occasion of speaking out in America. They have articulated a sense of understanding and compassion for the traditions of Judaism, Christianity, and Islam. Following are excerpts of presentations or statements made by some of those champions, who have espoused tolerance and interfaith trialogue as they acknowledge the three Abrahamic faiths:

Champions of Interfaith Trialogue in America

Jewish Americans
- Congressman Howard L. Berman
- New York City Mayor Michael R. Bloomberg
- Rabbi Amy Eilberg
- Dr. Yehezkel Landau
- Rabbi Allen S. Maller

Christian Americans
- Joseph L. Cumming
- Cardinal William Henry Keeler
- Former Senator John Kerry
- Dr. Joseph V. Montville
- President Barack Obama

Muslim Americans
- Imam Feisal Abdul Rauf
- Dr. Mahmoud Ayoub
- Imam Yahya Hendi
- Imam Hassan Qazwini
- Dr. Sayyid M. Syeed

Rep. Howard L. Berman
Chairman of the House Committee on Foreign Affairs
110th US Congress, Washington, DC

Rep. Howard L. Berman and Rep. Ileana Ros-Lehtinen, offered an amendment to H. Con. Res. 374, sponsored by Rep. Zach Wamp and cosponsored by Rep. Keith Ellison et al. The amendment was supported by the Senate, and the following concurrent resolution passed the House of Representatives on September 23, 2008:

Supporting Christian, Jewish, and Muslim interfaith dialogue that promotes peace, understanding, unity, and religious freedom.

Whereas interfaith dialogue among Christians, Jews, and Muslims is a powerful way to bridge the chasms of mistrust and misunderstanding that can divide adherents to the three Abrahamic faiths;

Whereas a number of important initiatives to enhance interfaith dialogue have been launched in recent years;

Whereas in 1997, the Three Faiths Forum was founded in London and has focused on "improving understanding between the Muslim, Christian, and Jewish communities";

Whereas in 1998, the Foundation for the Three Cultures of the Mediterranean was founded in Seville, Spain, by former Israeli Prime Minister Shimon Peres, King Juan Carlos I of Spain, and King Hassan II of Morocco, with the objective of promoting cooperation between Christians, Jews, and Muslims;

Whereas in 2005, King Abdullah II of the Hashemite Kingdom of Jordan launched the "Amman Interfaith Message" in order to "establish full acceptance and goodwill" between Christians, Jews, and Muslims;

Whereas in 2007, 138 Muslim scholars, leaders, and activists sent a letter to numerous Christian leaders expressing their support for peace, harmony, and goodwill between Christians, Jews, and Muslims;

Whereas in 2007, the Council of Religious Institutions of the Holy Land was founded "to advance [the] sacred values [of Christianity, Islam, and Judaism], to prevent religion from being used as a source of conflict, and instead serve the goals of just and comprehensive peace and reconciliation";

Whereas the Vatican has announced that the Pope intends to address a Catholic-Muslim summit of religious leaders in November 2008;

Whereas interfaith dialogue has the potential to inspire men and women around the world to appreciate the common values shared by adherents of different religions, thereby strengthening the bonds of respect, cooperation, and tolerance against the forces of radicalism, extremism, and hatred;

Whereas these initiatives provide an opportunity to elevate the voices of people of faith who, often at risk to themselves, advocate for peace and understanding, courageous positions too often drowned out by radical extremists; and

Whereas unity among leaders of different faiths is a powerful weapon to fight intolerance, marginalize extremism, and defeat the agents of terrorism: Now, therefore, be it *Resolved by the House of Representatives (the Senate concurring),* That it is the sense of Congress that—

(1) the United States supports the spirit of peace and desire for unity displayed in initiatives of interfaith dialogue among leaders of the three Abrahamic faiths;

(2) the United States further supports additional meetings of Christian, Jewish, and Muslim religious leaders aimed at greater dialogue between the religions;

(3) the United States encourages the many people of faith around the world who reject terrorism, radicalism, and extremism to join these and similar efforts in order to build a common bond based on peace, reconciliation, and a commitment to tolerance; and

(4) the United States appreciates those voices around the world who condemn terrorism, intolerance, genocide, and ethnic and religious hatred, and instead commit themselves to a global peace anchored in respect and understanding among adherents of the three Abrahamic faiths.

Amend the title so as to read: A resolution supporting Christian, Jewish, and Muslim interfaith dialogue that promotes peace, understanding, unity, and religious freedom.

New York City Mayor Michael R. Bloomberg
Remarks Delivered at Governors Island, August 3, 2010
New York, NY

"Defending Religious Tolerance: Remarks on the Mosque near Ground Zero"

... New York City was built by immigrants, and it is sustained by immigrants—by people from more than a hundred different countries speaking more than two hundred different languages and professing every faith.

We may not always agree with every one of our neighbors. That's life and it's part of living in such a diverse and dense city. But we also recognize that part of being a New Yorker is living with your neighbors in mutual respect and tolerance. It was exactly that spirit of openness and acceptance that was attacked on 9/11.

On that day, 3,000 people were killed because some murderous fanatics didn't want us to enjoy the freedom to profess our own faiths, to speak our own minds, to follow our own dreams and to live our own lives.

Of all our precious freedoms, the most important may be the freedom to worship as we wish ...

This morning, the City's Landmark Preservation Commission unanimously voted not to extend landmark status to the building on Park Place where the mosque and community center are planned ... The simple fact is this building is private property, and the owners have a right to use the building as a house of worship.

The government has no right whatsoever to deny that right—and if it were tried, the courts would almost certainly strike it down as a violation of the US Constitution. Whatever you may think of the proposed mosque and community center, lost in the heat of the debate has been a basic question—should government attempt to deny private citizens the right to build a house of worship on private property based on their particular religion? That may happen in other countries, but we should never allow it to happen here. This nation was founded on the principle that the government must never choose between religions, or favor one over another.

The World Trade Center Site will forever hold a special place in our City, in our hearts. But we would be untrue to the best part of ourselves—and who we are as New Yorkers and Americans—if we said "no" to a mosque in Lower Manhattan.

Let us not forget that Muslims were among those murdered on 9/11 and that our Muslim neighbors grieved with us as New Yorkers and as Americans. We would betray our values—and play into our enemies' hands—if we were to treat Muslims differently than anyone else. In fact, to cave to popular sentiment would be to hand a victory to the terrorists—and we should not stand for that ...

On September 11, 2001, thousands of first responders heroically rushed to the scene and saved tens of thousands of lives. More than 400 of those first responders did not make it out alive. In rushing into those burning buildings, not one of them asked "What God do you pray to?" "What beliefs do you hold?"

The attack was an act of war—and our first responders defended not only our City but also our country and our Constitution. We do not honor their lives by denying the very Constitutional rights they died protecting. We honor their lives by defending those rights—and the freedoms that the terrorists attacked ...

Muslims are as much a part of our City and our country as the people of any faith and they are as welcome to worship in Lower Manhattan as any other group. In fact, they have been worshipping at the site for the better part of a year, as is their right.

The local community board in Lower Manhattan voted overwhelming to support the proposal and if it moves forward, I expect the community center and mosque will add to the life and vitality of the neighborhood and the entire City.

Political controversies come and go, but our values and our traditions endure—and there is no neighborhood in this City that is off limits to God's love and mercy, as the religious leaders here with us today can attest.

Rabbi Amy Eilberg
Cofounder of the Bay Area Jewish Healing Center
San Francisco, CA

"Awake to Life's Pain, How Could We Hate?"
Posted on StarTribune, June 1, 2011

Fifty-some religious leaders gathered last night at Masjid Al-Rahman, the Muslim Community Center in Bloomington, to cultivate relationships with one another across religious divides ...

The event was convened by a remarkable coalition: the MN [Minnesota] Council of Churches, the Greater MN Evangelical Association, the MN Rabbinical Association, the Jewish Community Relations Council, the Islamic Center of MN and the Islamic Civic Society of America. The goal was to bring religious leaders together to deepen relationships with one another, to contemplate the upcoming tenth anniversary of September 11th, and to consider the role of religious leaders as the anniversary approaches.

There were many beautiful moments: colleagues of different religions and races greeting one another as old friends, others engaging in spirited and full-hearted communication with new friends, and many scenes of small groups of people leaning toward one another in engrossed and lively conversation. The spirit of openness to learning and gracious desire to know "the other" was palpable. We were of the whole world, and what a world it would be if it were characterized by such deep desire to connect, to learn, and to grow.

The imam and the host mosque taught that the diversity of Creation reflects God's desire that people of different "nations and tribes," religious and ethnic communities, come to "know another," to compete with one another only in righteousness (Qur'an 49:13). One rabbi shared that his memory of the Nazi Holocaust moved him to vow that he would not stand idly by as Muslims were targeted for discrimination and hate. We all received many eloquent blessings and moments of inspiration from around the room, from across the religious spectrum ...

After months of planning, it was my deep joy and pleasure to co-lead the gathering with my colleague and friend, Rev. Dr. Tom Duke, of SPIN, the Saint Paul Interfaith Network. But just before the event was to begin, I received a text message ... that my friend had lost his 25-year-old daughter to suicide. I had listened to my friend talk for years about his gifted daughter's struggle with depression, keenly aware that she was roughly my daughter's age.

The news took my breath away. I felt weak and disoriented, wondering how I would recover my focus and do my job as coleader of an important gathering. As people began to arrive, my energy returned, and the evening's many moments of joy and hope nourished my spirit ...

It was wonderful to spend the evening in such a powerful circle of good will and hope before descending fully into the reality of my friend's pain. I asked myself once again what the world might look like if we could more often remember the pain and fragility of those around us, and allow human compassion to direct our words and our actions. What would it take for us to ground our lives in the truth of human frailty ...

Dr. Yehezkel Landau
Faculty Associate in Interfaith Relations
Hartford Seminary, Hartford, CT

"Jewish-Muslim Relations in the 21st Century"
Posted on State of Formation, March 5, 2012

... Following the traumatic events of September 11, 2001, the outbreak of the second Intifada, and the war in Iraq that began in 2003, I coauthored a public statement with my Palestinian-American friend and colleague,

Imam Yahya Hendi, who serves as the Muslim chaplain at Georgetown University. We called on "our fellow Jews and Muslims to join forces with concerned Christians to transcend this cycle of death and destruction." In our joint statement, we asserted:

Jews and Muslims should be spiritual allies, not adversaries. Any student of comparative religion knows that Judaism and Islam are as close to one another as any two faith traditions can be ... It is only in the past hundred years that the conflict over the Holy Land, whether called Israel or Palestine, has engendered competing nationalisms and the violation of basic human rights affirmed as sacred by all three faith traditions. The conflict has also undermined the historic cross-fertilization of these traditions ...

Both communities, guided by wise leadership, need to overcome longstanding prejudices and resentments. Each tradition has sacred teachings that can be enlisted to build bridges of respect, reconciliation, and cooperation. Wise religious leadership consists of identifying those teachings and educating both peoples in that spirit. There will be no political peace in the Middle East without a spiritual underpinning reconciling Jews and Muslims. At this critical moment in our history, with heartbreaking suffering and loss on all sides, we need to be inspired by the Divine light that shines forth from the Qur'an and the Torah. They both affirm life, not death. They both teach compassion, not callousness or hatred. They both call for a richly diverse human family under the sovereignty of the One God.

Rabbi Allen S. Maller
Former Spiritual Leader of Temple Akiba, Culver City, CA
Past President of Southern California Association of Reform Rabbis

"A Jewish Rabbi Learns from Prophet Muhammad"
Posted on Khutbah Bank, July 22, 2012

... God's Messenger is so well known for his sense of justice that a Jew can appeal to him even in a conflict with a Muslim who has attacked a Jew. It is only natural for Jews to think that Moses is the best and for Muslims to think that Muhammad is the best. Muhammad rebukes the

Muslim, telling him not to claim that Muhammad is superior to Moses, because even on the day of resurrection, Muhammad himself will not know their relative merit ... Muhammad teaches us that claims of religious superiority are wrong ...

As a Reform Rabbi, I can state that all Reform Rabbis would applaud this teaching of Prophet Muhammad because we are all aware that during the Middle Ages all three religions claimed religious superiority over each other. If Jews, Christians, and Muslims had only followed this teaching of Prophet Muhammad, we could have avoided many centuries of bloodshed and massacres, three of the best known examples being the many Christian Crusades in Spain, Poland, and the Middle East; the Roman Catholic Inquisition in Spain and Portugal; and the thirty-year war between Catholics and Protestants in Germany and central Europe.

The Qur'an is the only book of revelation that includes within itself a theory of prophethood that includes other religions ... Of the twenty-five mentioned by name in the Qur'an only four (Moses, David, Jesus, and Muhammad) revealed books of sacred scripture that are the bases for three religions that still flourish today ... The Qur'an declares, "Mankind! We created you from a single male and female, and made you into nations and tribes, that you may know each other [and not despise each other]. Verily the most honored of you in the sight of Allah is the most righteous of you. Allah has full knowledge and is well acquainted" (49:13).

Most Americans would be amazed to hear such a liberal and tolerant statement coming from a religion that they think is rigid and fanatical, but the politicized Islam that has captured so much attention in the world today is not true Islam. It is the outgrowth of two recent factors. One is anti-Western reaction and scapegoating due to the great dislocations and upheavals occurring in Muslim societies as a result of the globalization taking place in all modernizing societies in the twentieth century. The second factor is the result of several previous centuries of socioeconomic decline in the Middle East. Jews and Christians have already had reforming and modernizing movements that have helped them break out of the narrow rigidity of the Middle Ages, but Muslims have not ...

I have considered myself to be a Reform Rabbi and a Muslim Jew. I am a Muslim Jew, that is, a faithful Jew submitting to the will of God, because I am a Reform Rabbi. As a Rabbi I am faithful to the covenant that God made with Abraham—the first Muslim Jew—and I submit to the commandments that God made with the people of Israel at Mount Sinai. As a Reform Rabbi I believe that Jewish spiritual leaders should modify Jewish tradition as social and historical circumstances change and develop. I also believe we should not make religion difficult for people to practice. These are lessons that Prophet Muhammad taught twelve centuries before the rise of Reform Judaism in the early nineteenth century ...

I believe that the Qur'an is as true for Muslims as the Torah is true for Jews ... Following Muhammad's teaching I neither believe nor disbelieve in the Qur'an. If I believed in the Qur'an I would be a member of the Muslim community. If I disbelieved in the Qur'an I would be a member of the atheist community or of those religious communities that think that only their religion is the one true religion ... There can be no religious conflict between religions like Judaism and Islam because neither of them declares that their scriptures are the only ones from God. The strong support that the Qur'an gives to religious pluralism is a lesson that is sorely needed by the religious fundamentalists of all religions in the world today ...

Joseph L. Cumming
Director of the Reconciliation Program
Yale Center for Faith and Culture
Yale Divinity School

"Religious Resources in Peacemaking between Muslims and Christians"
Fourth Forum for Al-Azhar Graduates, June 28–30, 2009

... Clearly religious leaders and religious convictions have an important role to play in peacemaking. They are not the only thing needed for peace: political leaders and diplomats also have a crucial role, and religious peace can lead to political peace only if it is accompanied by political will. But the role of religious leaders and religious beliefs is indispensable to peacemaking in today's world.

What can religious leaders uniquely bring to the table, apart from the fact that their peoples trust them more than they trust politicians? Several contributions might be mentioned here. For example religious leaders are often free to meet with one another across sharp lines of division, when political leaders are unable to do so. I have been present at very productive meetings between Iranian Muslim leaders and American Christian and Jewish leaders, including both conservative and progressive leaders on both sides, in which much progress was made toward mutual understanding. US government policy and Iranian government policy have sharply restricted contacts between American and Iranian political and diplomatic leaders, but religious leaders are able to meet together without compromising their deeply held convictions.

It is precisely those deeply held convictions that I wish to highlight as a key contribution that religious leaders can make toward peace. On certain matters we hold differing convictions, and none of us is interested in ignoring or minimizing those differences. But on other matters we hold to similar or common values and moral convictions, and those values and convictions can make an important contribution to peace. This is particularly true for Muslims, Christians and Jews, who among them constitute 55% of the human race.

Thus, Muslims, Christians and Jews agree that One God created the entire human race from one ancestor, and that therefore, in all our human diversity, we form a common family and we each have equal dignity before God. Christians and Jews would agree with the Qur'anic affirmation: "O people, we have created you from male and female and caused you to be peoples and tribes, so that you would come to know each other." We agree that God has put humankind on the Earth as stewards with a responsibility to care for Creation and not to destroy it. The recent Common Word initiative has called the world's attention to the fact that Islam, Christianity, and Judaism all call upon us to love God with all of our being and to love one another (including loving those who are different from us) as we love ourselves ...

Cardinal William Henry Keeler of Baltimore
Former President, National Conference of Catholic Bishops

"How Mary Holds Christians and Muslims in Conversation"
Speech given to the American Muslim Council,
Washington, DC, December 8, 1995

... Much more awaits us in the future. We need to keep looking for ways for our formal dialogue to continue so that we can move along, especially theologically, in our understanding of one another ...

Catholics are delighted to learn that there are more verses in the Qur'an—34 of them—which name the Blessed Virgin Mary than there are in the whole New Testament! They speak of her presentation in the temple of Jerusalem, which Christian tradition also records, of her purification, of the annunciation, of her virginal conception of Jesus and of the birth of her son, the Messiah ... What a propitious moment it is, therefore, that finds Christians and Muslims together on a major feast of the Virgin Mary to celebrate the mutual esteem for one another which befits men and women in the faith tradition of Abraham ...

Now the times call for renewed efforts on our part to foster a climate of mutual respect and tolerance, not only in a world grown largely impervious to faith, but sadly ever more ready to think in terms of racial and cultural stereotypes. There are those commentators who at the close of the 20th century envision a coming clash of civilizations which they are ever more ready to see as a confrontation between Islam and the West. But here in America, Muslims and Christians are factually in a position to show that the circumstances of democracy can just as well foster a dialogue among the believers in the one God ...

This fall I had the privilege of hosting His Holiness Pope John Paul II in Baltimore. One of the events we planned was a prayer service at the Cathedral of Mary Our Queen, which included guests from various Christian churches and our friends in the Muslim and Jewish communities. The Holy Father chose to speak on religious freedom:

> Today religious tolerance and cooperation among Americans cannot simply be a pragmatic or utilitarian

understanding, a mere accommodation to the fact of diversity. No, the source of your commitment to religious freedom is itself a deep religious conviction. Religious tolerance is based on the conviction that God wishes to be adored by people who are free: a conviction, which requires us to respect and honor the inner sanctuary of conscience in which each person meets God.

To all believers in the one true God I express the respect and esteem of the Catholic Church. As I said at the United Nations, the world must learn to live with *difference* if a century of coercion is to be followed by a century of persuasion. I assure you, dear friends, that the Catholic Church is committed to the path of dialogue in her relations with Judaism and Islam, and I pray that through that dialogue new understanding capable of securing peace for the new world may be forged.

... The times call for a new dedication to dialogue and cooperation between our faith communities ...

Former Senator John Kerry

Speech on Global Interfaith Dialogue
Yale Divinity School
July 29, 2008

... As a Catholic American politician ... I believe we have a duty to understand each other in the name of living peacefully. We have a duty to engage with each other. The Abrahamic faiths—Christianity, Judaism, and Islam—have to find new meaning in the old notion of our shared descent. What really is our common inheritance? What does it mean to be brothers? Are we responsible for each other, or are the exhortations of the Koran, the Torah, and the Bible just words?

Ultimately, our sense of kinship has to rest on something more basic than our common ancestry: an acknowledgement of our shared humanity.

The good news I see is that, for all the challenges our differences present, all of the major religions do have a sense of universal values—a moral truth based on the dignity of all human beings ...

Every religion embraces a form of the Golden Rule, and the supreme importance of charity, compassion, and human improvement ... The Talmud says that in Roman times a nonbeliever approached the famous Rabbi Hillel and challenged him to teach the meaning of the Torah while standing on one leg. Holding up one foot, Hillel replied: "what is hateful to yourself, do not do to another. That is the whole of the Torah ... the rest is commentary."

Prophet Muhammad said, "not one of you truly believes until you wish for others what you wish for yourself" ... anyone who adheres to these basic principles must acknowledge the moral challenges we all face today are immense, but also shared ... Demagogues misappropriate and distort religion to drive a wedge and gain a foothold—and failed states, failed civil societies, and frankly corruption in governance empower them to do so. The dialogue here must include ways in which we join to express a common moral responsibility to avoid that exploitation and find instead the governance that empowers people and liberates religion to live its true meaning ...

Whatever our differences among the Abrahamic faiths, we should be celebrating that we all believe in one God. All religions should be celebrating our agreement to put one thing above all else: worship. And at the same time, we must also welcome the secular among us to join in celebrating our common awe at the majestic fact of the universe we inhabit, however it may have originated.

We don't need to agree on everything to get along—instead, we need to ask ourselves tough questions about coexistence. I see at least two types of conversations to cultivate between the great Abrahamic faiths— and all faiths. The first I would call traditional interfaith dialogue. The second is a search for how we might live together in some sort of peace and harmony that respects our differences while fashioning a common effort for human dignity. We cannot wait for the theological conversation to finish before we move to pressing political and social questions.

Somehow, we have to find a way to agree that faith may be worth dying for, but it cannot be worth killing for. We have to strive for a global ethic that allows each of our religious faiths to express themselves fully but also allows us to unite around common ethical ground ...

All religions today include their moderate and extreme elements— those who value peaceful coexistence and those who don't. It's up to each of us to work within our faith communities and between them to push people toward expressing their beliefs in a manner compatible with a peaceful world ...

We have come together to make an honest effort at understanding. When you do so, whatever your faith, I believe you are doing God's work ...

We still need to set an example for the world. We have a lesson to teach humanity ... We must learn how to love our faiths and live them side by side ...

Dr. Joseph V. Montville
Chairman, Track Two
An Institute for Citizen Diplomacy

A Guidebook for Interfaith Organizations Seeking
Jewish, Christian and Muslim Community
October 2008

This Abrahamic Family Reunion Guidebook is offered to people who participate in voluntary activities that promote respectful relationships among Jews, Christians, and Muslims in the United States, and indeed, wherever Abrahamic peoples meet in the world ...

The last but perhaps most valuable part of this guidebook is a set of three independent but clearly serially connected papers on the pro-social or ethical values in Judaism, Christianity, and Islam that lay the irrefutable basis, we believe, for the conviction that the peoples of the three Abrahamic traditions are indeed a family. The dominant values are love of God and love and care for neighbors and strangers. More specifically, this faith-based caring extends to the least among us in society, the widows and orphans, the poor and the sick, the unemployed and the imprisoned. It is extraordinary how these caring values flow seamlessly from the Hebrew Bible through the New Testament and find themselves powerfully reaffirmed in the Qur'an ...

The ultimate message of the sacred literature is that all human beings are innately precious and valuable in God's eyes. God created no person, tribe, or nation to be despised. The logic of this conclusion is that all races and religions are equally valuable ... The Abrahamic Family Reunion project concentrates on Jews, Christians, and Muslims because their lack of reconciliation poses a serious threat to world peace. But success in the Abrahamic family reunion will be a model for all ethnic and sectarian conflict healing approaches ...

The Abrahamic Family Reunion project offers ways to use psychological and spiritual approaches in reconciling conflicts among Jews, Christians, and Muslims ... emphasizes our shared values of compassion and justice, explores positive historical precedents, and acknowledges collective traumas ... seeks to enhance the possibility of contrition and reconciliation among civil and religious representatives of the three Abrahamic traditions ...

The first task towards achieving the Project's goals is to establish a network of authentic representatives of religious and civil communities, synagogues, churches, mosques, and organizations that are willing to participate in discussions within their respective communities ... facilitators encourage participants to share candidly their feelings, beliefs, and preconceptions about the other two faith traditions based on a challenging history. Participants are then asked to discuss what they need to hear from the other two faiths to believe that the Abrahamic family reunion is possible. The next step will be to build relationships between and among local interfaith communities and extend the discussion between the faith groups ...

President Barack Obama

Speech to the Muslim World
Cairo, Egypt
June 4, 2009

... All of us share this world for but a brief moment in time. The question is whether we spend that time focused on what pushes us apart, or whether we commit ourselves to an effort—a sustained effort—to find common ground, to focus on the future we seek for our children, and to respect the dignity of all human beings.

It is easier to start wars than to end them. It is easier to blame others than to look inward; to see what is different about someone than to find the things we share. But we should choose the right path, not just the easy path. There is also one rule that lies at the heart of every religion—that we do unto others, as we would have them do unto us. This truth transcends nations and peoples—a belief that isn't new; that isn't black or white or brown; that isn't Christian, or Muslim, or Jew. It's a belief that pulsed in the cradle of civilization, and that still beats in the heart of billions. It's a faith in other people, and it's what brought me here today.

We have the power to make the world we seek, but only if we have the courage to make a new beginning, keeping in mind what has been written.

The Holy Koran tells us: "O mankind! We have created you male and a female; and we have made you into nations and tribes so that you may know one another."

The Talmud tells us: "The whole of the Torah is for the purpose of promoting peace."

The Holy Bible tells us: "Blessed are the peacemakers, for they shall be called sons of God."

The people of the world can live together in peace. We know that is God's vision. Now, that must be our work here on Earth …

Imam Feisal Abdul Rauf, PhD
Chairman, Cordoba Initiative
Imam, Masjid al-Farah, New York

"A Call to Bridge the Abrahamic Faiths: Judaism, Christianity and Islam" al-Farah Mosque, September 6, 2002

I begin by invoking the name of God, the God of Abraham, Ishmael, Isaac, Jacob and the Children of Israel, the God of Moses, Jesus and Muhammad, peace and blessings be upon them all. And I invoke the special blessings of God upon all three Prophets and Messengers, and greet them with the greetings of peace …

We recognize that all religions have the same relative value with respect to the high goal to be reached, and the same lack of value if they fail to call forth the love of God ...

Our voices, raised together to proclaim the recognition of the unity of God, serve to bring mankind together, while those voices that focus on the differences of our laws cause division and loss ...

We urgently need to establish discourse and dialogue not only at an interfaith level, but also at an intra-faith level, between those who have different perspectives and interpretations within the same religious tradition ...

Today, we are joined in our commemoration of 9/11 by some of our friends from the Jewish and Christian community, whose souls are aglow with the love of God ...

Islam relates itself to Jews and Christians on three levels: as humans, as heirs of the Semitic religious tradition, and as Jews and Christians. This relationship is on this account built into Islam's very nature and core. There is no Islam without it ... Islam relates itself to the religions of mankind, and through them to humanity ...

Islam recognizes all Jews and Christians as creatures of God, whom God had blessed with reason and understanding, sufficient to enable them to know God; that being so endowed, they must have recognized God, as one who is transcendent and ultimate. Moreover, Islam acknowledges that all Jews and Christians have received from God messages through their prophet's teaching of the same lesson, so that, if for some reason they have missed what is natural and hence necessary to them, they were given it gratuitously as a gift from Heaven, through prophecy. As such, Jews and Christians are people with the true religion, the din al-fitrah. No Muslim may deny this fact of nature without contradicting the Qur'an and hence abjuring Islam. Recognition of this truth is of his faith ...

Islam regards the God of Judaism and Christianity as its own God, their prophets as its own prophets, their revelations and scriptures as its own revelation and scripture. Together, Islam holds the two religions and itself to be one religious fraternity. Nothing more could be asked or desired ... This unity—even identity—of the three religions makes the Muslims regard the Jews and Christians as their brothers in faith, in submission to the one God of all ...

Mahmoud Ayoub, PhD
Professor and Director of Islamic Studies
Department of Religion, Temple University

"Religious Pluralism and the Qur'an"
Posted on International Institute of Islamic Thought, Herndon, VA

... The Qur'an lays down four basic principles, which are necessary for the truth-claim of any religion. The first is that a true religion must be enshrined in a divinely revealed scripture or sacred law (shari'a). Secondly, it must affirm God's absolute Oneness (Tawhid). Thirdly, it must profess active faith in God and the last day. Finally, it should foster righteous living (ihsan). On the basis of these four principles, the Qur'an affirms the truth of the faith of Muslims, Jews, Christians, and Sabaeans ...

The Qur'an enjoins Muslims to dialogue with Jews and Christians in the fairest manner. It sets forth both the etiquette and theology of dialogue: "Do not debate with the People of the Book save in the fairest manner, except those among them who do wrong; and say to them we accept faith in that which was sent down to us [that is the Qur'an] and that which was sent down to you [that is the Torah and the Gospel]. Our God and your God is one, and to Him we are submitters" (Qur'an 29:46) ...

It may be first concluded ... that neither the Qur'an nor the Prophetic tradition demands of Jews and Christians that they give up their religious identity and become Muslims unless they freely choose to do so. The basis of this religious freedom in Islam is the categorical Qur'anic assertion "... there is no compulsion in religion" (Qur'an 2:256). This is a categorical command, not a statement of fact.

Secondly, the Qur'an and Prophetic tradition only enjoined Muslims as well as the followers of other faiths to engage in meaningful dialogue, cooperation, and agreement on basic principles. This is what the Qur'an calls 'a just word of common ascent,' between the Muslims and the People of the Book to worship no one except God and not "take one another as Lords beside God" (Qur'an 3:64). This important call to a unity of faith across the diversity of religions is far more relevant to our time than it was to the time of the Prophet and his people ...

To conclude: what then is the challenge that the Qur'an presents to us today? The challenge is this, that we all have faith in God and compete with one another in righteous works. It follows from this challenge that all people of faith respect one another and that they believe in all of God's revelations.

The Qur'an presents the followers of all three monotheistic religions not only with a great challenge, but with a great promise as well. The promise is this:

"Were the People of the Book to abide by the Torah, the Gospel and that which was sent down to them from their Lord [i.e., the Qur'an], they would be nourished with provisions from above them and from beneath their feet" (Qur'an 5:65–66).

Imam Yahya Hendi
Muslim Chaplain at Georgetown University
Muslim Chaplain at the National Naval Medical Center, Bethesda, MD
Imam of the Islamic Society of Frederick, MD

"A Call for Dialogue"
Posted on fredericknewspost.com, September 3, 2006

... The three Middle Eastern and monotheistic religions have been used to advocate hate, when they can be used to advocate love and co-existence. We can make a historic decision to succeed in our dialogue efforts—if not internationally, at least here in our beautiful country.

Judaism, Christianity, and Islam each claim the same historical legacy within the prophetic tradition, although each may interpret specific historical and prophetic events differently. While each of the three religions has dogma unique to itself, the core is essentially similar ...

One would have to conclude that peace, reconciliation, and dialogue are an expression of faith. Peace building and reconciliation are values we all have to commit ourselves to and encourage because reality demands them and because our religious traditions require them.

It is true that ignorance, religious extremism, terrorism, and fears generated from past encounters have widened the gap between us and created a sense of mistrust and rejection ... There is another path we can model, the path of love, reconciliation, and dialogue which streams from our religious commitment to a God of love.

Yet, the fruits of religious convictions and our love of God are not achieved in a vacuum. They are achieved and found in the context of human relationships ...

All of us Americans, in general, and committed Jews, Christians and Muslims, in particular, must find within their own traditions sound reasons to value other faiths without compromising their own. We should not tolerate voices of divisiveness. We must use Sept. 11 to explore the best in each of us. So let us all choose to be united with all of our differences for the best of this nation and all of humanity.

The major burden, however, falls on all religious communities. Our communities, guided by wise leadership, need to overcome longstanding prejudices and resentments. Each tradition has sacred teachings that can be enlisted to build bridges of respect and reconciliation. Wise religious leadership consists of identifying those teachings and educating all peoples in that spirit.

Let today's events inspire us to find a common forum with a common action for the common good of all. Let dialogue become a part of our culture.

Imam Hassan Qazwini
Religious Leader
Islamic Center of America, Dearborn, MI

Opening Prayer Speech, 108th Session of Congress
Washington, DC, October 1, 2003

Respected Congressmen and Women. I would like to greet you with the greeting of Islam. Peace be with you in the name of Allah, the Compassionate, the Merciful.

Glory be to Allah, the Lord of Abraham, Moses, Jesus, and Muhammad. As we commence our legislative day in this 108th Congress, we ask You to bestow Your blessing upon us and help our legislators enact that which pleases You and ensures the interest of our people. Lend Your infinite wisdom to this Congress and allow them to embrace what is right, not what is popular.

As our Nation faces many challenges, we beseech Your guidance. And as we pursue those who intend harm to our country, let us seek justice rather than revenge. Guide our leaders to use the influence of their power as an instrument for the betterment of all humankind and peace throughout the world.

Oh, Allah, endow the people of this great land with a growing trust in one another and an increasing faith in You. Help us all uphold our God-given rights of freedom and equality. Allow us never to evoke Your law by embracing color or creed as tools for superiority. As You say in the Holy Koran, "Oh people, We had created you from one male and one female, and made you into nations and tribes so that you may know one another. Verily, the best amongst you are those who are the most pious."

Dr. Sayyid M. Syeed
National Director
Office for Interfaith & Community Alliances
Islamic Society of North America

"Anti-Semitism Has No Place in Islam"
Posted on the Jewish Daily Forward, March 23, 2011

... This spirit of cooperation has enabled us to strive shoulder to shoulder against both anti-Semitism and Islamophobia, leaving little room for hate mongers among our Jewish and Muslim communities in America. Leaders from all three Abrahamic faiths have visited the Holy Land together, returning with shared concerns as well as shared solutions.

The work we are doing is reinforced by our scriptures and by our American vision of pluralism and diversity. As Muslims, we must understand that there is absolutely no place for anti-Semitism in Islam, and we must speak out against all instances of anti-Semitism, wherever they may occur.

Our success in creating an atmosphere of cooperation in America enables us to carry this message to other parts of the world. We have already begun this process by inviting rabbis and imams from Europe to visit our Islamic centers and synagogues in America. We took delegations of Imams to Holocaust sites in Poland and Germany, in order to educate our community about a colossal tragedy that was inflicted on an entire community.

Summary

The statements listed above are a cross-section of the views of many staunch supporters of interfaith trialogue. The theme that permeates through each of their remarks is one of collaboration and cooperation among the three traditions. Interfaith trialogue occurs frequently in government, educational and other kinds of organizations, seminaries, and houses of worship. Since September 11, 2011, there has been a marked increase in interfaith trialogue, which has become a critical element for preserving stability in the domestic and international arenas.

We can no longer claim ignorance about other faith traditions. We can no longer claim to have a monopoly on the truth. We can no longer claim that God belongs to only one religion. The eloquent words of these prominent champions of interfaith remind us that we can no longer evangelize that there is one faith. While there are differences among the three Abrahamic traditions, there is dignity within these differences. And it is this dignity that is a dominant principle of interfaith trialogue. That principle is based on our coexistence with each other, irrespective of our beliefs, customs, and views. When we live in peace together, our own faith is strengthened and the covenant of Abraham is restored, as God ordained it to be.

Origins of the Abrahamic Faiths

Semitic Languages

A common connection between Judaism, Christianity, and Islam is the Semitic family of languages, which arose in the Middle East (Mullins 2005). The word Semitic derives from the Greek version of the Hebrew name, Shem, one of the three sons of Noah in the Jewish scriptures (Genesis 5:32). The term Semitic can be used as an adjective or as a noun when referring to languages. The noun Semite refers to the people. There is a significant common ancestry among Semitic people.

To understand the impact of Semitic languages on the world, let us first examine the number of believers among the major religions of the world.

Table 1
Number of Adherents among the Major Religions (circa mid-2010)

	in millions	%
Christians	2,281	32.5
Muslims	1,553	22.1
Hindus	943	13.4
Buddhists	463	6.6
Chinese (folk religionists)	454	6.5
Sikhs	24	0.3
Jews	15	0.2
Subtotal	5,733	81.6
Total World Population	7,023	100.0

Sources: Population Reference Bureau World Population Data Sheet 2011; World Factbook; World Almanac; and Book of Facts 2012.

As seen in table 1, Christians, Muslims, and Jews comprise 54.8 percent (3.9 billion) of the total world population of seven billion.

There are more than 6,500 known living languages in the world today (Grimes 1996). The current number of speakers of Semitic languages are shown in table 2.

Table 2
Semitic Languages by Number of Speakers
(circa 2005)

	in millions	%
Arabic	206.00	82.3
Amharic	27.00	10.8
Tigrinya	6.70	2.7
Hebrew	5.00	2.0
Neo-Aramaic	2.11	0.9
Silt'e	.83	0.4
Tigre	.80	0.3
Sebat Bet Gurage	.44	0.2
Maltese	.37	0.1
Modern South Arabian	.36	0.1
Inor	.28	0.1
Soddo	.25	0.1
Harari	.02	—
Total	250.16	100.0

Sources: Raymond G. Gordon, *Ethnologue: Languages of the World*, 15th ed. (Dallas: SIL International Publisher, 2005); and Ethnologue Report for Maltese (2008).

Today, the most widely spoken form of Semitic language is Arabic (206 million), followed by Amharic (27 million), Tigrinya (6.7 million), Hebrew (5 million), and Neo-Aramaic (2.1 million). Most Semitic speakers reside in the Middle East and North and East Africa. While the total number of speakers has been estimated at 250 million, the Arabic Language Institute, Katy, Texas, has set the number as high as 450 million. The Semitic languages constitute the northeastern subfamily of Afro-Asiatic languages (formerly called Hamito-Semitic) and the only branch of this group spoken in Asia (Hetzron 2006). Other branches of the Afro-Asiatic group include Ancient Egyptian and its successor, Coptic; the Berber languages of North Africa; the Cushitic languages of northern East Africa (such as Somali and Oromo); and the Chadic languages of West Africa (such as Hausa in Nigeria) (Huehnergard 2011).

Linguistically, the Semitic languages have the longest recorded history of any linguistic group. Arabic is spoken in a wide variety of dialects and is the official language in more than twenty countries throughout the Middle East and North Africa. Other countries with an official Semitic language include Ethiopia (Amharic); Israel (where Hebrew is one of the official languages); Malta (Maltese); and Eritrea (Tigrinya). Ancient Semitic languages include Phoenician (Canaanite) and its successor Punic, the language of Carthage; the languages of the neighbors of ancient Israelites, such as the Ammonites and Moabites; and Akkadian, the language of the ancient Babylonians and Assyrians. The Akkadian language was first attested in cuneiform writing on clay tablets from ancient Mesopotamia (modern Iraq) during the mid-third millennium BCE (Marcus 1978).

The vestiges of the past authenticate the importance of the Semitic languages and their impact on the Abrahamic faiths. For example, while the Old Testament is largely written in Hebrew, there are a few chapters written in Aramaic (*International Standard Bible Encyclopedia*). Old texts of the Ethiopian Christian church have roots in Ethiopic, a branch of the Semitic language (Harden 1926). The New Testament was originally written in Greek with a few passages in Aramaic (Zeolla 2005). South Arabian languages are attested in inscriptions found in modern Yemen, such as Sabaean, the language of ancient Sheba of the Bible (Simeone-Sinelle 1997). The Qur'an is written in classical Arabic, while other Muslim writings show an early Semitic influence.

Due to the similar origins of Aramaic, Hebrew, and Arabic, many of the terms are alike, including the words for *peace: shlama (šlām-ā')*, *shalom (šālôm)*, and *salaam (salām)*, respectively. Aramaic was the language spoken by Jesus. All religions, including Judaism, Christianity, and Islam, call for peace. Despite these common words and goals, peace has eluded mankind since the beginning of Creation. While followers of all three faiths believe that peace is an attainable goal, the grim reality is that they are too preoccupied with their differences, thereby creating impediments to the path for peace.

An examination into word usage in Aramaic, Hebrew, and Arabic reveal a common sharing of roots and meanings (Muller 1995). For example, the word *father* is translated as 'aḫ-ā' in Aramaic, 'āḫ-a in Hebrew, and 'ab in Arabic. The word *house* is translated as *bayt-ā'* in Aramaic; *báyiṯ* in Hebrew; and *bayt* in Arabic. To see how words can be misinterpreted, let us examine the various names or attributes used for God. The Aramaic El sounds more like the Arabic Allah than the English God. Similarly, the Hebrew words for God are El, Elah, and the plural form of Elohim (Warren 1998).

In addition, when the Christian Bible was being translated into English, the Aramaic or Hebrew word *El* was written variously as God, god, and angel. For example, the word *angel* ends in *el*, and the names of the archangels—Gabriel, Michael, and Raphael—all end in *el*, a Semitic name for God. The imprecise language allowed different translators to interpret the meaning of the Creator to fit their own views. As such, many believe that Allah is not the same as God, even though Allah is actually the Arabic name for God (Caner 2007). Because of this misconception, many non-Muslims are skeptical or cynical whenever Allah is mentioned. As each religion worships the Creator based on its own customs and traditions, its followers must personify the principles of peace and patience in the practice of their faith.

Demographic Data

As shown in table 3, with 2.3 billion believers, Christianity is the largest religion in the world, followed by Islam with 1.6 billion people. The sacred texts for Judaism, Christianity, and Islam are the Tanakh (including the Torah), Bible, and Qur'an, respectively. The original language of Judaism was Hebrew, while for Christianity, it was Aramaic and Greek. The Qur'an was written in Arabic. Abraham founded Judaism, and Moses followed in his footsteps. Saint Paul is credited with spreading and proliferating Christianity based on the teachings and inspiration of Jesus. Muhammad was the messenger of Islam.

All three Abrahamic religions were founded in the Middle East. The religious law that each adherent follows is Halakhah (Judaism),

Canon Law (Christianity), and Sharia (Islam). While Halakhah is a heritage that belongs to all Jews, it does not mean that rabbinic law and its literature function for Reform Jews in exactly the same way as they function for Orthodox and Conservative Jews. Canon Law is still relevant in certain branches of Christianity (e.g., Catholicism). But after the Reformation of the sixteenth and seventeenth centuries, most Protestants rejected it (Hartono 1996). Each religion has a special place and day of worship—synagogue on Saturday for Judaism, church on Sunday for Christianity, and mosque on Friday for Islam. The church and state are separate in Judaism and Christianity, but they are integrated in Islam. Notwithstanding these differences, the three traditions have a rich history of cooperation and coexistence.

Table 3
Demographics of the Abrahamic Faiths

Criteria	Judaism	Christianity	Islam
Adherents	Jews	Christians	Muslims
Population	15 million	2,281 million	1,553 million
Sacred Text	Tanakh (Torah, etc.)	Bible	Qur'an
Original Language	Hebrew	Aramaic, Greek	Arabic
Other Traditions	Talmud	Writings, Creeds	Hadiths
Founder	Abraham, Moses	Jesus, Saint Paul	Muhammad
Place Founded	Palestine	Palestine	Saudi Arabia
Religious Law	Halakhah	Canon law	Sharia
Clergy	Rabbis	Priests, ministers, etc.	Imams
House of Worship	Synagogue	Church	Mosque
Main Day of Worship	Saturday	Sunday	Friday
Church and State	Separate	Separate	Integrated

Sources: Data derived from Bibles, encyclopedias, literature, and religious clerics.

Case Studies of Coexistence

Over the centuries, examples abound as to actual occurrences of peaceful coexistence and cultural exchange among the followers of the Abrahamic faiths. For example, Andalusia Spain and much of the Iberian Peninsula were under Islamic rule for more than seven hundred years from the eighth to the fourteenth century. During that time, the Golden Age of Judaism perpetuated, and Jewish religious, cultural, and economic life flourished in that region. Indeed, it was a time of tolerance, mutual admiration, and consensus between Jews and Muslims. A great example of what can transpire through mutual cooperation was that Muslim scholars, with the aid of Jewish and Christian scholars, translated ancient Greek texts into Arabic. These scholarly works later helped Europe move out of the Dark Ages and into the Renaissance.

After the collapse of the Western Roman Empire in the fifth century, Europe had lost touch with much of its intellectual heritage. All that remained of the Greek sciences were Pliny's *Encyclopedia* and Boethius's treatises on logic and mathematics. Because the Latin library was so limited, European Christian theologians found it extremely difficult to expand their knowledge of their own scriptures. Furthermore, the church became the center of Europe's new worldview, whose leaders exerted profound influences in medicine but didn't know how to administer medicine for those who desperately needed it (Tschanz 1997).

The immense contributions of Muslim and non-Muslim scientists from Spain helped Europe move forward in the discipline of medicine as well as other sciences. They accomplished this monumental task by collecting, translating, augmenting, and codifying the classical Greco-Roman heritage that had been lost for centuries. They also disseminated this scientific knowledge to other regions of the world.

During Muslim rule in Spain, there were incidents of friction between Muslims and non-Muslims. However, Muslims did respect and honor the rights of Jews and Christians, as this golden age was one of religious and ethnic tolerance and interfaith harmony (Mahmood 2008). As such, non-Muslims were treated better than conquered people might have been expected. During the long time span of Muslim rule in Spain, there were periods of bias and narrowness. Nonetheless, non-Muslims were not prevented from following their faith or pressured to convert to Islam.

Christians always outnumbered both Muslims and Jews in Spain. After Christianity replaced Islam in Spain, the status of minority faith groups became much more precarious. In 1492, King Ferdinand and Queen Isabella issued an edict stating that any of Spain's two hundred thousand Jews who refused to convert to Christianity would be expelled from the country. Jews found sanctuary by escaping to Muslim countries in the Ottoman Empire (Telushkin 1991).

Maimonides, a famous Jewish physician, theologian, and scholar, lived in Spain during Muslim rule. He was also known as Musa ibn Maymun. He later migrated to Egypt and became the personal physician of Sultan Saladin the Great. He also became the head of the Jewish communities in Egypt (Frank 1981). His fourteen-volume *Mishnah Torah* still carries canonical authority as a codification of Talmudic law (Twersky 1980). In the twelfth century, after Saladin's army defeated the English King Richard the Lionheart, the two rulers signed the Treaty of Ramia, which led to the gates of Jerusalem being opened to Christians as well as Jews (Axelrod 2001).

Another example of cooperation between Muslims and Jews took place in the seventh century, during the onset of Islam. At that time, Muhammad had initiated the first-ever written interfaith constitution, the Charter of Medina. Muslims and Jews lived together in Medina, and constant warfare took a toll on both sides. The parties to this constitution agreed to help each other in the event of any violation. Both Jews and Muslims had the right to practice their own religions. Jews were entitled to the same rights as Muslims without any injustice or partisanship. Furthermore, Jews were considered a community of believers just as Muslims were.

Under the Charter of Medina, Muslim and non-Muslim citizens were protected and given rights and duties, and justice was secured via a legal system rather than through tribal military actions. The Charter of Medina is a model for creating and maintaining dialogue in a pluralistic society and nurturing and promoting sustainable political and social relationships among different groups (Yildirim 2005).

Summary

Judaism, Christianity, and Islam grew out of Semitic traditions, which arose in the Middle East and extended from Mesopotamia to the eastern coast of the Mediterranean Sea. Various forms of Semitic languages were spoken in this region. Jews are of Semitic origin and first settled in Canaan and later Israel. Although influenced by Semitic mythology and languages, they did not adhere to the pantheon of deities but to the one God of monotheism. Christianity was influenced by Jewish tradition and also followed the ideology of monotheism. Islam is also a monotheistic faith that developed from Semitic traditions.

A common thread that runs through all three monotheistic religions is a foundation in the Semitic languages. Study of the Abrahamic religions necessitates a proficiency in at least three Semitic languages—Hebrew, Aramaic, and Arabic—and one Indo-European language, Greek. Such knowledge can greatly enhance one's understanding of terms with similar meanings; for example, the Semitic term for *day* is *yom* in both Hebrew and Arabic.

Undoubtedly, Semitic languages have had a great influence in our understanding of biblical scriptures. Over time, God sent messengers to teach and guide the people about monotheistic beliefs and practices in their native languages.

3 Beliefs

Biblical Scriptures

Judaism, Christianity, and Islam were all revealed in the Middle East. Each messenger undertook a special covenant with God. The covenant was made with Moses (Judaism), Jesus (Christianity), and Muhammad (Islam), who all trace back to Abraham. All three religions are intimately connected to each other. Christianity emanated from within the Jewish tradition, and Islam augmented the precepts and ideologies of both Christianity and Judaism. This interconnectivity does not indicate sameness, but unique and diverse religions with discrete beliefs and principles.

As shown in table 4, there is strict adherence to monotheism in Judaism and Islam, while Christianity holds to the Trinitarian concept. All three religions believe in the one God, who has different names and attributes. Each accepts the existence of angels, while Islam also accepts the existence of jinn (unseen creatures made up of smokeless and scorching fire). While each religion has its own prophets, they share prophets as well. Christians believe in saints as revered humans, while Shi'a Muslims believe the Imams were Divinely inspired. Jews do not accept the concept of revered humans. Original sin is affirmed by Christianity but rejected by Judaism and Islam. The virgin birth of Jesus is affirmed by Christianity and Islam but rejected by Judaism. While Judaism and Christianity acknowledge that Jesus was crucified, Islam avows that Jesus is still living. Both Christianity and Islam believe in the second coming of Jesus, although this is denied by Judaism.

Table 4
Religious Beliefs

Following is a comparison of the religious beliefs of Judaism, Christianity, and Islam:

Criteria	Judaism	Christianity	Islam
Monotheism	Strict	Trinitarian	Strict
Ultimate Reality	One God	One God	One God
Creator	Yahweh, Elohim	God	Allah
Spiritual Beings	Angels	Angels	Angels, Jinn
Messengers	Prophets	Prophets	Prophets
Other Revered Humans	Nonexistent	Saints	Imams (Shi'a)
Original Sin	Rejected	Affirmed	Rejected
Jesus	Ordinary Jew	Son of God	Prophet
Birth of Jesus	Normal Birth	Virgin Birth	Virgin Birth
Death of Jesus	Crucifixion	Crucifixion	Not Crucified
Second Coming of Jesus	Denied	Affirmed	Affirmed
Afterlife	Heaven, Gehenna	Heaven, Hell	Heaven, Hell
Purgatory	Gehenna	Yes (Catholics)	Barzakh

Sources: Data derived from bibles, encyclopedias, and literature.

The eternal abode is Heaven or Hell for Christians and Muslims. Jews have varied beliefs regarding the afterlife. For example, some Jews reject the notion of an afterlife, while others affirm that there is a Heaven (Gan Eden) and a Gehenna (a purification place for souls before entering Heaven; souls that cannot be purified remain in Gehenna forever).

Catholics accept Purgatory, the place between death and the eternal abode, while many Protestant and Orthodox churches reject it. Roman Catholics believe that while some souls are not free of sin, those sins do not warrant eternity in Hell; therefore, the souls will be purified before entering Heaven. Hence, Purgatory is the purification or temporary punishment for those who are being made ready for Heaven. Roman Catholics further believe that the pious still living on Earth can offer prayers and perform deeds of charity to help purify the souls in Purgatory (Martens 2011).

Muslims believe in Barzakh, which is somewhat analogous to Purgatory. Barzakh is an intermediate state where the soul stays until the Qiyamah (Judgment Day). Muslims believe there are three groups of souls in Barzakh: 1) true believers, 2) confirmed unbelievers and hypocrites, and 3) those who are neither true believers nor confirmed believers. While the true believers are ready for Heaven, they must wait until Judgment Day. Unbelievers and hypocrites are questioned about their beliefs during their stay in Barzakh, and they too must wait until Judgment Day. Those who have not yet become true or confirmed believers (e.g., children, the insane, etc.) will not be questioned; rather, they will be left in a state of deep slumber until the Day of Judgment.

Belief in God

Judaism, Christianity, and Islam maintain that there is a common Creator and that their messengers descended through Abraham. Jews and Muslims greatly stress the oneness and unity of God. While Christians affirm the oneness of God, they also believe that the one God is a Holy Trinity.

Judaism is composed of three main groups: Orthodox, Conservative, and Reform. The Orthodox view God as spirit rather than form. He is a personal God—omnipotent, omnipresent, omniscient, eternal, and compassionate. The Conservative concept of God is nondogmatic, flexible, impersonal, and indescribable. Reform Judaism allows a varied interpretation of the concept of God, giving wide room to naturalists, mystics, supernaturalists, and religious humanists. It holds that the truth is that we do not know the truth (Kohler 2010).

In Judaism, the concept of God is that he is One:

> Hear, O Israel: the Lord our God, the Lord is One. (Deuteronomy 6:4)

> I am the Lord thy God, which have brought thee out of the land of Egypt, out of the house of bondage. Thou shall have no other gods before Me. (Exodus 20:2–3)

Any attempt to divide God into parts and claim to understand His structure, essence, and compassion runs counter to Jewish tradition.

Many Jews comprehend God to be the one supernatural being whose presence is acknowledged through Divine revelation and avowed through prayer. There are spiritual values that actually sustain life and can be seen as signs of the Divine; examples include justice, love, and freedom. These values are celebrated during the Jewish religious year.

Reform or Progressive Judaism relies on science and philosophy to help mold beliefs and religious perceptions. God is understood as infinite, and human beings as finite. Judaism speaks about the God of history and about a covenant between God and the Jewish people. Jews find religious inspiration in the concept of the moral and ethical imperative (MacDonald 1998).

Christianity has three main groups: Roman Catholicism, Orthodox, and Protestantism. Roman Catholics believe they have inherited an apostolic line of succession from the earliest Christian leaders. The pope leads this group.

The Orthodox see themselves as being in continuity with the undivided church before its separation into Eastern and Western traditions. Orthodox churches are independently governed, with leaders bound together by their recognition of the patriarch of Constantinople.

Protestants vary considerably, especially concerning forms of church organization and government. They emphasize the supremacy of scriptural authority and faith in Jesus. There are various denominations, including Anglican, Baptist, Brethren, Congregationalist, Lutheran, Methodist, Moravian, Pentecostal, Presbyterian or Reformed, and Salvationist.

Churches of the Anglican traditions see themselves as both Reformed and Catholic. They are autonomous churches that look to the archbishop of Canterbury for international leadership.

The Pentecostal tradition emerged within the broader Protestant tradition and emphasizes sharing the spiritual gifts and experiences of the earliest Christians.

Christians believe that there is but one God, and He alone is the object of their worship and service. They adhere to a pluralistic concept of God—that He is Three in One, the Holy Trinity: God the Father, God the Son, and God the Holy Spirit (Modi 2000). "Therefore go and make disciples of all nations, baptizing them in the name of the Father and of the Son and of the Holy Spirit" (Matthew 28:19). Though the word *trinity* does not occur in the Bible, Christians believe that this concept is the very fabric of the New Testament, a truth revealed by God. Belief in the Trinity is not acceptance of more than one God; rather, it is a belief that there are three entities sharing the one essence in perfect unity.

Islam has two major sects, Sunni and Shi'a, and they both believe in the one God, agree on the fundamentals of Islam, and share the same holy book, the Qur'an. But there are differences, mostly derived from their dissimilar historical experiences, political and social developments, and ethnic composition. The division originated over the question of who would lead the emerging Muslim community after Muhammad's death. While both Sunni and Shi'a Muslims follow the Hadiths of Muhammad, they disagree on which of these traditions are legal.

Four Sunni schools of thought—Hanafi, Maliki, Shafi'i, and Hanbali—formulated Islamic solutions to moral and religious questions. Sunni Muslims are the largest group in Islam, representing about 85 percent of total adherents. They believe that the first four elected caliphs were Muhammad's rightful successors, since God did not specify any particular successors. They argue that leadership is not a birthright but an earned trust that may be given or taken away by the people.

Shi'a Muslims constitute about 15 percent of the total followers of Islam. Their school of thought is derived from Imam Ja'far as-Sadiq. The largest sect of Shi'a Islam, known as the Twelvers, believe that Twelve Imams were chosen by God and foretold by Muhammad. The Shi'a community contends that these Imams were the true leaders and rightful rulers, as they held absolute spiritual authority among Muslims and had final say in matters of doctrine and revelation. Furthermore, Shi'a Muslims believe that the Twelve Imams are perfect, infallible, and sinless. They often revere the Imams by performing pilgrimages to their tombs and shrines in the hope of Divine intercession.

Shi'as believe that Imam Al Mahdi (Guided One), the living Twelfth Imam, is in a state in which he has been hidden by God. His occultation has currently lasted more than eleven centuries. When he emerges from his occultation, he will prevail over evil in an apocalyptic battle against the enemies of God. Thereafter, Jesus will appear and join forces with Imam Al Mahdi, and Jesus will slay the antichrist.

In Islam, the one true God is the almighty Creator and sustainer of the universe. He is similar to nothing and nothing is comparable to Him: "Say: He is God, the One and Only. God, Eternal, Absolute. He begets not, nor is He begotten. And there is none like unto Him" (Qur'an 112:1–4).

The unity of God means that He is not dependent on anything, and everything depends on Him. He is the Creator and the ultimate source of all existence. Since God is the cause of Creation, this universe has only one source, one end, and one truth. The universe and everything in it are the reflections of absolute unity, coherence, and discipline. All of the components in the universe have a common origin, a common purpose, and a common end, as they are creations of God. God has many attributes, all of which are linked together as one. There can be no pluralism in God's essence. Everything is dependent on Him. God has no partners and no associates in His Divine essence. All three Abrahamic religions believe that God is the origin and source of all Creation.

Big Bang Theory

According to the big bang theory, the universe once was a single entity, with matter and space joined together. Then a powerful force, a powerful explosion, separated it all around fifteen billion years ago. Since then, the universe has been expanding (Kanipe 2007).

The first law of thermodynamics (also known as the law of conservation of energy) states that energy can neither be created nor destroyed. Energy can only change forms—for example, from chemical-based energy to heat-based energy—and in any process, the total energy of the universe remains the same (Atkins 2007).

The second law of thermodynamics states that all energy is proceeding toward uniformity and neutrality. The universe had a beginning and will not exist forever. Eventually, everything will be at the same extremely low temperature, and the universe will weaken until energy is no longer available and life ceases to exist. Even within the concept of the big bang theory, there had to be a force to cause that explosion. That force is God. And it is God who will bring the universe to its termination.

The second law of thermodynamics supports the creation and eventual termination of the universe. While there was skepticism about the big bang theory in the past, scientists and theologians are coming to grips with the notion that this theory is conceivable (Magee 2007). Table 5 shows a comparison of the major religions regarding their acceptance or rejection of the theory:

Table 5
Acceptance or Rejection of the Big Bang Theory

Religion	Divine Scripture	Theologians (pre-20th century)	Theologians (post-20th century)
Islam	Yes	Yes	Yes
Christianity	No	No	Divided
Judaism	No	No	Divided
Hinduism	No	No	Divided
Buddhism	No	No	Divided

Sources: Data derived from bibles and literature.

Islam has always accepted the big bang theory, and it is so described in the Qur'an:

> Do not the unbelievers see that the Heavens and the Earth were joined together [as one unit of Creation], before we clove them asunder? We made from water every living thing. Will they not then believe? (Qur'an 21:30)

However, Christian, Jewish, Hindu, and Buddhist theologians are divided; some accept while others reject the big bang theory. Abbe Georges Lemaitre, a Belgian physicist, put forth the idea of a big bang theory in 1927 (Magee 2007). It is interesting to note that while theologians, other than Muslims, did not accept the occurrence of a big bang explosion before the twentieth century, many have since come to accept it due to scientific discoveries.

There are different views about the big bang theory, but the consensus in Judaism, Christianity, and Islam is that God created the universe. The Christian Bible states that the entire universe, including the Earth, came into being during the six days of the Creation (Genesis 1:31, Exodus 20:11). The Bible also states that man existed from the beginning of the Creation (Mark 10:6). Islam's view is that, perhaps, the six days were actually six periods that stretched across eons of Earth years. Since Genesis is an ancient Hebrew text, linguistic and contextual ambiguities may have entered into its interpretations. For example, the word *day* in Hebrew and Arabic is *yom*, which Jewish scholars have interpreted as twenty-four hours, a year, time in general, or a specific period.

Interestingly, science, Judaism, Christianity, Islam, Hinduism, and Buddhism agree that the universe continues to expand at an increasing rate. Moreover, whether it was the result of the big bang or some other means, the universe had to emerge from something, out of which came the Creation of the Earth and mankind.

For centuries, the creation of the universe has been a major topic of discussion among scientists and theologians, all of whom have various opinions and theories. Did our existence arise from the big bang?

There is consensus that God was the cause of our existence. God is just and merciful and has provided basic rules so that we may be good and righteous. God communicates to the people through the prophets, whose revelations are recorded in the holy scriptures of each religion. While the scriptures of the three religions are not the same, they all acknowledge God's truth. The Torah, Bible, and Qur'an are commandments and guidelines for our lives. All three religions promote modesty, moderation, moral values, and ethical principles.

God's Books (The Scriptures)

Divine revelation has given mankind the means to acquire true knowledge and understanding. The essence of unity is manifested in the fact that revelation must derive from a single author and a single unadulterated moral code. Furthermore, the revelation must have historical credibility, and it should stand the test when scholars evaluate it for accuracy, consistency, and reliability. One such test is the criterion of miracles. Divine revelation should be replete with historical and future accounts of miracles. Jews, Christians, and Muslims believe in the books that God has sent down to mankind through His prophets. These books all had the same source, God, and all were revealed in truth in their original form. Each of the Abrahamic faiths considers its books to be Divine revelation.

The religious texts of Judaism are the Torah, which focuses on law and the origin of the religion; Nevi'im, which is largely narratives of prophets following the death of Moses; and Ketuvim, which includes historical accounts of events that occurred after those described in the other two texts. The Old Testament is largely composed of the Tanakh (T for Torah, N for Nevi'im, K for Ketuvim) and shows the influence of Judaism's concepts in Christianity (Maddison 2007). Jews state that there is no mention of either Christianity or Islam in the Jewish scriptures, and they hold steadfast to their texts as the original and final revelation. The Torah reveals that God intervenes and interacts with mankind and the world. According to Jewish tradition, the true aspect of God is not known or comprehended, and only God's revealed aspect brought the universe into existence. The Jewish relationship with God is a covenant relationship (i.e., they keep God's laws and bring holiness into every aspect of their lives).

The Jewish Old Testament, notwithstanding the rearrangement of some biblical passages, influenced the Christian New Testament, which was revealed to Jesus and includes twenty-seven books and numerous writings attributed to apostles. The New Testament differs from the Old Testament in its proclamation that God chose to reveal Himself to mankind through Jesus. Christians believe that the one true God is composed of the Father, the Son, and the Holy Spirit; that Jesus was born through the Virgin Mary; that he suffered, was crucified, and died for the sins of mankind; that he was resurrected, ascended to Heaven, and will return to judge the living and the dead. Moreover, Christians maintain that God created all that is seen and unseen and that Islam and the emergence of Muhammad are not mentioned in either the Old or the New Testament.

The Qur'an acknowledges the existence of the Jewish and Christian scriptures. However, the Qur'an states that the Jewish and Christian scriptures have been tampered with due to translation and interpretation issues. It acknowledges the four holy books of Islam as the Torah, the Psalms (of David), the Gospel, and the Qur'an. Islam accepts the original Gospel, which does not break down into the four canonical Gospels or the Epistles of Paul. Muslims further contend that while Moses and Muhammad came with new laws (the Ten Commandments and the Qur'an), Jesus did not:

> Think not that I have come to abolish the Law and the Prophets; I have come not to abolish them but to fulfill them. For truly, I say to you, till Heaven and Earth pass away, not an iota, not a dot, will pass from the Law until all is accomplished. (Matthew 5:17–18)

Muslims believe that this verse from the book of Matthew clearly states that Jesus came to fulfill the law that had been revealed to Moses and that he made no mention of a new law. However, a vast majority of Christians do not support this premise. For example, one of the main principles of most Protestant theologies is that salvation comes through faith and grace and not through adherence to the law.

Translation into another language can be problematic. For example, in the English translation of John 2:4, Jesus is depicted as speaking harshly to his mother, Mary: "Woman, what have I to do with you? My hour is not yet come." Addressing or rebuking one's mother as "Woman" would have been considered impolite and disrespectful. However, Jesus and Mary spoke either Hebrew or Aramaic. As Jesus would not have been impolite to his mother, then the English translation must be incorrect and taken out of context. Jesus is a revered role model; thus, it would be highly unacceptable for us to speak to our mothers in a condescending tone.

Similarly, Muslims are very wary about the Qur'an being translated from Arabic into other languages. For example, an English translation of a Qur'anic verse depicts husbands as being authorized to beat their wives:

> Men are the protectors and maintainers of women, because God has given the one more [strength] than the

other, and because they support them from their means. Therefore, the righteous women are devoutly obedient, and guard in [the husband's] absence what God would have them guard. As to those women on whose part you fear disloyalty and ill conduct, admonish them [first, next] refuse to share their beds, [and last] beat them [lightly]; but if they return to obedience, seek not against them means [of annoyance]: for God is Most High, Great [above you all]. (Qur'an 4:34)

This verse was revealed in Arabic, and the Arabic word *daraba* has been translated into English as *to beat*. *Daraba* has been used in other verses to mean *ignore, condemn, get out, travel, strike*, etc. Before we examine the meaning of this verse, we first need to understand that the role of women in primitive societies of ancient times was to be completely obedient and dependent on their husbands. However, in modern societies, the condition of *daraba* may no longer be applicable. Today, a wife's contribution to the family extends beyond household chores and the rearing of children. Wives enhance the family structure on the basis of equal partnership with their husbands, may have dual role of wife and bread earner, engage in activities outside the home, share in family budgeting, and participate in intellectual discourse.

Women's Rights in Ancient Times

Women did not fully enjoy the same rights as men in ancient times. They were not even allowed to testify in courts of law. The scriptures of all three religions depict the wife as obedient to her husband.

When Moses came on the scene, how successful would he have been if he immediately preached about complete equality between the sexes? In ancient Jerusalem, the woman had rights only in the home and even those were very limited. However, "... according to traditional Judaism, women are endowed with a greater degree of 'binah' [intuition, understanding, intelligence] than men. The rabbis inferred this from the idea that woman was 'built' (Genesis 2:22) rather than 'formed' (Genesis 2:7), and the Hebrew root of 'build' has the same consonants as the word 'binah'" (Mamre 2013).

The same rationale regarding women may also apply to Jesus and Muhammad, although both did preach about the equality of the sexes. Jesus focused on women quite often and used women as illustrations of spiritual truths in his teachings. Muhammad also preached about equality between men and women, and the Qur'an mandates that the husband and wife are the "garments" of each other, thereby implying equality between them (Qur'an 2:187). While the Jewish and Christian scriptures both refer to the equality and the inequality of the sexes, the time in which these verses were revealed is not identified in either the Old Testament or the New Testament. To capture the mind-sets of the people to whom God conveyed His revelations, given the dominance of the men over the women, it makes sense that the original scriptures reflected the lifestyles and outlooks of the day.

Women had a very low status and were not protected by the courts. Their function was to obey. If they did not, they were punished. In Judaism, during the Second Temple period (lasted between circa 516 BCE and circa 70 CE), women were not allowed to testify in court trials. They could not go out in public or talk to strangers: "They had become second-class Jews, excluded from the worship and teaching of God, with status scarcely above that of slaves" (Metzger 1993).

In the Old Testament, a bride who had been presented as a virgin, and who could not be proven to be one, was stoned to death by the men of her village:

> If, however, the charge is true and no proof of the young woman's virginity can be found, she shall be brought to the door of her father's house and there the men of her town shall stone her to death. She has done an outrageous thing in Israel by being promiscuous while still in her father's house. You must purge the evil from among you. (Deuteronomy 22:20)

The men of Sodom gathered around Lot's house, and asked that he bring his two male guests out so that the men could "know" them. Lot offered his two virgin daughters to be raped instead, saying:

> Look! I have two daughters who have never slept with
> a man. Let me bring them out to you, and you can do
> what you like with them. But don't do anything to these
> men, for they have come under the protection of my
> roof. (Genesis 19:8)

Yet, even after this despicable act, Lot was still regarded as an honorable man, worth saving from the destruction of the city. Allowing one's daughters to be sexually assaulted by multiple rapists was treated as a minor transgression, because of the young women's low status. However, Islam takes exception to this interpretation, as the Qur'an states that Lot was honorable and offered his daughters only for marriage: "He said, 'There are my daughters [to marry], if you must act [so]'" (Qur'an 15:71).

The New Testament stipulates that a wife should obey her husband:

> Wives, submit yourselves to your own husbands as you
> do to the Lord. For the husband is the head of the wife as
> Christ is the head of the church, his body, of which he is
> the Savior. Now as the church submits to Christ, so also
> wives should submit to their husbands in everything.
> (Ephesians 5:22–24)

Similarly, the meaning of the Qur'anic verse relating to *daraba* has to be understood in conjunction with its time period. Wives in the ancient Islamic world also had to submit to their husbands in everything. During quarrels, emotions can run rampant. In Islam, there is a process by which the husband must treat his unruly wife. First, he must speak to her lovingly. If this does not resolve the situation, then he must speak to her politely. If this does not work, then he must speak to her using religious terms. If this fails, then he can speak to her harshly. If there is no reconciliation, the husband is prohibited from beating his wife. Reconciliation is seen as a solution to the quarrel:

> If you fear a breach between them twain, appoint
> arbiters, one from his family, and the other from hers; if
> they wish for peace, God will cause their reconciliation:

for God has full knowledge and is acquainted with all things. (Qur'an 4:35)

However, even in ancient times or in primitive societies, beating one's wife was not meant to inflict physical harm, but only to cause her some emotional pain. Therefore, the husband must avoid her face and other sensitive parts of the body to not cause scars, wounds, or bruises. Beating represents ethical opposition to one's wife rather than physical punishment. For example, an ethical punishment would be to admonish her and refuse to share the bed with her until she reconciles. The beating of one's wife is optional and should only be administered if the husband believes it will save the marriage. The husband cannot beat his wife to unleash his anger or exhibit his manliness. The slightest physical violence towards one's wife, if it bruises her skin, is forbidden in Islam. Prophet Muhammad stated: "I am astonished at a man who beats his wife, whereas it is he himself, more than his wife, who deserves a beating" (Majilsi 1983).

The Qur'an and New Testament have many examples of treating one's wife with kindness:

O you who believe! You are forbidden to inherit women against their will, nor shall you treat them with harshness, that you may take away part of the dowry you have given them, except where they have been guilty of open lewdness; on the contrary live with them on a footing of kindness and equity ..." (Qur'an 4:19)

Husbands, love your wives and do not be harsh with them. (Colossians 3:19)

Certainly, there will always be questions as to the validity and authentic meaning of scriptural verses once they have been translated into another language. Can translations be made without altering the fundamental message? Can we adjust our translations of the scriptures to accommodate the constantly changing social, political, and economic conditions—now and in the future?

Of course, there will always be pessimists who hold to their own distinct views, shutting the door to any possibility of interfaith dialogue. Monotheism will become vulnerable to attacks and threats from those who wish to destroy it, unless there is a genuine effort among Jews, Christians, and Muslims to cooperate with one another. Toward this end, we need to find ways to engage in meaningful dialogue with each other. Interfaith dialogue is not a debate but rather a mutual exchange of ideas and discussion. Listening to each other with openness and empathy creates an atmosphere of understanding. Those who come to the dialogue must be immersed in integrity and sincerity and allow others to genuinely express their points of view. Effective dialogue can be achieved only when a foundation of mutual trust is first established. Participants must first seek to understand before they seek to be understood.

The seeds of Abraham gave mankind the Torah, Bible, and Qur'an as revealed books of instructions from God. Each of these scriptures is a system of beliefs that guides its followers toward a relationship with the same God. As such, their devotion, obedience, and submission should inspire those followers to unify their efforts toward peace, reconciliation, and conflict-resolution.

Every light has its shadow. Differences among one another arise out of aloofness, mutual ignorance, and intolerance. Unity in diversity is the highest possible attainment, made possible through passion and trust. For unity to prevail, we need to make a great deal of effort in order to put away prejudices, traditional rivalries, and authoritarianism. The challenge is to find the common ground and principles that unite the Abrahamic faiths, even as we uphold their individual beliefs and traditions.

Common Ground, Common Principles

Despite differences in opinion and interpretations within each of the Abrahamic faiths, we need to avoid discord. We can agree on many issues. When interfaith dialogue takes place, all participants should proceed from the point of harmony. There is commonality among us, and we should build an alliance on those issues. We are all part and parcel of God's Creation. Only by achieving unity can we thwart the evils of those who wish to drive a wedge between us and eventually destroy us.

The three Abrahamic faiths have similarities. All are monotheistic and believe God to be the Creator and source of moral law. Their sacrosanct stories and passages contain many of the same figures, histories, and places, although with different roles, perspectives, and meanings. It is not the differences that separate us but the unwillingness to recognize the many instances in which we agree.

Let us examine some of the doctrines in which Jews, Christians, and Muslims agree, admittedly with different interpretations.

The Afterlife (Hereafter)

Judaism, Christianity, and Islam each are based on a linear concept of time (i.e., one's time spent on the Earth is followed by one's time in the afterlife).

Although not accepted by some Jewish sects (e.g., the Sadducees), resurrection of the soul is a key belief of Judaism. Prior to resurrection, the soul rests in a place known as Sheol ("grave"). Jews believe that there are two places in the afterlife. The soul that has done good deeds is considered righteous but needs to be purified of any sinful deed. This soul enters Gehenna, reviews the sins of its earthly life, and then is purified for a period of up to one year, at which point the soul enters Heaven. However, if the soul is too wicked to be purified, it will remain in Gehenna forever (Cohen 1995).

A review of the literature does not reveal much about the Jewish concept of Heaven (Gan Eden), except that it is a place where God resides and the soul finds its eternal resting place. The amount of good deeds performed on the Earth will determine how close the Jewish soul is to God in Heaven. Judaism is mainly concerned with life on the Earth. Because Jewish people have been given promises in this life, the afterlife is less essential in Judaism than it is in other religions (Williams 2008).

Christians believe in the immortality of the soul (i.e., the soul that is saved enters Heaven while the soul that is not saved enters Hell). The soul in Heaven resides eternally in the presence of God. The soul in Hell either receives eternal punishment or ceases to exist. In Catholicism, the soul may be saved depending on its stay in Purgatory, where the soul may or may not be cleansed of its past sins. Cleansed souls enter Heaven; those that are not cleansed enter Hell, which is a place of fire, darkness, and punishment. However, many Protestants and Orthodox Christians do not accept the concept of Purgatory.

In Christianity, Heaven is described as a place of ultimate bliss and beauty, free of pain and sorrow, where there is only joy and constant worship of God. Christians are saved when they accept Jesus as their Savior. However, depending on which Christian denomination one follows, salvation can be lost because of sinful behavior. Because the spiritual connection between good deeds and the refusal to commit sin motivates Christians to uphold their faith and beliefs, they believe that Heaven will be their final destination. As a result, thoughts of the afterlife greatly affects their actions in this life (Kardec 2008).

Islam has similar views regarding Heaven and Hell. However, Islam differs from Christianity substantially in doctrine and practice. Muslims believe that Heaven can be attained by following God's will and living a holy life. Muslims do not claim to know whether God will allow them to enter Heaven, which is a place of eternal bliss and pleasure. Hell is a place of eternal punishment and suffering.

According to Islam, time and space will end, and a new life will begin. Patience and perseverance in one's previous life will be rewarded in the next. Those who do not pay heed to self-sacrifice and constancy will pay the immeasurable price. In this world, fifty thousand years seems a very long time. In the afterlife, it may be the equivalent of a mere moment. In this world, with all its misfortunes, Muslims should be patient and have faith and trust in God. To Muslims, resurrection may seem a very far-off event. The nearness becomes more profound when one realizes that he cannot go back to the previous life to correct his wrongs. He rests in his grave until summoned by God for his accountability. The end result for the winners is a garden that awaits them as a reward for their patience. For the transgressors, the supreme penalty of Hell awaits them (Turfe 1996).

Instead of nourishing him, the sinner's food chokes him, and the result is perpetual pain and suffering in Hell. In Heaven, the faithful are nourished with the blessings of God as a reward for their perseverance. The spiritual good that a Muslim performs in this temporal life will endure forever. With faith, one can accomplish spiritual good, and God will reward people's best actions. In this world, every soul shall be given a body, and that being will have the free will and volition to do as he pleases. On the day of resurrection, each person will be summoned to witness his own actions on Earth. The end result is reward or punishment for one's earthly actions. In Islam, attaining the highest spiritual level does not happen automatically. Man must prove himself worthy of this level. Angels are sent to protect man and to record his deeds—good and bad. The angel on the right notes the good deeds; the angel on the left records the bad deeds (Turfe 1996).

How a Muslim chooses to utilize the blessings of God in the physical life will determine what lies ahead—Heaven or Hell. Peace will be for those who lived a good life, while punishment awaits those who lived a bad life. Man is an everlasting being, and death is only a step toward eternal life. The eternal future rests on the deeds and actions of one's stay in the earthly existence.

In Islam, once death separates the soul from the physical body, the soul travels to a partition between the current life and the resurrection (*barzakh*), when it becomes more aware of the facts of existence. In the resurrection, every soul will be given a visible body, and everyone will be aware of the existence of God. On the Day of Judgment, the earthly actions (good and bad) of everyone will be unfolded in their presence. It is only those who patiently persevered in the previous life who will reach happiness in the Eternal Garden (Turfe 1996).

According to the Qur'an, life after death is a second Creation. Birth and rebirth are blessings from God. The human hope to transcend death is not the hope to escape death, but the hope of the resurrection. At the resurrection, human beings will be given a new body to participate in the new Creation. The resurrection of the body is not in any way conditioned upon the immortality of the soul. Both body and soul are dependent on the creative will of God.

The Abrahamic faiths hold that the dead go to a specific place after death, based on their beliefs and actions during life. Judaism, Christianity, and Islam try to give their followers an explanation of the world on the other side of life. Although they differ in the details, each of these faiths advises their followers that good actions and intentions in this life will be rewarded in the next world. Similarly, the wicked shall be punished for eternity.

Angels

Angels are the unseen spiritual creatures mentioned in Jewish, Christian, and Islamic scriptures. Their primary function is to praise and serve God and do His will. Angels play an essential role in the relationship between God and humans. All three religions believe that angels follow God's commands, including serving as intermediaries in His communication with humans, although there are variations about what angels are and what they do. In addition, all three faiths believe in the existence of demons.

Angels' role in bridging the gap between God and mankind may be to teach, command, or inform individuals of their destiny. They reward the faithful, punish the unjust, and help people in need. They help people establish relationships or connections with God and cope with life's situations. As the conduit in the revelation of Divine truths to mankind, angels help people understand how these truths apply to everyday life. They transport the souls of the dead to the afterlife.

Table 6
Existence of Angels

	Judaism	Christianity	Islam
Angels	Yes	Yes	Yes
Archangels	Yes	Yes	Yes
—Gabriel	Yes	Yes	Yes
—Michael	Yes	Yes	Yes
—Raphael	Yes	Yes	Yes
—Uriel	Yes	Yes	—
—Azrael	—	—	Yes
Fallen Angels (Lucifer)	Yes	Yes	No (jinn)
Demons	Yes	Yes	Yes

Sources: Data derived from scriptures and literature.

As noted in table 6, each of the three religions believes that angels exist. Angels are described in the canon laws of monotheism. The scriptures within each religion refer to the same archangels—Gabriel, Michael, and Raphael. Judaism and Christianity also include Uriel, while

Islam includes Azrael. Fallen angels (e.g., Lucifer) also appear in Jewish and Christian scriptures, but the concept of fallen angels is rejected in Islam. Each religion accepts that demons exist.

Let us examine the impact these archangels had on mankind. Each of the three religions affirms that the archangel Gabriel destroyed Sodom and Gomorrah as well as their inhabitants because they transgressed against the restrictions and constraints of God. Christians and Muslims also believe that Gabriel told Mary that she would bear a son, Jesus, although she would be untouched by any man. Furthermore, Muslims contend that Gabriel revealed the Qur'an to Muhammad.

According to Jews, the archangel Michael is the guardian of Israel (Daniel 12:1). Christians believe Lucifer (Satan) and his followers were thrown out of Heaven (Revelation 12:7–9). Muslims believe that whoever is an enemy of God's angels (e.g., Michael and Gabriel) is an enemy of God (Qur'an 2:98). Lucifer is considered an archangel in Judaism and Christianity, but not in Islam, where he is *Iblis*, a jinn (genie) made out of fire. Iblis did not prostrate to the acceptance of Adam (Qur'an 18:50), because he considered himself to be superior to Adam who was made out of clay.

The archangel Raphael is the healer, according to Jews and Christians (Tobit 3:17). According to Muslims, Raphael will twice herald the final days with his trumpet. After the first blow, all will be destroyed, and after the second, all the dead will be resurrected (Qur'an 39:68).

The Abrahamic religions hold different views about the nature of angels. While some regard angels as God's messengers, others believe that they merit worship. Some believe angels have physical bodies, while others believe they assume material bodies when necessary.

In Judaism, angels are the connection between God's laws in Heaven and humans on the Earth. As angels serve God, they also help people understand His will. Angels reward goodness and punish evildoers. As such, they also take the souls of righteous believers to Heaven. Two superior types of winged angels, known as cherubim (Ezekiel 10:1–22) and seraphim (Isaiah 6:1–13), guard the throne of God. Some angels, such as Lucifer, are believed to have fallen from a position of proximity to God, because of pride or because they tried to usurp the position of God. To draw a wedge between God and man, these fallen angels provoke humans to commit sin. In addition, they are viewed as agents of war, disease, earthly disasters, and other disorders.

The two archangels mentioned in the canonical Old Testament are Michael, the warrior leader of the Heavenly hosts, and Gabriel, the Heavenly messenger. The two archangels mentioned in the apocryphal Old Testament are Raphael, God's healer or helper, and Uriel (meaning fire of God), the watcher over the world and the lowest part of Hell (Sparks 1985). Seven archangels in total are noted in the Old Testament.

In Christianity, angels are the messengers of God. Angels declared the birth of Jesus. They play an active role in the daily lives of Christians, transmitting the prayers of the faithful to God and providing comfort and strength to those in need. Celestial beings are grouped into seven ranks in the New Testament: angels, archangels, principalities, powers, virtues, dominions, and thrones. Adding the cherubim and seraphim from the Old Testament to this group brings the total number of angelic groups to nine. According to this system, the first circle of angels—the seraphim, cherubim, and thrones—devote their time to contemplating God. The second circle—the dominions, virtues, and powers—govern the universe. The third circle—principalities, archangels, and angels—carry out the orders of the superior angels (Browne 2003).

The notion of angels in Islam is akin to the views in Judaism and Christianity. However, while Judaism and Christianity generally divide spiritual beings into those who are with or against God, Islam divides such beings into angels (*mala'ikah*), demons (*shayatin*), and genies (jinn), the latter of which may be either good or evil. The jinn were created out of fire, and they can be visible, invisible, or assume various human or animal forms. According to Islam, angels always obey God's commands and, therefore, can never disobey Him. The jinn are another matter; they are capable of disobeying God, as did Satan.

In Islam, angels serve God and carry out His will. Angels do not have free will or the ability to disobey God. Belief in angels is an article of faith. Four archangels are well known. The most important is Gabriel, the angel of revelation, who made the Qur'an known to Muhammad and also conveyed the messages of God to Abraham, Moses, and Jesus. Michael, the angel of nature and mercy, provides man with rainfall and sustenance and rewards righteous people for doing good deeds.

The archangel Raphael is the one who will blow the trumpet twice to herald the Day of Judgment, the first blow announces the destruction of everything, and second indicates the resurrection of the dead. The angel of death is the archangel Azrael (Malak al-Maut), who separates the soul from the body at the moment of death (Qur'an 32:11).

There are lower ranking angels who guard and maintain Heaven (Ridwan); supervise, guard, and punish the unjust in Hell (Malik); and two angels (Munkar and Nakeer) who record the good deeds on the right shoulder and the bad deeds on the left shoulder of each human. There are also guardian angels who pray for and help protect mankind.

The Qur'an states that God created more angels than humans, as groups of angels have been guardians over each individual person on Earth since the beginning of mankind (Qur'an 13:11). The Qur'an doesn't directly describe the hierarchy of angels in detail. However, archangels do hold the highest positions, as they rule over the operations of the universe and deliver revelations to mankind.

In summary, there is commonality among Judaism, Christianity, and Islam about the belief in angels. Even the names of some of the archangels are the same. Before the Creation of the world, God created angels and spiritual beings. The primary role of angels is to praise and serve God and do His will. They also act as God's messengers to mankind and as helpers and guardians of the faithful.

Summary

The essence of Judaism, Christianity, and Islam is the worship of the one God, and that God created the universe and mankind. Each religion adheres to religious credos that substantiates and confirms the oneness of God, and that He creates and rules all that is in existence. Although the details of each Creation differ marginally, many of the fundamental doctrines and principles of theology are shared by each, for example, the belief in God, the afterlife, and angels. In addition, there is a growing trend in the acceptance of the big bang theory.

Although the three religions were revealed thousands of years ago, the adherents of Judaism, Christianity, and Islam still base their religious faith on the Torah, Bible, and Qur'an, respectively. Each of the three religions reveres its scriptures as unique, complete, authoritative, and universal, regulating the metaphysical role and conduct of mankind toward God. The concept of stewardship is part and parcel of each religion, as the followers are entrusted to protect each other, plants and animals, resources, and the environment. The concept of equality is prevalent in each of the faith traditions. The status of women has changed over the centuries. Today, women are reclaiming religious power, as they actively assert their influence in their respective synagogues, churches, and mosques.

Prophets were inspired by God to speak for Him and be His messenger. They received God's revelations, prophecies, and commandments, which were later written in biblical scriptures for the benefit of mankind.

4 Messages of the Prophets

One of the basic tenets in religion is the acceptance of prophets and their contributions to mankind. Judaism, Christianity, and Islam mention, describe, chronicle, or relate stories about some of these prophets.

While the three religions refer to thousands of prophets, only a few are mentioned specifically. For example, Islam states that there are some 124,000 prophets, but only twenty-five are mentioned by name in the Qur'an. Therefore, only those named in the scriptures or approved religious texts are included in this analysis.

Table 7
Prophets Mentioned in Jewish, Christian, and Islamic Scriptures

- Aaron
- Abraham
- David
- Elijah (Elias)
- Elisha
- Ezekiel
- Jacob
- Jonah
- Moses
- Solomon

Sources: Biblical scriptures, religious texts, encyclopedias, literature, and *Table of Prophets of Abrahamic Religions.*

Table 7 shows the prophets mentioned in the scriptures of all three religions. Other prophets—those mentioned in the scriptures of only one or two of the three religions—include Adam, Amos, Daniel, Enoch, Ezra, Isaac, Isaiah, Jesus, Job, Joel, John, Joseph, Joshua, Malachi, Micah, Micaiah, Muhammad, Nahum, Nathan, Noah, Obadiah, and Samuel.

Judaism uses religious texts other than the Hebrew Bible to define prophets. Moreover, Orthodox rabbis use different criteria to classify someone as a prophet; e.g., Enoch is not considered a prophet.

Judaism and Christianity include female prophets; Islam only refers to male prophets. As a representative of God, each prophet had a role to perform, for example, to warn, direct, encourage, intercede, teach, counsel, and, if necessary, admonish the inhabitants of the community in which they lived. By conveying the message of God to the people, the prophets expected people to respond by fulfilling their religious obligations. Jews, Christians, and Muslims believe that God revealed himself to mankind via the prophets.

According to Judaism, Christianity, and Islam, God chose Moses, Jesus, and Muhammad, respectively, to deliver His revelations to mankind. They in turn memorized and recited those revelations, which were written down in the Torah, Bible, and Qur'an, respectively. The role of the other prophets was to teach mankind about the revelations and scriptures. While Abraham is the father of the Abrahamic faiths, others before him also received revelation from God (e.g., Adam and Noah).

The Covenant of Abraham

There are a number of views on the meaning and principle of the word *covenant* in secular and religious literature. It may derive from the notion of obligation, perception, or bond. It assumes a vow of some kind as well as contractual obligations and conditions. While a covenant can be made as a bond between a man and woman in marriage, for example, the intent of this analysis is to examine God's covenant with the prophets to convey His will to mankind. While God made covenants with various prophets, we will examine His agreement with Abraham.

God communicated His messages to the prophets in actions and words that people could comprehend. These messages underscored the importance of worshipping the one God, just and merciful; the purpose of the universe and Creation; reward and punishment in the hereafter; and a code of ethics to follow. In addition, God also sent His revelations to some prophets via angels (e.g., the archangel Gabriel).

All three Abrahamic faiths affirm that Abraham was a dominant figure in God's revelation to mankind. Jews, Christians, and Muslims believe that God made a covenant with Abraham and other prophets to uphold the belief in the one God and to worship Him. This covenant became the legacy that Abraham's children would continue. Symbolically, Jews, Christians, and Muslims are called the children of Abraham. Promises of the covenant were made not only to Abraham but to his descendants as well. Genesis and the Qur'an affirm the Covenant between God and Abraham:

> On that day the Lord made a Covenant with Abram [Abraham] and said, "To your offspring I give this land, from the river of Egypt to the great river, the Euphrates— the land of the Kenites, Kenizzites, Kadmonites, Hittites, Perizzites, Rephaim, Amorites, Canaanites, Girgashites and Jebusites." (Genesis 15:18–21)

> After these things God tested Abraham and said to him, "Abraham!" And he said, "Here I am." He said, "Take your son, your only son Isaac, whom you love, and go to the land of Moriah, and offer him there as a burnt offering on one of the mountains of which I shall tell you." (Genesis, 22:1–2)

> When they came to the place of which God had told him, Abraham built the altar there and laid the wood in order and bound Isaac his son and laid him on the altar, on top of the wood. Then Abraham reached out his hand and took the knife to slaughter his son. But the angel of the Lord called to him from Heaven and said, "Abraham, Abraham!" And he said, "Here I am." He said, "Do not lay your hand on the boy or do anything to him, for now I know that you fear God, seeing you have not withheld your son, your only son, from me." And Abraham lifted up his eyes and looked, and behold, behind him was a ram, caught in a thicket by his horns. And Abraham went and took the ram and offered it up as a burnt offering instead of his son. (Genesis 22:9–13)

And remember that Abraham was tried by his Lord with certain Commands, which he fulfilled. He said, "I will make thee an Imam to the Nations." He pleaded: "And also [Imams] from my offspring!" He answered: "But My Promise is not within the reach of evil-doers." Remember We made the House a place of assembly for men and a place of safety; and take you the Station of Abraham as a place of prayer; and We Covenanted with Abraham and Ishmael that they should sanctify My House for those who compass it round, or use it as a retreat, or bow, or prostrate themselves [therein in prayer]. (Qur'an 2:124–25)

He said: "I will go to my Lord! He will surely guide me! O my Lord! Grant me a righteous [son]!" So We gave him the good news of a boy ready to suffer and forbear. Then, when [the son] reached [the age of serious] work with him, he said: "O my son! I see in vision that I offer thee in sacrifice: now see what is thy view!" [The son] said: "O my father! Do as thou art commanded: thou will find me, if God so wills, one practicing patience and constancy!" So when they had both submitted their wills [to God], and he had laid him prostrate on his forehead (for sacrifice), We called out to him, "O Abraham! Thou hast already fulfilled the vision!" Thus indeed do We reward those who do right. For this was obviously a trial. And We ransomed him with a momentous sacrifice [ram]: and We left [this blessing] for him among generations [to come] in later times. (Qur'an 37:99–108)

From these passages in Genesis and the Qur'an, we see a similar theme: the story of Abraham and his covenant with God regarding the sacrifice of Abraham's first-born son. While Jews and Christians believe that Isaac was to be sacrificed, Muslims believe that Ishmael was the son to be sacrificed. Genesis 22:1–2 mentions that Abraham is to take "his only son" to the altar. Yet Genesis also mentions that Abraham was eighty-six years old when Ishmael was born (Genesis 16:16) and one hundred years old when Isaac (Genesis 21:5) was born. Thus, all three faiths are in agreement that Ishmael was born before Isaac.

The three religions agree that God revealed himself to Abraham and commanded him to sacrifice his son as a test of faith and obedience. God promised Abraham that his descendants would inherit his legacy and become the fathers of great nations.

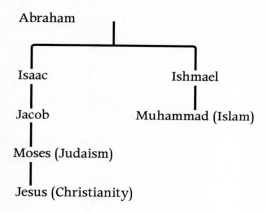

The children of Abraham became a monotheistic family of Jews, Christians, and Muslims who believe in one God, the Creator of the universe and everything in it. Because Abraham's obedience to God was the seed from which these great nations sprung, they have a common linkage and can engage in interfaith dialogue to cement and restore the great heritage he left. God's promises to Abraham concerned not only Abraham but also the nations of the Earth.

Obedience to God is the unifying thread of the three faiths. Witness God testing Abraham by ordering him to sacrifice his son. Abraham set the tone by responding to his Lord, "Here I am" (Genesis 22:1). God then had Abraham sacrifice a ram instead. The meaning of this event is that God does not demand human sacrifice, only the will to obey Him. Jews and Christians adhere to the biblical scriptures by acknowledging their presence to the Lord in prayer. Similarly, Muslims utter this sense of obedience by saying, "... I bow [my will] to the Lord and Cherisher of the Universe" (Qur'an 2:131). Muslims also make a pilgrimage to the

Sacred Mosque in Mecca, the holy shrine founded by Abraham, where they utter the words, "Labaik! Allahuma labaik!" (I am ready to obey your orders, O God!).

Covenant and promise are linked together. Without a covenant, there is no promise. Without a promise, the covenant is not binding. The Abrahamic covenant is a universal one in which God promises to bless Abraham's children and all nations. The covenant was sealed, as God made His promises to Abraham, who was in complete obedience. As a condition of obedience, Abraham was to sacrifice his son. The agreement to sacrifice his son indicates a very high level of obedience, and God rewarded Abraham for his obedience. Simultaneously, God promised to multiply Abraham's descendants and grant them the highest levels of leadership all over the world.

As the prophets, beginning with Adam, received their covenants, they made God's revelations progressively known over the course of history. Judaism originated with the covenant between God and Abraham, which was inherited by Isaac, then by Jacob, and then by the Israelites. The covenant was then reformulated with Moses. Judaism focused on the act of sacrifice at the Temple of Solomon in Jerusalem, but various Israelites strayed from observance of the covenant. As a result, God sent the prophets, who reaffirmed the Mosaic Covenant, but neither added to nor modified it. This state of affairs continued until a new covenant was formed with Jesus, from which Christianity emerged (Dirks 2007). Six centuries later, Muhammad, as God's messenger, conveyed to mankind the faith of Islam and the Qur'an.

Essentially, God made a covenant—not just with the prophets but with all mankind—to practice fundamental ethical laws. We are separate and distinct; each of us has his or her own religious preference. If we uphold God's laws and honor His covenant, as Abraham did, then the end result will be unity. We will understand the oneness that unites every human being on Earth.

The Ten Commandments

A commandment is a doctrine that is taught. It is also a direct order or injunction as well as an authority or control over someone. In a religious context, commandments can be positive or negative. "Thou shall" is a positive commandment, an order to do something. "Thou shall not" is a negative commandment, a prohibition from doing something.

The Ten Commandments—inscribed on tablets given to Moses by God—are a set of religious rules for how mankind should behave. They are an example of commandments that tell us what we should not do (i.e., "thou shall not ..."). According to Exodus (32:19) of the Torah, when Moses descended from Mount Sinai, he saw the golden calf his people had created. Shocked with anger at the false idol of worship, Moses smashed the original tablets, so God gave him a second set of Ten Commandments. According to the Qur'an (7:154), the tablets were not smashed but picked up later. Jews and Christians adhere to the Torah scriptures of the books of Deuteronomy and Exodus, while Muslims follow the Qur'an. Table 8 shows a comparative analysis of the Ten Commandments, as revealed in the book of Deuteronomy and the Qur'an.

Table 8
Comparative Analysis of the Ten Commandments
Deuteronomy versus the Qur'an

Deuteronomy	*Qur'an*
1. "You shall have no other Gods before Me." (5:7)	"Take not with God another object of worship ..." (17:22)
2. "You shall not make yourself an image in the form of anything in Heaven or above or on the Earth beneath or in the waters below." (5:8)	"No vision can grasp Him, but His grasp is over all vision ..." (6:103)
3. "You shall not misuse the name of the Lord ..." (5:11)	"And make not God's name an excuse in your oaths against doing good, or acting rightly, or making peace between persons ..." (2:224)

4. "Observe the Sabbath day by keeping it holy ..." (5:12)

"... We commanded them: 'Transgress not in the matter of the Sabbath.' And we took from them a solemn Covenant." (4:154)

5. "Honor your father and your mother ..." (5:16)

"... And that you be kind to parents ..." (17:23)

6. "You shall not murder." (5:17)

"Nor take life which God has made sacred, except for just cause ..." (17:33)

7. "Thou shall not commit adultery." (5:18)

"Nor come nigh to adultery: for it is a shameful deed and an evil, opening the road to other evils." (17:32)

8. "Thou shall not steal." (5:19)

"As for the man who steals and the woman who steals, cut you off their right hands; as a recompense for what they two have earned; as an exemplary punishment from God ..." (5:38)

9. "Thou shall not give false testimony ..." (5:20)

"Those who witness no falsehood, and, if they pass by futility, they pass by it with honorable (avoidance)." (25:72)

10. "You shall not covet your neighbor's wife." (5:21)

"And in no wise covet those things in which God hath bestowed His gifts more freely on some of you than on others ..." (4:32)

Based on the above comparison, we can see that there is a great deal of similarity between both scriptures. What is important is that the Ten Commandments revealed to Moses are the cornerstones of morality in Judaism, Christianity, and Islam. The three faiths agree that the Ten

Commandments were inscribed on tablets by God, given to Moses, and do not change based on time or place. They are a set of rules that define duties toward God and to each other with the highest level of ethical standards. Their focus is to encourage people to develop outward actions to improve their inner selves.

Unfortunately, in today's society, there appears to be a rejection or negligence of the commandments. Many people cannot recite them from memory, comprehend their true meaning, or even live according to their rules. True, these commandments were revealed in ancient times when societal conditions were different from today. Nonetheless, their relevance has not diminished but is vital to our moral integrity, to our ability to discern between right and wrong. Ours is a very troubled society, suffering from a disintegration of moral standards that has led to social problems such as suicide, murder, violence, crime, adultery, and sexual disorientation. In America, we have laws that maintain order and address a myriad of social problems. Likewise, the Ten Commandments maintain ethics and morality. The reality is that both are needed.

The challenge for the adherents of the Abrahamic faiths is to be able to address today's social problems while at the same time uphold the ethical standards God etched into the stone tablets. Cases in point are the issues of homosexuality and euthanasia, which are considered sins in the scriptures of Judaism, Christianity, and Islam. Yet, laws of our American society allow homosexuality and assisted suicide to be practiced. Assisted suicide is currently legal in the states of Oregon and Washington. While there is separation between church and state in the United States, we cannot just entomb the Ten Commandments because they are no longer practical or suitable for contemporary life.

We can bridge the gap by encouraging theologians to meet with senators and congressmen to discuss these types of issues, while observing the separation of church and state. However, much advance groundwork will be needed. Interfaith dialogue must take place in an atmosphere of trust and cooperation. We have shown the similarities among the Ten Commandments in Judaism, Christianity, and Islam. Each religious cleric must be committed to lay aside his prejudices if we are to achieve unity. Reliance is the start of the journey, and commitment is its result. Prepare for the dialogue by thinking ahead about group dynamics and the direction in which the discussions might go. Establish an atmosphere of trust and relaxation by focusing on differences of ideas rather than on personalities. Institute clear guidelines for discussion by encouraging openness and respect for honest opinions.

Bridging this gap will be difficult but necessary. Enacting changes or amendments in our legal process to retain the doctrines of the Ten Commandments is an obstacle that we must overcome. For example, how do we communicate the necessity of including the Ten Commandments when some of the commandments are outmoded in modern America? The first commandment prohibits the worship of any deity other than God. The second commandment prohibits the use of religious statues. These two commandments are in direct conflict with the First Amendment of the US Constitution, which guarantees freedom of religious belief.

Other commandments are not in direct opposition to the US Constitution. For example, the sixth commandment forbids murder, and the ninth commandment and our court system are in agreement on perjury. It is one thing to know the Ten Commandments and another to always have them in our minds and hearts. We must remember them and make them part of our daily lives. We should strive for a moral way of life with the highest level of ethical standards. The Ten Commandments have shown us the way. Now we must truly follow the rules that God has ordained for us.

The Patience of Job

Patience is a virtue, a quality of doing what is right and avoiding what is wrong. Patience is associated with confidence, tolerance, tranquility, and restraint. Impatience is associated with fear, intolerance, apprehension, and failure. While the general notion of patience is waiting calmly for something to happen, a deeper meaning suggests that one is proactive rather than passive. Spiritually, patience is a remedy for the self-centered ego. It is interwoven into the fabric of Judaism, Christianity, and Islam. The most popular example of patience in the scriptures is the story of Job. A devout man, Job suffered greatly despite his good deeds. Yet he patiently endured this suffering and anguish by holding steadfast to his faith. He remained resolute as he overcame adversity while good triumphed over evil:

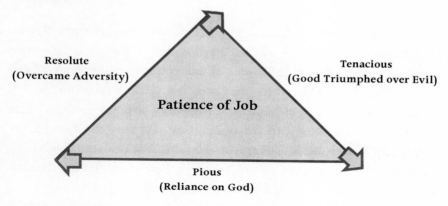

The story of Job is recounted in the scriptures of the three Abrahamic religions with remarkable similarity. Satan had challenged God that he could take his most devout servant and turn him from good to evil. God allowed Satan to test Job's faith and virtuousness:

> "Does Job fear God for nothing?" Satan replied. "Have you not put a hedge around him and his household and everything he has? You have blessed the work of his hands, so that his flocks and herds are spread throughout the land. But now stretch out your hand and strike everything he has, and he will surely curse you to your face." The Lord said to Satan, "Very well, then, everything he has in your power, but on the man himself do not lay a finger." (Job 1:9–12)

> O you who believe! Seek help with patient perseverance and prayer: for God is with those who patiently persevere ... Be sure We shall test you with something of fear and hunger, some loss in goods or lives or the fruits [of your toil], but give glad tidings to those who patiently persevere, who say, when afflicted with calamity: "To God we belong, and to Him is our return." They are those on whom [descend] blessings from God,

and Mercy, and they are the ones that receive guidance.
(Qur'an 2:153–57)

Job was a prosperous man who fell victim to misfortune. But he held steadfast to his faith in God, irrespective of Satan's interference and continuous adverse inflictions of calamities that devastated him. After losing his children, his servants, his cattle and property, his false friends, his peace of mind, and becoming afflicted with physical maladies, Job humbled himself before God. He was constant in his prayer. Never once did Job falter from his faith. More calamities hit him. He acquired a severe skin disease, perhaps leprosy or another form of lupus. Still he did not utter a word of complaint.

Adversity did not break Job's spirit. He humbled himself in prayer and asked God to restore him back to health. God did so, and also granted Job wealth and many children. God recalled to Job His mercy and restored him with twice as much as he had before. Job had fought off evil with the best of weapons: humility, patience, and faith:

> After Job had prayed for his friends, the Lord restored his fortunes and gave him twice as much as he had before ... The Lord blessed the latter part of Job's life more than the former part. He had fourteen thousand sheep, six thousand camels, a thousand yoke of oxen and a thousand donkeys. And he also had seven sons and three daughters ... (Job 42:10–13)

> And [remember] Job, when he cried to his Lord, "Truly distress has seized me, but Thou art the Most Merciful of those that are merciful." So We listened to him. We removed the distress that was on him, and We restored his people to him, and doubled their number—as a Grace from Ourselves, and a thing for commemoration, for all who serve Us. (Qur'an 21:83–84)

Islam maintains that Job refused to complain, rebel in deed, in word, or even in thought. Traditionally, all three faiths regard Job as an example of patience and forbearance, a representation of the pious virtue. All three faiths hold to the premise that Job is a paradigm of perfect charity, hospitality, and generosity and stands as a model beneficiary of Divine grace and recompense.

Pious, resolute, and tenacious—Job is an example for all people, teaching us how to address adversity, intellectually as well as morally. His story depicts man at the extreme limits of endurance and shows that there is no excuse for the neglect of God's worship. For no one will ever be more sorely afflicted than Job was.

The Psalms of David

Psalms are sacred songs or hymns, poetical compositions that praise or worship God. Psalms help the pious meditate and reflect on the inner self. Various authors compiled the Psalms, an anthology of collections, over the course of history, the most famous of whom was David.

David was a prophet, a king, and a great warrior, who defeated the giant Goliath in a legendary battle as a youth. Judaism and Christianity hold to the belief that David committed adultery, while Islam refutes this notion, stating that as a prophet he could not have committed this sin. God revealed the Psalms to David, and this is part of Jewish, Christian, and Muslim theology.

The book of Psalms is a collection of 150 hymnal pieces divided into five books, which are the chief hymns of Jews and Christians. The hymns are of varying date and authorship, but many are ascribed to David, and some to Asaph, Solomon, Moses, and the sons of Korah. Many scholars believe that some of the Psalms originated in David's time and some even earlier. Most of them, however, took their present form between circa 538 BCE and circa 100 BCE. The hymns or poems vary significantly in tone and subject. Many Psalms can be classified into major literary types: (a) laments, (b) declarations of praise, and (c) liturgical rituals. Leading us through valleys and peaks of human experiences, the Psalms express the passions of humanity—cries, praises, joys, or confessions.

Muslims believe that the book of Psalms (Zabur) was revealed to David and is one of God's holy books. The Qur'an mentions the Psalms three times:

> We have sent thee [Muhammad] inspiration, as we
> sent it to Noah and the Messengers after him. We sent
> inspiration to Abraham, Ishmael, Isaac, Jacob, and the
> Tribes, to Jesus, Job, Jonah, Aaron, and Solomon, and
> to David We gave the Psalms. (Qur'an 4:163)

Clearly, God revealed the inspiration to David, as he did to other prophets before him. In Islam, the Psalms are one of the four holy books; the others are the Torah, Gospel, and Qur'an. Another Qur'anic verse mentions God giving David the Psalms as a gift:

> And it is your Lord that knoweth best all beings that are
> in the Heavens and on Earth: We did bestow on some
> Prophets more [and other] gifts than on others: and We
> gave to David [the gift of] the Psalms. (Qur'an 17:55)

The third passage in the Qur'an that mentions the Psalms is, "Before this We wrote in the Psalms, after the Message [given to Moses]: My servants, the righteous shall inherit the Earth" (Qur'an 21:105).

While the Qur'an gives no specific reference to the Psalms mentioned in this verse, there is no question that it corresponds to the language found in the Old Testament: "The righteous shall inherit the land, and dwell therein forever" (Psalms 37:29).

What we learn from the Psalms of the three Abrahamic faiths is that they are a guide to our spiritual life as well as an inspiration to better understand the theological importance of our working together for a better and safer world.

The Great Flood

Judaism, Christianity, and Islam all believe that the Great Flood took place. During the time of Noah, society became infested with wickedness that angered God. Grieved that His Creation had gone astray, God unleashed a Great Flood on mankind. He gave Noah, a righteous man, detailed instructions for building an ark. Those who had faith in God found refuge on the ark, while those who were wicked or who had lost faith did not. People and animals embarked on the ark, and the flood arrived thereafter. Noah set sail, and the flood rose until all the mountains were covered and life, except for those on board the ark, was destroyed. As the water subsided and dry land reappeared, the ark rested on a mountain. When it was determined that the water had indeed subsided and land was visible, Noah and all those on the ark disembarked and began a new life.

Table 9 compares dates and criteria for the Great Flood, as disclosed in Genesis and the Qur'an.

Table 9
The Great Flood
Comparison between Genesis and Qur'an

Criteria	Genesis	Qur'an
Biblical passages	Chapters 6–9	Various verses
Date	ca. 1000–500 BCE	ca. 600 CE
Destroyer	YHWH (God)	Allah (God)
Savior	YHWH (God)	Allah (God)
Hero	Noah	Noah
Warning	Direct order	Direct order
Reason	Sin	Sin
Cause	Rain, fountains	Rain, springs
Destruction	Worldwide	Localized
Size of ark	Dimensions	Not mentioned
Ark sealant	Tree resin	Palm fiber
Animals	Pairs of male and female	Pairs of male and female
Total duration	370 days	Not mentioned
Duration of rain	40 days/nights	Not mentioned
Time afloat	150 days	Not mentioned
Destination	Ararat	Judi

The above comparison shows that the major criteria (e.g., warning, reason, cause, and animals) are the same in Genesis and the Qur'an. However, the Qur'an differs from Genesis in some key criteria, including the dimensions and the location of the flood. Another difference is the name of the mountain where the ark landed. According to Genesis 8:4, it landed on Mount Ararat, while Qur'an 11:44 states that it landed on Mount Judi. Some literary sources indicate that Mount Judi has been mistaken for Mount Ararat and vice versa, while geographical sources state that Mount Judi is two hundred miles south of Mount Ararat in southern Turkey (Weaver 2006).

Often interpreting passages from biblical literature can be very difficult and may lead to different views about what is fact and what is fiction. Nonetheless, it is vital to remember that the flood was real and that Judaism, Christianity, and Islam all hold that a valuable lesson was learned from this event. The story of the flood recounts God's purpose for mankind through the moral and spiritual lessons that were taught and experienced. For Noah and his followers, the waters of the flood were symbolic of a purification process that cleansed the soul. Only with patient perseverance can mankind hope to attain salvation.

The Repentance of Jonah

Repentance is an action one takes for moral shortcomings or misdeeds. It implies that one feels a sense of remorse for sins committed in the past and now has the desire to change for the better. The one who repents seeks God's mercy. Jonah was a prophet who repented and received God's mercy.

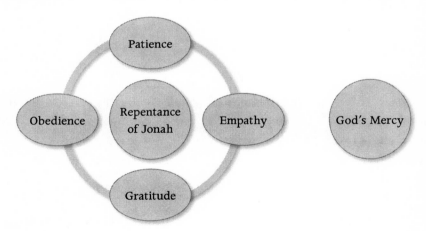

As we shall see, God's mercy was not that easy to come by. Jonah had to learn the hard way that there are prerequisites to achieving God's mercy. Obedience to God is mandated, and there must be no compromise of a person's—particularly a prophet's—commitment to follow God's orders. Exercising empathy, even to those one dislikes intensely, is an attribute that reaches the highest level of moral excellence. Patience and gratitude complement each other. Jonah realized that the performance of a good deed required a patience that emanated from the thanks and gratitude he extended to God. As the attributes of obedience, empathy, patience, and gratitude restored Jonah's dignity and self-respect, God accepted his repentance.

According to biblical passages in Judeo-Christian and Islamic theology, God demanded that Jonah teach the inhabitants of Nineveh, the capital of Assyria, how to repent from their wickedness and worship God. God wanted to tell the Ninevites that if they did not repent, they would suffer the consequences. Assyria was a powerful and evil nation that was disliked by Jonah because of its atrocities against his people. Jonah would have preferred that God punish these idolaters, including those living in Nineveh. Nonetheless, he eventually obeyed God and delivered God's message to the people of Nineveh, who repented.

The timing of this repentance differs in Islamic theology and Judeo-Christian theology. Muslims believe that Jonah carried out God's order immediately, but the inhabitants of Nineveh ignored him and were not afraid of his threats. Feeling dejected, Jonah left, not knowing that the Ninevites would soon repent. God struck fear in them by changing the skies to the color of fire. Filled with fear, they repented and asked God for his mercy and forgiveness. God granted them His blessings.

Jews and Christians, however, believe that Jonah did not go to Nineveh immediately to deliver God's message of repentance. Rather, he took off for Spain, because he felt that if the people repented, God would spare them. And Jonah did not want these people to be spared. He detested them.

Muslims agree that Jonah boarded a ship headed for Spain. At sea, a vicious storm took place, and the sailors were terrified. The sailors, including Jonah, cast lots, and the lot fell on Jonah. When he confessed that he'd incurred the wrath of God, the sailors threw him overboard. But he did not sink; a whale or big fish swallowed him, an act of God's mercy saved his life. Jonah sat in the whale's body for three days and nights. Realizing that God had saved him, he didn't complain; rather he repented and prayed. God then had the whale eject Jonah onto a remote island.

Jews and Christians believe that God then ordered Jonah to go to Nineveh and fulfill his mission. Jonah did so, and the Ninevites repented and were spared. However, Jonah was angry because he would have preferred the Ninevites to suffer.

Jonah's mission, his incarceration by the whale, and the outcome of his dilemma are the same in each of the three Abrahamic religions. The importance of obedience, empathy, patience, and gratitude are lessons Jonah learns in his efforts to seek God's mercy. These are also lessons we must follow, as we learn to cope with and understand one another for the betterment of humanity.

The Wisdom of Solomon

Wisdom is the mental enlightenment that transcends knowledge and is goal oriented with a desired end. It is the integration of organized knowledge, but it is more than the accumulation of information. The connection between wisdom and knowledge is the value-added understanding of how applied knowledge fits into the big picture. Understanding is the ability to evaluate that knowledge in order to reach the high levels of wisdom.

Self-Actualization

Wisdom

Applied Knowledge

Organized Knowledge

Solomon had the innate ability and God-inspired power to self-actualize in wisdom. He was able to synthesize, integrate, and interpret God's revelations and life's situations, all of which molded his mind and personality, allowing him to attain the highest level of wisdom. His wisdom enabled him to recognize the difference between good and evil.

Solomon, son of King David, was the builder of the first temple in Jerusalem. He had sound judgment and the competence to administer the affairs of people in a just manner. He became King Solomon when he took over for his father. At that time, he led the children of Israel into a golden age. From an early age, Solomon had wise qualities, and he earned the respect of his father and the community.

Jews, Christians, and Muslims agree that God granted Solomon the power of wisdom:

> At Gibeon the Lord appeared to Solomon during the night in a dream, and God said, "Ask for whatever you want me to give you." (1 Kings 3:5)

> So give your servant a discerning heart to govern your people and to distinguish between right and wrong. For who is able to govern this great people of yours? (1 Kings 3:9)

> So God said to him, "Since you have asked for this and not for long life or wealth for yourself, nor have asked for the death of your enemies but for discernment in administering justice, I will do what you have asked. I will give you a wise and discerning heart, so that there will never have been anyone like you, nor will there ever be. Moreover, I will give you what you have not asked for—both wealth and honor—so that in your lifetime you will have no equal among kings." (1 Kings 3:11–14)

> He described plant life, from the cedar of Lebanon to the hyssop that grows out of walls. He also taught about animals and birds, reptiles and fish. (1 Kings 4:33)

> He said, "O my Lord! Forgive me, and grant me a Kingdom which [it may be], suits not another after me: for Thou art the Grantor of Bounties [without measure]." Then We subjected the wind to his power, to flow gently to his order, withersoever he willed—as also the evil ones,

(including) every kind of builder and diver—as also others bound together in fetters. "Such are Our Bounties: whether thou bestow them (on others) or withhold them, no account will be asked." (Qur'an 38:35–39)

To Solomon We inspired the [right] understanding of the matter: to each [of them] We gave wisdom and knowledge; it was Our power that made the hills and the birds celebrate Our praises, with David: it was We Who did [all these things]. (Qur'an 21:79)

It was Our power that made the violent unruly wind flow tamely for Solomon, to his order, to the land which We had blessed: for We do know all things. (Qur'an 21:81)

And to Solomon We made the wind obedient: its early morning stride was a month's journey, and its evening stride was a month's journey ... (Qur'an 34:12)

And Solomon was David's heir. He said: "O you people! We have been taught the speech of birds, and on us has been bestowed (a little) of all things: this is indeed Grace manifest from God." (Qur'an 27:16)

This comparison of biblical passages clearly shows the remarkable similarities regarding the wisdom of Solomon among the three faiths. The Qur'an also states that Solomon communicated with ants (Qur'an 27:18–31). Ants are mentioned in the Bible, which states, "The ants are a people not strong, yet they prepare their meat in the summer" (Proverbs 30:25, KJV).

Solomon was wise and noble, as he ruled with wisdom and justice. Acknowledging that all his power, wisdom, knowledge, and strength came from God alone, he spent his life pleasing God. While Solomon has been criticized in Judeo-Christian history because of his excesses, Islam rejects the notion that Solomon disobeyed the laws of God or that he worshipped idols. Islam believes he embraced wisdom with humility and the greatest sense of piety.

Wisdom is knowledge embodied within us. The challenge for the followers of the three Abrahamic faiths is to cultivate that wisdom by recognizing and embracing each other's intelligence, as we try to achieve a mutual balance of cooperation, harmony, and respect. The aim of interfaith dialogue is to reveal the wisdom within each participant. Wisdom is the vehicle that unleashes the innate empathy that allows the individual to understand the faiths of others. It allows one to have a deeper understanding of one's own faith, which leads to greater mutual respect.

By seeking common principles within each of the Judaic, Christian, and Islamic scriptures, we must organize, apply, and integrate the requisite knowledge that strives for peace, tranquility, and safety. The example of Solomon's wisdom can be the driving force behind an effort that embraces diversity and culminates in reaching self-actualization. As Solomon sought wisdom for the right reasons, so can we. Unity is the door, and wisdom is its key. Wisdom with knowledge molds a person into becoming more aware of the common principles and practices of his faith.

Summary

Prophets are intermediaries who deliver God's revelations and commandments to mankind. Abraham is considered the father of the prophets and a pivotal figure in the shared history of the three faith traditions. Still, Judaism, Christianity, and Islam may each interpret specific historical events differently. Moses is a prophet of Judaism; Jesus is the holy savior of Christianity; and Muhammad is the prophet of Islam.

The consensus among the three faith traditions is that each stresses adherence and obedience to God's revelations and commandments. Moses, Jesus, and Muhammad established a proper relationship with God and with their communities of followers. There are far more similarities than differences among the three religions. For example, they share common values and common obligations as stewards to their fellow man.

While Judaism, Christianity, and Islam all recognize Jesus, his importance varies greatly in each religion. Islam considers Jesus to be a prophet, but does not believe that he died for our sins. Judaism does not believe Jesus played any important role. Only Christianity and Islam affirm the second coming of Jesus and his ascension into Heaven.

Nonetheless, each of the Abrahamic faiths has similar practices of prayer, fasting, charity, and pilgrimage.

Principles and Practices

Prayer

The common thread that permeates through all three Abrahamic faiths is prayer. Some of the common practices in prayer are shown in table 10.

Table 10
Prayer Practices in Judaism, Christianity, and Islam

Prayer Practice	Judaism	Christianity	Islam
Ablution	Exodus 40:31–32	Acts 21:26	Qur'an 5:6
Remove shoes	Exodus 3:5	Acts 7:33	Qur'an 20:12
Prostration	Genesis 17:3 Numbers 20:6 Joshua 5:14	Matthew 26:39	Qur'an 3:43 Qur'an 22:77
Main day of worship	Saturday	Sunday	Friday

Ablution, the washing and cleansing of certain parts of the body, is a ritual purification that removes any uncleanliness. It prepares us mentally for prayer. It allows us to cool the nerves in our bodies so we can concentrate when we humble ourselves before God. When a person faints, water is sprinkled on his face and other parts of the body to awaken him. The same is true of ablution. Applying water to parts of our bodies awakens us, enabling our thoughts to be in harmony with our prayers.

Removing one's shoes is an act of respect, as one humbles oneself before God. Moses was ordered to remove his shoes before he entered hallowed ground. Likewise, we remove our shoes prior to entering a room that is holy and consecrated.

Prostration heightens our awareness, love, and remembrance of God, as we bow and kneel to Him in submission, obedience, humility, adoration, and honor. When we bow or lie down, we humble ourselves before God. It shows our appreciation, respect, and gratitude to Him. Prostration in prayer follows the traditions established by the prophets.

One day each week is set aside for collective prayer. For Jews, it is Saturday; for Christians, Sunday; and for Muslims, Friday. Getting together once a week fosters unity, cooperation, and cohesiveness as well as a demonstration of equality. In a congregation, worshippers have the opportunity to listen to a sermon together and reflect on how they can identify with its message.

Each faith has similar themes in prayer: adoration, submission, and supplication. Let us examine each of these themes in the Jewish Kaddish Prayer, the Christian Lord's Prayer, and the Muslim al-Fatiha (Opening) Prayer.

Table 11
Prayer Themes in the Kaddish Prayer, Lord's Prayer, and al-Fatiha Prayer

Prayer	Adoration	Submission	Supplication
Kaddish Prayer (Judaism)	Exalted and Sanctified	According to His will	Grant peace upon us
Lord's Prayer (Christianity)	Hallowed be Thy name	Thy will be done	Lead us not into temptation
al-Fatiha Prayer (Islam)	Beneficent and Merciful	Thee do we worship	Show us the straight way

The Kaddish Prayer, Lord's Prayer, and al-Fatiha Prayer are universal prayers. Each of them emphasizes adoration, submission, and supplication.

There are a number of Jewish prayers. In a dream, Jacob envisioned a "ladder" that connected the Earth with Heaven (Genesis 28:12). Each upward step of prayer in the ladder represented a greater inspiration, a time of self-judgment and self-evaluation, until one wanted nothing but the feeling of attachment with God. The Kaddish Prayer resembles Christian and Muslim prayers on the themes of adoration, submission, and supplication. Another Jewish prayer is David's Psalm 23, "The Lord Is My Shepherd." It is also a Christian prayer. It emphasizes morality, happiness, humility, calm, comfort, hope, blessing, and forgiveness. The general themes of Psalm 23 are that God supplies His followers' needs as He leads and guides them. It also implies a celebration for its adherents—a great feast and a glimpse into eternity. One of the four books of Islam is the Psalms of David, unchanged and as it was revealed in its original form.

Prayer is voluntary for Christians and mandatory for Muslims, who must pray facing Mecca at specific times of the day. This does not mean that Christians should avoid prayer. Although the Bible does not list a set time for, direction of, or amount of prayer, it does state that Christians should pray regularly. Christian prayers are often for relief or forgiveness, or to praise the Lord.

Muslims pray five times daily, and their prayers differ from Christian prayers in style and intention. Muslims use the whole body when praying (i.e., they stand, they prostrate themselves, they sit up). They repeat these motions while reciting Qur'anic verses and supplications.

Prayer, as the cornerstone of one's faith, often is aligned with fasting, another religious doctrine practiced by the three traditions.

Fasting

Table 12 lists notable Jews, Christians, and Muslims who fasted for a continuous period of three days or more.

Table 12
Historical Figures Who Fasted in
Judaism, Christianity, and Islam

Reference	Person Fasting	Duration of Fast
Judaism:		
Deuteronomy 9:9; 9:18; 10:10; Exodus 24:18; 34:28	Moses	40 days
1 Kings 19:8	Elijah	40 days
Daniel 10:2–3	Daniel	3 weeks
1 Chronicles 10:12; 1 Samuel 31:13	Men of Jabesh	7 days
2 Samuel 12:16–20	David	7 days
Esther 4:16	Esther	3 days
Nehemiah 1:4	Nehemiah	Unspecified
Christianity:		
Luke 4:2; Matthew 4:2	Jesus	40 days
Acts 27:33	Paul's crew	14 days
Acts 9:9	Saul	3 days
Islam:		
Qur'an 2:183–85	All Muslims	Month of Ramadan

The principle of self-denial is common among the three faiths. Self-restraint is the manifestation of piety. During the period of fasting, there is a control of one's natural desires as well as an abstention of carnal desires. Fasting is a time of reflection and meditation. It is when one guards against one's temptations and frailties of character. It is a time to cement one's metaphysical relationship with God. During the fasting period, it is highly recommended to pray, irrespective of one's religion. While prayer during the fasting period is voluntary in Judaism and Christianity, there were times in the course of history that prayer was always connected to fasting.

The Old Testament law specifically required prayer and fasting for only one occasion—the Day of Atonement. This custom became known as "the day of fasting" (Jeremiah 36:6) or "the Fast" (Acts 27:9). Moses fasted during the forty days and forty nights he was on Mount Sinai receiving the Law from God (Exodus 34:28). Prayer and fasting were often done in times of distress or trouble. David fasted when he learned that Saul and Jonathan had been killed (2 Samuel 1:12). Nehemiah prayed and fasted when he learned that Jerusalem was still in ruins (Nehemiah 1:4).

Prayer and fasting are also described in the New Testament. Jesus fasted for forty days and forty nights before he was tempted by Satan (Matthew 4:2). Paul and Barnabas spent time in prayer and fasting before appointing the elders in the churches (Acts 14:23).

Daily prayer is required in Islam, and the month of Ramadan is no exception. In Islam, prayer is not voluntary, but mandatory. Fasting during Ramadan typically includes an increased offering of prayers and greater recitation of the Qur'an.

While all three faiths require fasting, the period of fasting varies. There are a few regular, fixed fast days in Judaism. The Talmud lists two mandatory fasts and five voluntary fasts. The two mandatory fasts are the Day of Atonement (Yom Kippur, tenth of Tishri) and Tishah B'Av (ninth of Av). The five voluntary traditional fasts are: Ta'anit Bechorim (fourteenth of Nissan), Tzom Tammuz (seventeenth of Tammuz), Tzom Gedaliah (third of Tishri), Asarah B'Tevet (tenth of Tevet), and Ta'anit Esther (thirteenth of Adar) (Parsons, n.d.).

An additional twenty-five nonobligatory fasts are observed on different dates; there are also private fasts. All Jewish fasts begin at sunrise and end with the appearance of the first stars of the evening, except those of the Day of Atonement and the Tishah B'av, which last from nightfall to nightfall. The Day of Atonement and Tishah B'Av fasts last twenty-four hours, during which no food or water is taken. Reform Jews do not observe Tishah B'Av as a mandatory fast (*Jewish Encyclopedia* 1906).

There are four fasting seasons in Christianity: Lent (forty days) and Holy Week (seven days), Nativity (forty days), Apostles' Fast (variable length), and Dormition Fast (two weeks) (Dictionary.com). The forty-day Lenten fast is observed by the Roman Catholic Church and the Eastern Orthodox Church. Roman Catholics fast and abstain from meat on Ash Wednesday and Good Friday, and they abstain from meat on all Fridays during Lent. Eastern Orthodox Catholics observe Lent, the Apostles' Fast, the Dormition Fast, the Nativity Fast, and several one-day fasts. Every Wednesday and Friday is considered a fast day, except those that fall during designated "fast-free weeks."

While fasting is not a major part of the mainstream Protestant tradition, it can be done at the discretion of communities, churches, other groups, and individuals. There are no specific times in the day for beginning and ending a fast. It is up to the person fasting to set the time. The fast is not a complete abstention from food and drink. Moreover, one can decide how much to fast—one meal, one day, one week, several weeks, forty days, etc.

While fasting during the month of Ramadan is considered obligatory, Islam also prescribes certain days for nonobligatory, voluntary fasting, such as: (a) the thirteenth, fourteenth, and fifteenth of every lunar month; (b) each Monday and Thursday; (c) six days in Shawwal (the month following Ramadan); (d) the day of Arafat (ninth of Dhu al-Hijjah); (e) first ten days of Dhu al-Hijjah; and (f) as often as possible in the months of Rajab and Sha'ban before Ramadan. Each day of fasting starts at dawn, defined as the moment when the human eye can distinguish a white thread from a black one, and ends at dusk, when the eye is no longer able to distinguish the difference.

Sunnis fast on the tenth day of Ashura in commemoration of the victory God gave to Moses as well as the day of victory for Islam and its resurgence resulting from the martyrdom of Imam Hussein, the grandson of Prophet Muhammad.

Table 13 is a summary of current fasting practices among Jews, Christians, and Muslims.

Table 13
Current Fasting Practices in Judaism, Christianity, and Islam

Religion	Mandatory Fast	Duration of Fast
Judaism	Yom Kippur	1 day
	Tishah B'Av*	1 day
Christianity	Day of Atonement	1 day
	Lent (partial fast)**	40 days
Islam	Ramadan	1 month

*Reform Jews do not recognize it as a mandatory fast day.
**Observed by the Catholic Church and the Eastern Orthodox Church.

Sources: Scriptures from Judaism, Christianity, and Islam; literature.

Fasting stimulates concentration, which can help people discover the similarities among the three religious traditions. The combination of fasting and prayer removes hindrances to peace and opens a window of opportunity to engage in fruitful discussions and relationships with others. While each fast may be different in duration and practice, what is the same is the result: self-awareness.

Fasting serves a dual purpose. It stimulates the mind and brings about a state of consciousness that draws us nearer to the Divine. We become more aware of ourselves as we experience self-restraint, reflection, meditation, and the remembrance of God. The peak of awareness is when one attains self-actualization in his faith. A test of that self-actualization is the empathy we share with each other.

When we fast, our senses are heightened to the needs of others. As we reflect and empathize on those in need, we become proactive by extending a helping hand.

Charity

The concept of charity (giving alms) is common to Judaism, Christianity, and Islam. The charitable amounts may vary, but they typically are given to a religious institution or project, orphans, those in dire need, or some other charitable endeavor.

Table 14
Charitable Requirements in Judaism, Christianity, and Islam

Religion	Charitable Requirement	Charitable Amount	Payment Method
Judaism	Tithe	10.0%	After-tax earnings
Christianity	Tithe	10.0%	Pretax income
Islam	Zakat	2.5%	Total wealth
	Khums (Shi'as)	20.0%	Net profit on earnings

Sources: Literature and religious texts.

In Judaism, charity follows the concept of *ma'aser* (tithe). A tithe is one-tenth of something (money, property, etc.) paid to support a charitable, usually religious, cause. Jews are required to set aside 10 percent of their wages after taxes for *tzedakah* (charity). Business expenses and educational costs may be deducted from the 10 percent. Based on Leviticus 25:35 of the Old Testament, Jews are to help and provide for the poor and the needy. The suggested range of charitable contributions is 10 percent to 20 percent (Domb 1982).

In Christianity, tithes—10 percent of one's pretax income—are paid to the church for church expenses, community-outreach programs, and foreign missions (Burg 2003). It is an Old Testament concept, which required multiple tithes that would have pushed the total to around 23.3 percent, not the 10 percent that is generally accepted today. However, the New Testament does not designate a percentage of income; rather, it states that a person "... should set aside a sum of money in keeping with your income" (1 Corinthians 16:2; Burkett 1998).

In Islam, there are two forms of obligatory charitable payments: *Zakat* and *Khums*. *Zakat* is a compulsory act. Every Muslim has to pay *Zakat* (i.e., 2.5 percent of his or her total accumulated wealth beyond one's personal needs). It is paid annually. It serves as the welfare contribution to poor and deprived Muslims. It is payable in three kinds of assets: wealth, production, and animals. *Zakat* is one of the five pillars of Islam. Sunnis adhere to the *Zakat* principle.

Khums requires an obligatory charitable payment of 20 percent of the net profit of one's annual earnings or surplus of the past year's income. Generally, *Khums* is given to the poor and needy, orphans, and pilgrims. Shi'as adhere to the principle of *Khums* and *Zakat*. Although the composition of payment differs, *Khums* and *Zakat* generally serve the same purpose. They both assist the poor and needy. *Zakat* is obligatory for every Muslim. Part of the *Khums* is also given to descendants of Prophet Muhammad who are in need.

All Muslims are also encouraged to participate in voluntary charity (*sadaqah*). Charitable deeds are of value when they are done without any self-serving motives. Voluntary charity does not have to be monetary. It can be a kind gesture, word, smile, or warm embrace. To judge a dispute between two people fairly is a form of voluntary charity. Helping an elderly person who has trouble walking is yet another example.

Several verses in the Qur'an justify the charitable tax:

> ... They ask you how much they are to spend [in the way of charity]. Say, "What is beyond your needs ..." (Qur'an 2:219)

> Who believe in the Unseen, are steadfast in prayer, and spend out of what We have provided for them. (Qur'an 2:3)

> Those who spend [freely], whether in prosperity, or in adversity; who restrain anger, and pardon [all] men— for God loves those who do good. (Qur'an 3:134)

> And know that out of all the booty that you may acquire, a fifth share is assigned to God—and to the

> Messenger, and to near relatives, orphans, the needy,
> and the wayfarer ... (Qur'an 8:41)

As noted, all three religions adhere to the concept of charitable tax or payment. Charity is akin to justice, in that the Creator mandates that the poor and needy are cared for. Whether it is a tithe, *Zakat*, or *Khums*, justice is served via charity. The essence of giving rekindles the spirit of mankind in the direction of good deeds. Charity, or almsgiving, is universal. Followers of the three religions meeting and engaging in a dialogue of respect and tolerance is an example of voluntary charity, perhaps the panacea in the quest for unity.

Prayer, fasting, and charity are conduits and practices for the purification of the soul. The binding tie to these practices is pilgrimage, as visits to holy sites and shrines heighten our awareness of the Creator.

Pilgrimage

Each of the three Abrahamic religions has a legacy from all the ancient cultures and requires its adherents to visit the holy places. These visits, or pilgrimages, to the sacred and holy sites are reinforcements of one's beliefs. They are opportunities to reflect upon and relate to those who sacrificed so much to establish and sustain a religious identity. There are numerous holy sites in the world, and each one may have a different cultural or ethnic meaning.

Table 15
Selected Holy Cities in Judaism, Christianity, and Islam

Judaism	*Christianity*	*Islam*
Jerusalem	Jerusalem	Jerusalem
Hebron	Bethlehem	Mecca
Safed	Nazareth	Medina
Tiberius	Rome (the Vatican)	
	Lourdes	

Pilgrimage is one of the oldest and most basic forms of travel known to human society, and its political, social, cultural, and economic implications have always been and continue to be substantial (Collins-Kreiner 2010). Pilgrimage can be defined as "a journey resulting from religious causes, externally to a holy site and internally for spiritual purposes and internal understanding" (Barber 1993). It can also indicate the destiny of the person making the journey. The experience involves not only movement but also a spiritual response, as one encounters both the journey and the goal.

During the Middle Ages, pilgrimage journeys were long and arduous. Today, with airplanes, travel time is considerably shorter. Pilgrimage is performed in all three religions, Judaism, Christianity, and Islam, and all three share the holy city, Jerusalem.

For Jews, the central focus of pilgrimage is Jerusalem, particularly the Temple, until it was destroyed, and the Wailing Wall. Since ancient times, the annual practice has been to perform three pilgrimages. However, today, that may not be practical since the Temple no longer stands. Nonetheless, the Torah mandates the three pilgrimages:

> Three times a year all your men must appear before the
> Lord your God at the place He will choose: at the Feast
> of Unleavened Bread, the Feast of Weeks and the Feast
> of Tabernacles. No man should appear before the Lord
> empty handed. (Deuteronomy 16:16)

The four holy cities of Judaism are Jerusalem, Hebron, Safed, and Tiberius. A number of Jews still travel to Jerusalem, but mostly on a smaller scale during the three festivals. Others make pilgrimages to lesser holy places or tombs of the Tzaddiqim, the sages, well-known rabbis, and cities that are less sacred than Jerusalem, such as Nablus (Doumani 1995).

Jerusalem, Bethlehem, Nazareth, Rome, and Lourdes are some of Christianity's major holy cities. Jerusalem and Rome (including Vatican City) draw the greatest number of pilgrims. Lourdes, France, attracts more than four million Christians each year. They go because it was the site of a vision of the Virgin Mary, and miraculous healings have been experienced there. Some make pilgrimages to the Holy Land, to visit the same places Jesus did or walk in his footsteps (Disney 2007). There are many other Christian sacred sites around the world, and pilgrimage has become an important type of tourism. In addition to looking forward to their journeys, tourist-pilgrims are instilled with a strong sense of religious motivation.

Christian pilgrimage is often an attempt to follow the footsteps of Jesus. In doing this, pilgrims believe they have approached the texts of the Bible more closely, showed their love to God, gotten near to something sacred, or showed God their gratitude. Or they may use the pilgrimage to ask for pardon or a miracle (Post 1999). Christian pilgrims are invited to enter into their own time of sacredness so that the experience will represent not only movement of the body but also an itinerary for the soul. The journey becomes a paradigm of the whole life of faith. The departure represents the decision to go forward and achieve the spiritual objectives of one's baptismal vocation. Walking leads to solidarity with one's brothers and sisters and to the necessary preparation for the meeting with the Lord. The visit to the shrines invites the pilgrim to listen to the word of God and celebrate the sacraments. The return is a reminder of one's mission in the world, as a witness to salvation and builder of peace (Harrigan 2010).

Some of the holy sites frequently visited by Christians include the Church of the Holy Sepulcher, Church of the Ascension, and Garden Tomb in Jerusalem; Church of the Nativity in Bethlehem; Church of the Annunciation in Nazareth; Saint Peter's Square and the Basilica in Vatican City; Canterbury Cathedral in England; and the Cathedral of Santiago de Compostela in Spain.

Mecca and Medina are the places of pilgrimage (*hajj*) for Muslims. It is obligatory for all Muslims to make a pilgrimage at least once in their lifetimes, as long as they fulfill the conditions of age, health, sanity, and affordability. If possible, Muslims also should make a pilgrimage to Jerusalem, also considered a holy city in Islam. Circumambulation around the Holy Shrine (Ka'bah) in Mecca both signifies the broader idea of journeying and the sacred stone that is the goal of the pilgrimage. The Qur'an states that Prophet Abraham and his son, Ishmael, constructed the Ka'bah, which houses the celestial Black Stone that had descended from Heaven. The Black Stone dates back before the creation of mankind. It is a revered object set in a corner wall of the Ka'bah, a sanctuary

Muslims believe to be the holiest place on Earth. Tradition holds that it was a meteorite and the Stone was white in color when it first landed and then blackened. The faithful attribute this change in color to the belief that the Stone absorbs the sins of the pilgrims (Trubshaw 2008).

The complete pilgrimage for Muslims is performed during the first ten days of Zul-hajj (the last month of the Islamic calendar), while the less formal pilgrimage (*'umra*) can be done at any time of the year. During the pilgrimage, Muslims visit many holy shrines in Mecca and Medina. Pilgrimage is a place and time when one expresses his gratitude to God for His blessings by submitting to Him. Muslims from all over the world gather together in unity and humility to purify their faith through prayer. There is no distinction between race, color, sex, rank, or nationality; all are equal, and each has the opportunity to express his or her gratitude and love for God.

Table 16
Typical Experiences during Pilgrimage
Judaism, Christianity, and Islam

Spiritual awakening	Submission to God	Covenant with God
Purification of the soul	Supplication	Enlightenment
Inner peace	Reflection	Meditation
Introspection	Humility	Wisdom
Knowledge	Hope	Patience
Self-restraint	Tolerance	Brotherhood

Table 16 lists some experiences common to those performing a pilgrimage, no matter what their religion. The actions listed must continuously be practiced after the pilgrimage; otherwise, the result will be just a short-term phenomenon.

The Temple Mount in Jerusalem is a holy site that is revered in Judaism, Christianity, and Islam. It is known as Har haBayith in Hebrew and Haram Ash-Sharif in Arabic. The first Temple was built by Solomon, son of David, and destroyed by the Babylonians. The second Temple was destroyed by the Romans. Jewish tradition maintains it is on that site that the third and final Temple will be built. The Western Wall (Wailing

Wall) is the one part of the old Temple that is still standing. Muslims believe that the Temple is the location of Prophet Muhammad's journey to Jerusalem and ascent to Heaven. The al-Aqsa Mosque and the Dome of the Rock are located at the site.

While each faith has its own rituals during pilgrimage, the ultimate goal is the same—to extend gratitude and love to God and seek His blessings. Since Jerusalem is the holy city that is revered by all faiths, it can be the place where an enhanced interfaith dialogue can take place and usher in peace, stability, security, and unity. While on a pilgrimage, we should honor the past and celebrate the present, as a constant reminder that Abraham was the inspiration for and connection between the three faiths. As children of Abraham, we likewise have an obligation and duty to surrender our will to God. The lesson we learn from this great trial and test of Abraham is that we must be faithful and obedient to God, embrace brotherhood, and love and respect one another. If we transgress, then we need to atone for our sins and improve our way of life.

Summary

Judaism, Christianity, and Islam adhere to similar practices, including praying, fasting, charity, and pilgrimage. The need to worship is common to all three faiths, and each prescribes specific words and requirements for prayer, which is performed at appointed times. All three religions believe prayer is a way to communicate with God. However, they differ in how people should approach God in prayer.

Jews and Muslims have to pray a certain number of times a day; Christians do not. Jews are supposed to pray three times a day; Muslims are supposed to pray five times a day. All three groups believe that the more they pray, the closer they get to God. Some Jews and Christians use prayer books or prewritten prayers, while others simply speak to God from their heart. Prayer takes on a personal meaning, as each believer is humble in his private obedience to God.

Fasting has always represented spiritual cleansing for Jews, Christians, and Muslims. It reminds us to feel empathy for the needy. It is also a common form of worship, as fasts are often related to holy days. Periods of fasting differ in each of the faiths.

Charity is a form of purification as well as an act of kindness in the Abrahamic faiths. Each faith adheres to providing relief for the poor, although other forms of charity are also encouraged, such as mediating between two people and empathizing with the distressed and depressed. Followers of each religion are required to share their wealth with those who are disadvantaged, which exemplifies compassion and a love for humanity. Judaism, Christianity, and Islam each have charitable directives for collecting and redistributing donations to those in need.

While pilgrimage requirements of each of the Abrahamic faiths involve different destinations and holy shrines, the followers all seek forgiveness in their spiritual connectivity with God. They also try to make the pilgrimage to Jerusalem, the binding tie of the three traditions and the city of Abraham. Jerusalem is a contested city, because the followers of each religion are separated by the differences in their beliefs. Unfortunately, the city has become an area of discord, conflict, and fragmentation among the competing religions. Nevertheless, the idea of pilgrimage is ingrained in human thought and offers a sense of inspiration, healing, and oneness.

Unquestionably, the Abrahamic faiths adhere to common principles of prayer, fasting, charity, and pilgrimage, even though their followers fail to understand that is the case. Unfortunately, these misunderstandings have generated a great deal of hatred and suspicion in America (e.g., Islamophobia).

6 Misunderstandings

Atonement

Atonement is the act of reconciliation with God after one has transgressed or sinned. One may reconcile by reaffirming one's faith and obeying God's commandments. In ancient times, the ritual sacrifice of a human or an animal was also required.

Atonement in Judaism is observed by fasting on Yom Kippur. On this day of humiliation and repentance, Jewish people atone for the sins of the past year and ask for God's forgiveness. If a person committed transgressions against another person, then he or she is required to reconcile with that person prior to the Day of Atonement. Blood used to be offered as atonement for one's sins; such was the case in ancient times.

> For the life of a creature is in the blood, and I have given it to you to make atonement for yourselves on the altar; it is the blood that makes atonement for one's life. (Leviticus 17:11)

> The Lord spoke to Moses after the death of the two sons of Aaron who died when they approached the Lord. The Lord said to Moses: "Tell your brother Aaron that he is not to come whenever he chooses into the Most Holy Place behind the curtain in front of the atonement cover on the ark, or else he will die. For I will appear in the cloud over the atonement cover … This is to be a lasting

> ordinance for you: atonement is to be made once a year
> for all the sins of the Israelites." And it was done, as the
> Lord commanded Moses. (Leviticus 16:1–2, 34)

According to Jewish law, the blood of the atoning sacrifice was to be offered on the altar of the Temple: "Once a year Aaron shall make atonement on its horns. This annual atonement must be made with the blood of the atoning sin offering for the generations to come. It is most holy to the Lord" (Exodus 30:10). Today, penitence is done usually without shedding of blood. Animal sacrifices—which represented drawing closer to God—stopped when the second Temple was destroyed. They actually can't take place anywhere else.

In Judaism, three basic concepts underlie the concept of *qorbanot* (sacrifices or offerings) in atonement: giving, substitution, and coming closer. *Qorbanot* only expiate unintentional sins; they cannot atone for a malicious, deliberate sin. No atonement is needed for violations committed under duress or because of lack of knowledge. Some types of *qorbanot* are burnt offerings, peace offerings, sin offerings, guilt offerings, and food and drink offerings. A sin offering is an offering to atone for and purge a sin. It is an expression of sorrow for the error and a desire to be reconciled with God. A guilt offering is an offering to atone for sins of stealing things from the altar or for breach of trust. When giving, a person is supposed to renounce something that belongs to him or her. That is why people sacrifice domestic animals or make offerings of food in the form of flour or meal. The thing being offered is a substitute for the person making the offering, which is in some sense punished instead (Etshalom 1998).

In Christianity, atonement has been linked to the death of Jesus. However, some Christians now link it to his life rather than to his death. Some denominations believe that people must accept Jesus as their savior. Other denominations state that people must first repent for past sins. Still others feel that salvation can be attained via baptism and confession, while others uphold that atonement can occur through good deeds and adherence to church rules (Robinson 2007). Catholics believe that atonement comes with confessing one's sins to a priest, thereby receiving penance, then forgiveness, and returning to God's good grace.

Christianity is tied to the Old Testament. However, the Christian perspective of atonement differs from the Jewish view. In Christianity, at least in some denominations, atonement—the pardoning of sin—was granted through the death of Jesus on the cross. Some Christians believe that Jesus's death was a human sacrifice, while Jews state that human sacrifice is an outrage in the sight of God: "Do not give any of your children to be sacrificed to Molek, for you must not profane the name of your God. I am the Lord" (Leviticus 18:21).

Good Friday symbolizes the final atonement, as Christians believe that Jesus died for the sins of mankind: "At that moment the curtain of the temple was torn in two from top to bottom. The earth shook, the rocks split" (Matthew 27:51). Christians further believe that Jesus became the high priest and entered Heaven, not because of the blood shed by sacrificial animals, but because his own blood was shed on the cross. In so doing, he obtained eternal redemption for mankind. As such, Christians accept Jesus's sacrifice as the fulfillment of Yom Kippur, the final atonement for sin (Fairchild, n.d.).

The concepts of sacrifice, atonement, and repentance (*tawbah*) are also followed in Islam. During the annual pilgrimage (*hajj*), the Feast of Sacrifice (Eid al-Adha) is held at Mecca and throughout the Muslim communities around the world. This event commemorates Abraham's willingness to sacrifice his first son. Yom Kippur and the Feast of Sacrifice have much in common. Both date back to Abraham. While the Jewish high priest offers an annual sacrifice for himself and for all people, Muslims observe an annual sacrifice in Mecca.

Relative to repentance, the Qur'an states:

> Say: "O my servants who have transgressed against their souls! Do not despair of the Mercy of God: for God forgives all sins: for He is Oft-Forgiving, Most Merciful. You turn to your Lord (in repentance) and bow to His (Will), before the Penalty comes on you: after that you shall not be helped." (Qur'an 39:53–54)

> God accepts the repentance of those who do evil in ignorance and repent soon afterwards; to them will God turn in mercy: for God is full of knowledge and

wisdom. Of no effect is the repentance of those who continue to do evil, until death faces one of them, and he says, "Now have I repented indeed"; nor of those who die rejecting faith: for them We have prepared a punishment most grievous. (Qur'an 4:17–18)

According to Imam Ali Ibn Abi Talib, son-in-law of Prophet Muhammad:

> ... one who repents for his thoughts and deeds will not be refused acceptance of the repentance; one who has atoned for his sins will not be debarred from salvation and one who thanks God for the Blessings and Bounties will not be denied the increase in them ... Whoever has done a bad deed or has indulged in sin and then repents and asks for forgiveness will find God most Forgiving and Merciful ... About atonement of sin, God accepts the repentance of those who have ignorantly committed vice and then soon repent for it; God accepts such repentances. (Ibn Abi Talib 1999)

Islam does not accept animal or blood sacrifices for the atonement of one's sins. However, the sacrifice of a lamb during the Feast of Sacrifice is done to feed the poor and to remember Abraham's willingness to sacrifice his son at God's command. Atonement can be achieved by one's piety to God, prayers, fasting, and good deeds.

When people atone for their sins in prayer, they are required to dress properly when entering a house of worship or making a pilgrimage. These requirements include the wearing of a head covering for women.

Head Covering

Jewish, Christian, and Muslim women have worn scarves or other types of head covering since ancient times. Nonetheless, today, much consternation and media coverage have been directed at Muslim women who wear headscarves that cover their hair, neck, and ears, leaving only the face showing (Mernissi 1987). The headscarf has been stereotyped as threatening and offensive to non-Muslims, increasing the hostility toward Islam. Islamophobia is an ideology based on prejudice, hatred, irrational fear, and negative stereotyping that has resulted in attacks on Muslims (Lowe 1985).

Passages in the Old Testament and New Testament state that God has mandated that women should wear headscarves and veils:

> Rebekah also looked up and saw Isaac. She got down from her camel and asked the servant, "Who is that man in the field coming to meet us?" "He is my master," the servant answered. So she took her veil and covered herself. (Genesis 24:64–65)

> She took off her widow's clothes, covered herself with a veil to disguise herself, and then sat down at the entrance to Enaim, which is on the road to Timnah. For she saw that, though Shelah had now grown up, she had not been given to him as his wife. (Genesis 38:14)

> Every man who prays or prophesies with his head covered dishonors his head. But every woman who prays or prophesies with her head uncovered dishonors her head—it is the same as having her head shaved. For if a woman does not cover her head, she might as well have her hair cut off; but if it is a disgrace for a woman to have her hair cut off or her head shaved, then she should cover her head. (1 Corinthians 11:4–6)

For many centuries, wearing the veil was considered part of a modest woman's attire. Women wore the veil not as a fashionable item but because they were obedient to God's command. In ancient times, Jewish and Christian women who did not wear the veil in public were considered immoral. Today, the scriptures have not changed; the commandments about the wearing of veils and headscarves are still in effect. Catholic nuns still wear a very distinct coif and veil and some Christian women wear a head covering or bonnet.

The Qur'an also tells women to cover themselves when in public:

> O Prophet! Tell your wives and daughters, and the believing women, that they should cast their outer garments over their persons [when abroad]: that is most convenient, that they should be known (as such) and not molested. And God is Oft-Forgiving, Most Merciful. (Qur'an 33:59)

> And say to the believing women that they should lower their gaze and guard their modesty; that they should not display their beauty and ornaments except what [must ordinarily] appear thereof; that they should draw their veils over their bosoms and not display their beauty ... and that they should not strike their feet in order to draw attention to their hidden ornaments ..." (Qur'an 24:31)

Many of the stereotypes and misinformation associated with the wearing of the headscarf are rooted in a particular perception of Islam, such as the notion that it promotes terrorism, especially prevalent after the September 11, 2001 attacks on America (Peedin 2011). As such, Muslims are portrayed as "... alien and foreign to Western society, backward, uneducated, vulgar, and violent which has resulted in immense tension between Muslims and non-Muslims" (Lowe 1985). There are opposing views by Muslim and non-Muslim Americans about whether or not the headscarf should be worn in public.

Muslims are adamant that the headscarf protects women from the lack of sexual morals in America. Their assessment of contemporary American society seems to be a basic distrust of human nature and the ability to resist sexual impulses. The sexualized culture in American society is a significant problem for Muslims and a threat to their well-being. A study revealed that this produces a contested space for ethnic, religious, and gender identity development. Religious understanding plays an important mediating role in how gender is configured. Islam's increasingly public and controversial place in American life and the importance attached to the headscarf make this particularly sensitive

(Ajrouch 2004). Muslims have their own unique nature, illustrated by varying origins, ethnic and racial make-up, and political beliefs.

Non-Muslims believe the headscarf underscores Islam's inherent violation of women's equal rights and are a sign of the religion's oppression against women, despite the fact that many wear it voluntarily (Read 2000). Equality is a core American value and people are free to make independent decisions. Another dimension of equal rights is the concept of treating all people the same.

According to this interpretation, responding to gender inequality means dismantling barriers to women in public life. Many Americans view any outward manifestations of difference as inequality. As such, it is not difficult to see that the headscarf can be considered as a demonstration of inequality; women wear it, but men do not. In addition, the American media are full of stories about Islam's oppression of women, such as the prohibition on women driving automobiles in Saudi Arabia and the Taliban's vicious treatment of women in Afghanistan. Operating from this perspective, many Americans do not understand why second-generation Muslim-American women wear headscarves, which seem to be an open admission of second-class status (Shakeri 1998).

The American media has created a negative image of the headscarf, which makes it harder for Muslim women to cover their hair and be accepted in American society. In France, for example, the government has banned the wearing of headscarves. Rather than a symbol of piety and obedience to God, the scarf was associated with those who have declared war on America. As a result, Muslim women are often taunted and discriminated at work and on the street. They face sexual harassment, and often their physical safety is at risk. However, the backlash from September 11, 2001 made Muslim women step up and assume an activist role. They recognized that they needed to participate actively in American society and work to increase public understanding of Islam (Haddad 2007).

The headscarf is a social symbol as well. Women use it to fulfill other needs. American society puts great emphasis on equality, independence, and the establishment of autonomous personal identity. And the decision to wear the headscarf can work in this way for many second-generation Muslim-American women, who are creating cultural space for themselves through the use of this religious symbol. It emphasizes their Muslim identity and gives them some measure of autonomy (Seikaly 1998). Wearing the headscarf is a practical and useful response to living as women between two cultures and as members of a minority faith. It is a public symbol that visibly rejects the excessive individualized culture of dominant American society, giving Muslim women some room to feel at home and prosper in both worlds.

The headscarf also can cover a woman's ego: "By the soul, and the proportion and order given to it; and its enlightenment as to its wrong and its right; truly he succeeds that purifies it, and he fails that corrupts it!" (Qur'an 91:7–10). God endows the self with the possibilities of both integration and disruption. A person has the moral choice between good and evil. Containment of the ego is not only encouraged in Islam but mandated as well. Those who stereotype the headscarf as bad are practically saying the ego is good. Quite the opposite is true. It is the headscarf that symbolizes the containment of the ego, and through it, we are able to exercise self-control in our daily lives.

Similarly, Judaism and Christianity make it a high priority to contain the ego:

> Like a city whose walls are broken down is a man who lacks self-control. (Proverbs 25:28)

> Anyone who wants to follow me must put aside his own desires and conveniences and carry his cross with him every day and keep close to me! Whoever loses his life for my sake will save it, but whoever insists on keeping his life will lose it; and what profit is there in gaining the whole world when it means forfeiting one's self? (Luke 9:23)

Both of the aforementioned verses refer to the ego. Lacking self-control makes one defenseless, while self-discipline builds up a spiritual defense system against evil. The ego is worried about the material things of this world, its riches and pleasures. If the ego is not contained, then the fruit of life will have no meaning. Our egos constantly get in the way, as we lose sight of what is most important—the spiritual well-being of our souls. The ego only looks out for itself, but our true reward is when the soul is in charge.

Throughout the world, the Arabic term, hijab, has come to mean head covering, but it actually means barrier or partition. The more precise term for head covering is *khimar*, or cloth that covers the hair, ears, and neck. There is a strong connection between head covering and modesty in Islam. The head covering affords women modesty, respect, and dignity as well as a sense of purification. It protects them from harm and the evils of society by covering their beauty. Both men and women practice modesty by lowering their gaze when in the presence of the opposite sex.

In the early days of Islam, the hijab was a screen or partition that was placed between women and men to allow them to speak to each other without changing clothes. The hijab was also used by Prophet Muhammad's wives as protection against visitors and people who were looking to gossip about them.

Perhaps, the reason why many Americans and Europeans see the headscarf and veil as a symbol of inferiority, subservience, and degradation is because the New Testament states that the veil is a sign of man's authority over a woman (1 Corinthians 11:1–16). While the issue of the headscarf has taken center stage in America, there is another issue that historically has been common practice among the Abrahamic faiths: polygamy.

Polygamy

Polygamy is a marriage among more than two partners. There are three different types. Polygyny occurs when a man has multiple wives at the same time. Polyandry is when a woman has multiple husbands at the same time. Group marriages occur when a family unit has multiple husbands and wives at the same time.

While polygamy is neither encouraged nor mandatory in the three Abrahamic faiths, it is permitted. Many Jewish prophets were polygamous. Because Sarah was barren, she gave her handmaid, Hagar, in marriage to Abraham (Genesis 16:3). In fact, Abraham had three wives: Sarah, Hagar, and Keturah, as well as a number of concubines (Genesis 25:6).

Jacob, father of the twelve tribes of Israel, married Rachel and Leah, who were sisters (Genesis 29), and their servants, Bilhah and

Zilpah (Genesis 30). David had at least seven wives and concubines (1 Chronicles 3). While some believe that David had one hundred wives, this number is not verified in the Old Testament. Solomon had seven hundred wives and three hundred concubines (1 Kings 11:3). Moses had two wives (Numbers 12:1, Exodus 2:21). Polygamy was recognized and regulated by the law of Moses:

> If a man has two wives, and he loves one but not the other, and both bear him sons but the firstborn is the son of the wife he does not love, when he wills his property to his sons, he must not give the rights of the firstborn to the son of the wife he loves in preference to his actual firstborn, the son of the wife he does not love. He must acknowledge the son of his unloved wife as the firstborn by giving him a double share of all he has. That son is the first sign of his father's strength. The right of the firstborn belongs to him. (Deuteronomy 21:15–17)

Polygamy was also practiced in Christianity and Islam. If polygamy is immoral, then how do we assess the morality of the biblical prophets? Over the course of history, the number of wives allowed in polygamy was modified in the Old Testament: "He [the king] must not take many wives, or his heart will be led astray. He must not accumulate large amounts of silver and gold" (Deuteronomy 17:17). The Old Testament also provides protection to unmarried women:

> If a man happens to meet a virgin who is not pledged to be married and rapes her and they are discovered, he shall pay her father fifty shekels of silver. He must marry the young woman, for he has violated her. He can never divorce her as long as he lives. (Deuteronomy 22:28–29)

There is nothing in the Old Testament that indicates an exception was made if the man were married. So, if a married man had an affair with a single woman, then the law demanded he become a polygamist.

In Judaism, the practice of polygamy continued through the first millennium AD, until Rabbi Gershom ben Judah issued an edict that substantively discontinued it. The one exception was if a man received special permission from one hundred rabbis from three different countries. With few exceptions, most Jews accepted the edict throughout the Western world. Today, modern Jewish polygamy is limited to Yemenite Jews (Faigin 2009).

After the death of Jesus, Paul settled the question regarding the practice of polygamy for Christians. Several references indicate that he believed the practice was inappropriate:

> An elder must be blameless, faithful to his wife, a man whose children believe and are not open to the charge of being wild and disobedient. (Titus 1:6)

> For this reason a man will leave his father and mother and be united to his wife, and the two will become one flesh. (Ephesians 5:31)

> Now the overseer is to be above reproach, faithful to his wife, temperate, self-controlled, respectable, hospitable, able to teach, not given to drunkenness, not violent but gentle, not quarrelsome, not a lover of money. (1 Timothy 3:2–3)

> A deacon must be faithful to his wife and must manage his children and his household well. (1 Timothy 3:12)

Polygamy is practiced in America today, but it is difficult to collect accurate data from polygamous sects. Polygamy, once required by the founder of the Church of Jesus Christ of Latter-day Saints (the Mormons), Joseph Smith, was abolished in 1890, under pressure from the US government as a prerequisite for admitting Utah to the Union (Orsi 2012).

Polygamy is not condemned or outlawed in the New Testament. While it is not mentioned a great deal, there are a number of teachings and clarifications that are of assistance to the polygamist. For example, the following verse indicates that polyandry may be acceptable:

> So then, if she has sexual relations with another man while her husband is still alive, she is called an adulteress. But if her husband dies, she is released from that law and is not an adulteress if she marries another man. (Romans 7:3)

According to research by Dr. Ahmed Ali Sawad, polygamy is permitted under Sharia Law, not as an absolute privilege of men but as a legal right exercisable under strict conditions of justice as required by the Qur'an. Islamic law states clearly that every man and woman has a right to marry. The Sharia rule on the practice of polygamy is contained in the following verse of the Qur'an:

> If you fear that you shall not be able to deal justly with the orphans, marry women of your choice, two, or three, or four; but if you fear that you shall not be able to deal justly [with them], then only one, or [a captive] that your right hand possesses that will be more suitable, to prevent you from doing injustice. (Qur'an 4:3)

However, this rule is based on the precondition that the man who has more than one wife is "able to deal justly" with them:

> You are never able to be fair and just as between women, even if it is your ardent desire: but do not turn away [from a woman] altogether, so as to leave her [as it were] hanging [in the air]. If you come to a friendly understanding, and practice self-restraint, God is Oft-Forgiving, Most Merciful. (Qur'an 4:129)

These two verses of the Qur'an may be said to lay down the parameters within which the rule of polygamy operates in Islamic law.

Justice has an overwhelming interest in protecting the rights and affairs of women in a polygamous marriage. Moreover, Sharia Law allows women to make monogamy a precondition of their marriage contracts. Islamic law permits women to include in the marital contract an optional right of divorce in case the husband enters into a second marriage. The law considers marriage as a "solemn covenant" between a man and a woman, based on their free and full consent. Any coercion negates this basic understanding of marriage in Sharia Law. Every eligible woman has the right not only to give her free and full consent to a marriage she desires but also to include conditions and stipulations to the marriage covenant in order to ensure that her rights and privileges are protected (Sawad 2008).

Polygamy in Islam depends on several factors. For example, if the man lacks the material and moral conditions, or he is not competent to satisfy all of them, then he will not be eligible to take more than one wife. In addition, a healthy married life comes from the mutual love and kindness between husband and wife that are found in a monogamous relationship.

Religions that preceded Islam recognized no limit to the number of wives a man could marry. However, Islam severely restricted the number. If the husband cannot exercise equality among all the wives, then he is not allowed to marry more than one (Qur'an 4:3). Fairness and justice are required in marriage. Therefore, the husband must be able to economically provide for all of his wives: give each one food and clothing; provide a separate house for each of them; spend an equal amount of time with each wife, etc. Deciding which wife will be visited first renders a preference that negates equality. Therefore, the imposition of these severe conditions encourages a monogamous marriage (Qur'an 4:3).

Human Rights

The concept of human rights is understood as the absolute and inalienable basic rights to which a person is inherently entitled. President Franklin D. Roosevelt summarized the preconditions of human rights in his "Four Freedoms Speech" to the United States Congress on January 26, 1941:

- Freedom of speech and expression;
- Freedom of every person to worship God in his or her own way;

- Freedom from want ... economic understandings which will secure to every nation a healthy peacetime life for its inhabitants; and
- Freedom from fear ... a worldwide reduction of armaments [so] that no nation will be in a position to commit an act of physical aggression against any neighbor.

President Roosevelt implied that a dignified human existence requires not only protection from oppression and arbitrariness, but also access to the primary necessities of life.

Judaism, Christianity, and Islam all uphold human rights. When Jews, Christians, and Muslims violate human rights, it is done by individuals and not the religion.

> Human rights are an integral part of the faith and tradition of Judaism. The beliefs that man was created in the Divine image, that the human family is one, and that every person is obliged to deal justly with every other person are basic sources of the Jewish commitment to human rights. (McGill 1974)

> Learn to do right; seek justice. Defend the oppressed. Take up the cause of the fatherless; plead the case of the widow. (Isaiah 1:17)

> Woe to those who make unjust laws, to those who issue oppressive decrees, to deprive the poor of their rights and withhold justice from the oppressed of my people, making widows their prey and robbing the fatherless. (Isaiah 10:1–2)

Other passages from the Old Testament underscore the importance of human rights and that everyone, including immigrants and the poor, should be treated humanely:

> Do not mistreat or oppress a foreigner ... (Exodus 22:21)

> When a foreigner resides among you in your land, do not mistreat them. The foreigner residing among you must be treated as your native-born. Love them as yourself ... (Leviticus 19:33–34)

> If anyone is poor ... do not be hardhearted or tightfisted toward them ... be openhanded and freely lend them whatever they need. (Deuteronomy 15:7–8)

Over the course of history, Jews, Christians, and Muslims have fought each other in the name of religion. Contrary to religious doctrine, some have even inflicted undue harm on others by violating human rights. For example, while the Christian church is a champion of human rights, it has been a major violator of those rights:

> The historic relationship between Christianity and human rights is an ambiguous one. For hundreds of years the Christian Church actively promoted religious intolerance and persecuted those who failed to accept its moral values and customs. (Villa-Vicencio 2004)

However, it was not the religion that violated human rights but those who ran the Christian church at that time. Undeniably, Jesus stood for truth, morality, and steadfastness in the face of danger. His life was a call for love, freedom, and justice. The New Testament affirms the rights of humans:

> For I was hungry and you gave me something to eat, I was thirsty and you gave me something to drink, I was a stranger and you invited me in, I needed clothes and you clothed me, I was sick and you looked after me, I was in prison and you came to visit me ... "The King will reply ... whatever you did for one of the least of these brothers and sisters of mine, you did for me." (Matthew 25:35–40)

> There is neither Jew nor Gentile, neither slave nor free, nor is there male and female, for you are all one in Christ Jesus. (Galatians 3:28)

> Here there is no Gentile or Jew, circumcised or uncircumcised, barbarian, Scythian, slave or free, but Christ in all, and is in all. (Colossians 3:11)

Article 1 of the United Nations Universal Declaration of Human Rights states, "All human beings are born free and equal in dignity and rights. They are endowed with reason and conscience and should act towards one another in a spirit of brotherhood" (United Nations 1948). While the Universal Declaration of Human Rights is a significant step, God has already mandated human rights, as is evidenced in the tenets of Islam. Human rights granted by governments, organizations, or other entities can be given and later withdrawn. But, according to Islam, human rights granted by God can never be withdrawn or revoked by anyone. In Islam, the foremost basic right is to live and respect human life:

> ... if anyone slew a person—unless it be for murder or for spreading mischief in the land—it would be as if he slew the whole people; and if anyone saved a life, it would be as if he saved the life of the whole people ... (Qur'an 5:32)

> ... take not life, which God has made sacred, except by way of justice and law ... (Qur'an 6:151)

While Islam maintains that every human has the right to safety and security, it also obligates Muslims to uphold the economic rights and honor of mankind: "And in their wealth and possessions [was remembered] the right of the [needy] ..." (Qur'an 51:19). Equality is another fundamental human right in Islam, as all human beings are equal in their submission and obedience to God:

> O mankind! We created you from a single [pair] of a

male and a female, and made you into nations and tribes,
that you may know each other [not that you may despise
each other] ... (Qur'an 49:13)

... nor defame nor be sarcastic to each other, nor call
each other by [offensive] nicknames: ill-seeming is a
name connoting wickedness ... and spy not on each
other, nor speak ill of each other behind their backs ...
(Qur'an 49:11–12)

Because equality and freedom are guaranteed in Islam, it is forbidden
and highly detestable to force anyone to convert against his or her will
or to force anyone to bear the burden of others:

Let there be no compulsion in religion ... (Qur'an 2:256)

Nor can a bearer of burdens bear another's burden. If
one heavily laden should call another to [bear] his load,
not the least portion of it can be carried [by the other],
even though he be nearly related ... (Qur'an 35:18)

Justice is the cornerstone in upholding the rights of others:

God commands you to render back your trusts to those
to whom they are due; and when you judge between man
and man, that you judge with justice ... (Qur'an 4:58)

O you who believe! Stand out firmly for God, as witnesses
to fair dealing, and let not the hatred of others to you
make you swerve to wrong and depart from justice. Be
just: that is next to piety: and fear God ... (Qur'an 5:8)

As noted, human rights are compulsory and mandated in the
doctrines of Judaism, Christianity, and Islam. This requires believers
to truly engage in fulfilling this obligation, contain their egos, and
respect one another.

Jihad

Jihad (struggle) is one of the most misunderstood concepts in the world. As a result, unjust accusations have been leveled against Islam. The following will shed some light on the significance and meaning of *struggle* within each of the Abrahamic faiths.

Judaism

The Old Testament refers to struggling or striving on a spiritual level and a physical level, which are similar to the concept of jihad:

> And now, Israel, what does the Lord your God ask of you but to fear the Lord your God, to walk in obedience to him, to love him, to serve the Lord your God with all your heart and with all your soul … (Deuteronomy 10:12)

> Do not allow a sorceress to live. Anyone who has sexual relations with an animal is to be put to death. Whoever sacrifices to any god other than the Lord must be destroyed. (Exodus 22:18–20)

> Then he said to them, "This is what the Lord, the God of Israel, says: Each man strap a sword to his side. Go back and forth through the camp from one end to the other, each killing his brother and friend and neighbor." The Levites did as Moses commanded, and that day about three thousand of the people died. (Exodus 32:27–28)

> They devoted the city to the Lord and destroyed with the sword every living thing in it—men and women, young and old, cattle, sheep and donkeys. (Joshua 6:21)

> You will pursue your enemies, and they will fall by the sword before you. Five of you will chase a hundred, and a hundred of you will chase ten thousand, and your enemies will fall by the sword before you. (Leviticus 26:7–8)

My son, pay attention to what I say; turn your ear to my words. Do not let them out of your sight, keep them within your heart; for they are life to those who find them and health to one's whole body. Above all else, guard your heart, for everything you do flows from it. (Proverbs 4:20–23)

Blessed is the one who does not walk in step with the wicked or stand in the way that sinners take or sit in the company of mockers, but whose delight is in the law of the Lord, and who meditates on his law day and night. That person is like a tree planted by streams of water, which yields its fruit in season and whose leaf does not wither—whatever they do prospers. (Psalm 1:1–3)

May the praise of God be in their mouths and a double-edged sword in their hands, to inflict vengeance on the nations and punishment on the peoples, to bind their kings with fetters, their nobles with shackles of iron, to carry out the sentence written against them—this is the glory of all his faithful people. (Psalm 149:6–9)

In Judaism, life presents itself in a manner in which people have frequent, continuing struggles with God and with other people. However, the Divine promise is that they will overcome their struggles and have a rebirth of greater dimensions as a result of these difficulties. That was the case with Jacob, who struggled with difficulties in his life, as did his children. Sibling rivalries among Jacob's children encouraged them to search for ultimate meaning in their own lives. Jews are faced with many difficulties and struggles in today's world and strive to overcome them, as they transform their inner selves into a higher level.

Christianity

The New Testament refers to struggle or striving that is tied to the spiritual life. It teaches that God gives greater favor to those who are faithful and that believers should strive for the godly life. Jesus wanted the people to have faith in him and in his life; as such, the Christian gate is narrow. This spiritual striving is a form of jihad, in that Jesus asked his followers to love their enemies. The Bible refers to both spiritual struggle and physical struggle in the following passages:

> You were taught, with regard to your former way of life, to put off your old self, which is being corrupted by its deceitful desires; to be made new in the attitude of your minds; and to put on the new self, created to be like God in true righteousness and holiness. Therefore each of you must put off falsehood and speak truthfully to your neighbor, for we are all members of one body. (Ephesians 4:22–25)

> Make every effort to enter through the narrow door, because many, I tell you, will try to enter and will not be able to. (Luke 13:24)

> But those enemies of mine who did not want me to be king over them—bring them here and kill them in front of me. (Luke 19:27)

> He said to them, "But now if you have a purse, take it, and also a bag; and if you don't have a sword, sell your cloak and buy one." (Luke 22:36)

> Do not suppose that I have come to bring peace to the Earth. I did not come to bring peace, but a sword. (Matthew 10:34)

> For this very reason, make every effort to add to your faith goodness; and to goodness, knowledge; and to knowledge, self-control; and to self-control, perseverance; and to perseverance, godliness; and to godliness, mutual affection, and to mutual affection, love. (2 Peter 1:5–7)

> Fight the good fight of the faith. Take hold of the eternal
> life to which you were called when you made your
> good confession in the presence of many witnesses.
> (1 Timothy 6:12)

For Christians, struggle is necessary to enhance the development of one's self-being. As Christians struggle to better themselves in life, they seek self-reflection to overcome their difficulties. They have the same life experiences and spiritual, social, and physical struggles as other people in the world, including Jews and Muslims.

Islam

Throughout the world, Islam is inaccurately viewed as a complex, inhumane, and backward religion that promotes violence and terrorism. It is incorrectly perceived as a religion in which suicide is the easiest way to paradise and where the concept of jihad is related to terror. Some terrorists do try to justify their violence in the name of Islam, and it is unfortunate that this numerically insignificant minority can exert considerable influence over the majority, who tend to remain silent spectators. A sad situation indeed!

In Islam, jihad opposes all forms of violence and terrorism, and it defends the homeland against occupation, plunder, and colonialism. Jihad is waged against those who support others in driving people out of their homes as well as against those who are in breach of their covenants. Jihad is a struggle against oppression, exploitation, tyranny, fear, corruption, and denial of basic human rights:

> And why should you not fight in the cause of God and
> of those who, being weak, are ill-treated [and oppressed]
> men, women, and children, whose cry is: "Our Lord!
> Rescue us from this town, whose people are oppressors,
> and raise for us from You one who will protect; and raise
> for us from You one who will help!" Those who believe
> fight in the cause of God, and those who reject faith fight in
> the cause of evil: so you fight against the friends of Satan:
> feeble, indeed is the cunning of Satan. (Qur'an 4:75–76)

Jihad is called for to establish peace and justice, freedom of religion and security, compassion and equity:

> And fight them on until there is no more tumult or oppression, and there prevail justice and faith in God; but if they cease, let there be no hostility except to those who practice oppression. (Qur'an 2:193)

It is not meant for domination; to achieve personal, territorial, and economic gains; or to exercise power and control. Those who perform jihad must spiritually and morally reform themselves, as they struggle to overcome the self:

> And strive in His cause as you ought to strive [with sincerity and under discipline]. He has chosen you, and has imposed no difficulties on you in religion; it is the cult of your father Abraham ..." (Qur'an 22:78)

However, some Muslims must bear responsibility for the bad name given to jihad. Some governments and groups in Muslim countries have used jihad to hide their moral, social, and political bankruptcy. In the process, they have killed the innocent, caused destruction, and have not advanced the cause of peace and justice. But regrettably they are the ones who show up regularly in the media.

A great misconception equates jihad with war. The word jihad sends shivers down the spines of many non-Muslims. It is looked upon as a holy war against non-Muslims, a kind of Crusade in reverse. This is contrary to Islamic teachings. The true jihad is when one controls his own desires and self-actualizes himself in the virtues of tolerance, empathy, reconciliation, and forgiveness.

There are various levels of jihad. A personal struggle to submit to God, fight evil within oneself, and achieve higher moral standards is called an inner jihad. A struggle against evil, injustice, and oppression within oneself, one's family, and one's society is called social jihad. Physical jihad is against all that prevents Muslims from servitude to God, people from knowing Islam, defense of Muslims, retribution against tyranny, and the protection of Muslims being forcibly removed from their homeland. It is physical jihad that receives so much criticism; those who do not understand it equate it with terror. However, its very purpose is to answer the call of those who cry out for freedom and yearn to be liberated from tyranny and bondage. It is a means of defense, but only for the cause of righteousness and justice.

Other types of jihad are charity, empathy, and scholarly works, and the self-sacrifice one makes in terms of wealth, property, or forgiveness. For example, to reconcile differences with another is the pinnacle of jihad. Prophet Muhammad said, "Reconciliation of your differences is more worthy than all prayers and all fasting" (Ibn Abi Talib 1999).

Aggression against innocent people is strongly denounced by all religions including Islam, which condemns extremism and violence and stands firmly against terrorist practices. However, we must not confuse terrorism with freedom fighters. Islam regards the fight against aggression and occupation as a legitimate right. While Muslims must defend themselves, they must not be antagonistic. Islam requires its believers to be strong, but this strength should be used to achieve peace and security for society.

Some Muslim groups, who have been hoodwinked by fraudulent leaders, continue their acts of aggression against innocent civilians. Let there be no misunderstanding: Islam condemns these acts. Islam does not punish those who embrace a different faith or allow Muslims to fight against those who disagree with them on religious questions. Islam does not change; people do. Those who perpetrate such terrorist acts are not following Islam, even though they profess to do so. Prophet Muhammad said, "Whoever hurts a non-Muslim citizen of a Muslim state hurts me, and he who hurts me annoys God" (Khan 1994).

Often, poor communication leads to animosity and distrust. Some non-Muslim clerics are ill informed about Islam, as they continue to spread lies in their sermons. As a result, seeds of hatred and enmity are planted in the minds of their congregations, and when they air their sermons on television, the impact of this repugnance has a far-reaching audience. Such distortions about Islam may lead non-Muslims to violence and terrorism.

The media paints a bleak picture of Islam, as it misrepresents what Islam is in the minds of its audiences. People are being deceived, and they have a right to know what is really going on. Certainly, the misuse and abuse of jihad by terrorists and extremists has led to negative portrayals of Islam. However, the media should use caution and discretion when they make their reports, as acts of terrorism are committed by a relatively small number of those who call themselves Muslims.

The media is awash with tales of terror and oppression. The word jihad frightens a lot of people, and the media capitalizes on this fear. To them, this term means bloodshed and violence. Yet to the overwhelming majority of Muslims, the word jihad means the struggle to be good.

The present manifestation of jihad by terrorists has great audience appeal. Action, suspense, exhilaration, and damnation are what audiences appeal to. The media follows suit. In this way jihad, as it is presented, will always have a place in the media as long as terrorists choose to represent it in this way.

To combat terrorism, we must understand it. To understand it, we must study it. We must identify the real terrorists and bring them to justice, and those who protect and nurture them must be held accountable. Terrorism negates our most basic and treasured principles and values. We need to address the evils of terrorism and dispense justice with impartiality. The real cure for terrorism consists in removing the conditions, circumstances, and motives that have brought it about.

Usury

Usury is the practice of making loans with excessive or abusive interest rates. From a moral perspective, usury creates excessive profit and gain, without the labor that is deemed work in the context of biblical scriptures. As such, profits from usury are driven by greed and manipulation. Usury is forbidden in Judaism, Christianity, and Islam, with certain stipulations.

In ancient times, usury was acceptable in Judaism, but only when charged against a non-Jew. According to the rabbis of the Talmud, the prohibition of usury applies to the borrower as well as to the lender (i.e., it is not only forbidden to lend with interest but also to borrow with interest). The prohibition against usury does not seem to be violated by investment in business, since the money is used to increase profits and both parties hope to make a gain (Jacobs 1995). There are also rabbis who say there is no problem with taking or giving interest from a corporation, only from individuals (Simmons, n.d.).

Do not charge a fellow Israelite interest, whether on money or food or anything else that may earn interest. (Deuteronomy 23:19)

You may charge a foreigner interest, but not a fellow Israelite, so that the Lord your God may bless you in everything you put your hand to in the land you are entering to possess. If you make a vow to the Lord your God, do not be slow to pay it, for the Lord your God will certainly demand it of you and you will be guilty of sin. (Deuteronomy 23:20–21)

If you lend money to one of my people among you who is needy, do not treat it like a business deal; charge no interest. (Exodus 22:25)

He lends at interest and takes a profit. Will such a man live? He will not! Because he has done all these detestable things, he is to be put to death; his blood will be on his own head. (Ezekiel 18:13)

Do not take interest or any profit from them, but fear your God, so that they may continue to live among you. You must not lend them money at interest or sell them food at a profit. (Leviticus 25:36–37)

In Christianity, usury is permissible within strict provisions and guidelines. However, lending and charging interest to family, friends, and the poor is disallowed. Lending with interest must not be done for unjust gain. A lender should not take advantage of the uninformed, the disadvantaged, or the coerced to charge excessive rates of interest.

His master replied, "I will judge you by your own words, you wicked servant! You knew, did you, that I am a hard man, taking out what I did not put in, and reaping what I did not sow? Why then didn't you put my money on deposit, so that when I came back, I could have collected it with interest?" (Luke 19:22–23)

Well then you should have put my money on deposit with the bankers, so that when I returned I would have received it back with interest. (Matthew 25:27)

In Islam, usury is to be avoided in any form, even though it is the basic foundation of global economics. Unlike Judaism and Christianity, there are no exceptions to usury in Islam; it is entirely prohibited. Earnings and profit have to be in accordance with Islam.

Those who devour usury will not stand except as stands one whom the Evil One by his touch has driven to madness. That is because they say: "Trade is like usury," but God has permitted trade and forbidden usury. Those who after receiving direction from their Lord, desist, shall be pardoned for the past; their case is for God [to judge]; but those who repeat [the offence] are Companions of the Fire: they will abide therein [forever]. God will deprive usury of all blessing, but will give increase for deeds of charity: for He does not love ungrateful and wicked creatures. (Qur'an 2:275–76)

O you who believe! Fear God, and give up what remains of your demand for usury, if you are indeed believers. If you do it not, take notice of war from God and His Messenger: but if you turn back, you shall have your capital sums; deal not unjustly, and you shall not be dealt with unjustly. (Qur'an 2:278–79)

O you who believe! Devour not usury, doubled and multiplied; but fear God; that you may [really] prosper. (Qur'an 3:130)

Pork

Consumption of pigs or blood is strictly forbidden in Judaism and Islam, as evidenced by the Old Testament and Qur'an, respectively. Since pigs do not chew the cud, even though they have a divided hoof, it is unlawful to eat pork. The New Testament does not contain any passages prohibiting the eating of swine or pig. Although many Christians refer to the Old Testament and the Law of Moses, they do not support the edict that pork is forbidden. According to the New Testament, all food is clean for consumption. Following are passages from the Old Testament, New Testament, and Qur'an addressing the issue of pork consumption:

The pig is also unclean; although it has a divided hoof, it does not chew the cud. You are not to eat their meat or touch their carcasses. (Deuteronomy 14:8)

But you must not eat meat that has its lifeblood still in it. (Genesis 9:4)

Those who consecrate and purify themselves to go into the gardens, following one who is among those who eat the flesh of pigs, rats and other unclean things—they will meet their end together with the one they follow, declares the Lord. (Isaiah 66:17)

And the pig, though it has a divided hoof, does not chew the cud; it is unclean for you. You must not eat their meat or touch their carcasses; they are unclean for you. (Leviticus 11:7–8)

You are to abstain from food sacrificed to idols, from blood, from the meat of strangled animals and from sexual immorality. You will do well to avoid these things. (Acts 15:29)

> Do not destroy the work of God for the sake of food. All food is clean, but it is wrong for a person to eat anything that causes someone else to stumble. (Romans 14:20)

> He has only forbidden you dead meat, and blood, and the flesh of swine, and that on which any other name has been invoked besides that of God. But if one is forced by necessity, without willful disobedience, nor transgressing due limits, then is he guiltless, for God is Oft-Forgiving, Most Merciful. (Qur'an 2:173)

> Forbidden to you are: dead meat, blood, the flesh of swine, and that on which the name of other than God has been invoked; that which has been killed by strangling, or by a violent blow, or by a headlong fall, or by being gored to death; that which has been [partly] eaten by a wild animal; unless you are able to slaughter it [in due form]; that which is sacrificed on stone [altars]; [forbidden] also is the division [of meat] by raffling with arrows: that is impiety ... (Qur'an 5:3)

Interestingly, Joel Osteen, senior pastor of Lakewood Church in Houston, Texas, warns his Christian congregation about the dangers of consuming pork. His ministry reaches more than seven million broadcast media viewers weekly in over one hundred nations around the world. He believes that God is honored when we do not eat pork, that pigs are unclean, and that the consumption of pork can cause serious health problems (Zaimov 2012).

Medical research confirms that the pig is an omnivorous scavenger that eats everything. The number of patients suffering from tapeworm disease is the highest among pork-eating nations. In a 1952 study by Dr. Glen Shepherd, which was published in the *Washington Post*, "One in six people in [the] USA and Canada have germs in their muscles— trichinosis from eating pork infected with trichina worms ... No one is immune from the disease and there is no cure. Neither antibiotics nor drugs or vaccines affect these tiny deadly worms" (Shamsi 1999).

Shaving the Beard

Scriptures from each of the three monotheistic traditions affirm that the shaving of the beard is prohibited. Today, many Jews, Christians, and Muslims do not practice this directive, which was commanded by God. The Old Testament clearly states that shaving the beard is forbidden: "Do not cut the hair at the sides of your head or clip off the edges of your beard" (Leviticus 19:27). "Priests must not shave their heads or shave off the edges of their beards or cut their bodies" (Leviticus 21:5). Orthodox Jews refuse to shave their beards. However, other Jews opt to shave the beard.

The Torah prohibits "shaving," which involves "destroying." Whether it is wrong for a man to be clean-shaven depends on the interpretation of scriptures. However, the general consensus is that only the facial hair must not be removed with a razor. Destroying involves the removal of facial hair together with the roots. This does not apply to the mustache, which is not connected to the beard. Trimming the beard with scissors is permissible, since it does not destroy the roots.

There are varying opinions about whether using an electric shaver is acceptable. The distinction between a razor and scissors is based on the fact that scissors cut the hair using two blades, while a razor cuts it with a single blade. The question is whether an electric shaver cuts with one or two blades (a blade and protective metal screen). Moreover, does the electric shaver cut the hair solely with the blade like a lawnmower, or with a scissors-like action, with the protective screen functioning as a second blade? Whether or not to use an electric shaver is still open to clarification, which has resulted in the individual making the choice (Rosen 2002). Most Conservative Jews have no restrictions or requirements about beards. However, many Orthodox Jews shave with an electric razor on the grounds that technically this machine, with its two blades, is not to be treated as a razor. Reform Jews do not consider the prohibition on shaving with a razor as compulsory (Jacobs 1995).

In Judaism, it once was considered a disgrace for an adult man not to have a beard:

> So Hanun seized David's envoys, shaved off half of each
> man's beard, cut off their garments at the buttocks, and

sent them away. When David was told about this, he sent messengers to meet the men, for they were greatly humiliated. The king said, "Stay at Jericho till your beards have grown, and then come back." (2 Samuel 10:4–5)

According to this passage from the Old Testament, it was a humiliation to shave the heads and beards of captives. In addition, the traditional manner of expressing anguish was to shave the head and beard.

Jewish prophets had beards. For example, Aaron, the brother of Moses, had a beard: "It is like precious oil poured on the head, running down on the beard, running down on Aaron's beard, down upon the collar of his robe" (Psalm 133:2). Beards are seen as a mark of Jewish identity. Beards are also a physical link to Jewish tradition, lifestyle, and its history.

In Judaism, there are certain days when shaving and trimming beards or cutting hair is not allowed. For example, it is forbidden to shave on Shabbat and biblical holidays (Rosh Hashanah, Yom Kippur, the first and last days of Sukkot and Passover, and Shavuot). Cutting the hair on these days falls under the category of shearing, which is also forbidden (Posner 2012).

In the New Testament, shaving only applies to the head, not the beard (Acts 21:24). The New Testament does not mention anyone having or shaving a beard, or if Jesus had a beard. However, since Jesus maintained the commandments of the law, one might conclude that he did wear a beard.

There are reasons why God gave man a beard. The first was to distinguish man from woman. The beard is a clear mark of masculinity, a distinction between the sexes that was made by God. Similarly, the lion wears a majestic and full mane to distinguish him from the lioness. If the lion's mane were removed, what would happen to his masculinity? Second, the beard was the badge of manly dignity, respect, and honor. In the Old Testament, the shaving of the beard was done during the treatment of leprosy (Leviticus 14:8–9) or the taking of special vows; or as a sign of grief, judgment, shame, humility, conquest, or enslavement. Under normal circumstances, the beard was never shaved (Reed 2008).

Saint Augustine of Hippo argued, "The beard signifies the courageous; the beard distinguishes the grown men, the earnest, the active, the vigorous. So that when we describe such, we say, he is a bearded man" (Augustine of Hippo 2012). The beard also signifies submission to God. A shaven face signifies submission to man. Orthodox Christian piety begins in the holy tradition of the Old Testament. The relationship to God, holiness, worship, and morality was formed in ancient times (Leviticus 19:27; Leviticus 21:5). Orthodox Christian priests wear beards, which comes from their desire to physically resemble Jesus (Durham 1998).

On the other hand, Roman Catholics shave their beards, which is contrary to the Old Testament. Until the beginning of the eleventh century, most Roman Catholic bishops were still bearded. By the end of the eleventh century, most priests and monks were shaving regularly. In 1080, Pope Gregory VII tried to enforce shaving, and even resorted to force to make bishops and priests shave off their beards. However, there were bearded popes after Gregory VII. In the sixteenth century, further canons barred Roman Catholic clergy from keeping their beards. This prohibition was not dropped officially until the Second Vatican Council convened in the early 1960s (Comerford 2009).

Protestant denominations were influenced by the Roman Catholics, who already had a tradition of clergy who shaved. As such, there was no issue over Protestant pastors shaving their beards.

Whether or not to shave a beard has long been argued among Muslim scholars. Since Prophet Muhammad and his followers wore beards, some scholars believe that shaving the beard is forbidden. Other scholars argue that shaving is merely *makruh* (undesirable or reprehensible), because there isn't a specific verse in the Qur'an that prohibits it. However, it is mentioned in the Hadiths of Muhammad, so scholars argue that the act is prohibited.

There are three views. First, shaving the beard is prohibited. Second, it is *makruh*. Third, there is no problem in shaving the beard, a view that is held by many contemporary scholars. Muslims try to follow the example of Prophet Muhammad in lifestyle and behavior. Since he never shaved his beard, then logically that would be the example to follow. Even so, scholars acknowledge that the act of shaving the beard is reprehensible but does not constitute a sin.

According to Allamah Murtada Al-Baghdadi, in his book titled *Tahrim Halq Al-Lihyah* (Unlawfulness of the Shaving of the Beard), the decision about whether to shave the beard can be examined from four Islamic sources: (a) Qur'an, (b) Hadiths, (c) consensus, and (d) intellect. According to the Qur'anic verse (4:119) that states "altering the creation of God" is unlawful, shaving the beard is an unnatural alteration of what God has created naturally. No one has the authority to alter what God has created except God. Why? God considered the beard to be a thing of adornment and beauty for Adam and his male descendants.

A verse in the Qur'an mandates Muslims to follow the Hadiths of Prophet Muhammad:

> ... your Companion [Muhammad] is neither astray nor being misled. Nor does he say [anything] of [his own] desire. It is no less than Inspiration sent down to him: he was taught by the one Mighty in Power, endued with Wisdom ... While he was in the highest part of the horizon ... so did [God] convey the Inspiration to His Servant ... the [Prophet's mind and] heart in no way falsified that which he saw. Will you then dispute with him concerning what he saw? (Qur'an 53:1–12)

Sunni and Shi'a scholars agree that a verdict arrived at through consensus is well founded. During consensus, a jurist may give a ruling concerning an Islamic issue, particularly when a verdict cannot be found through any other available source. However, the Shi'as state that an Infallible Imam must be an integral part of the consensus for it to be considered a valid source. The Sunnis do not agree with the Shi'as on this point.

We can also rely on the intellect. God granted Adam and his male descendants beards. Why? The appearance of the beard on the face would be a clear distinction between the male and female until Judgment Day. According to Imam Ja'far As-Sadiq, "From amongst the laws of the Lord of the Universe was that He granted the male gender from amongst the humans a beard so that there may be a difference [in appearance] between them" (Al-Baghdadi 1999). The Qur'an states, "What God has bestowed on His Messenger [Muhammad] ... belongs to God ... So take what the Messenger assigns to you, and deny yourselves that which he withholds from you ..." (Qur'an 59:7). Therefore, using the power of the intellect, Muslims must follow Prophet Muhammad, which means that the beard should not be shaved.

Summary

Why do some followers of Judaism, Christianity, and Islam continue to believe that they are so different? Because they perceive each other differently, they often misunderstand each other. True, there may be differences in the practice; however, for the most part, there is agreement on their underlying significance. For example, in the concept of atonement, the underlying themes of reconciliation, sacrifice, forgiveness, fasting, and prayer are evident in each of the faith traditions, although the methods by which these themes are fulfilled or satisfied may differ.

The headscarf is another case in point. Scriptures from each of the religions mandate the wearing of headscarves by women. That followers of these faiths choose not to wear headscarves does not mean that it is not an obligation. And some women in each of these faiths do, in fact, cover their heads today. Yet there is so much demeaning and denigrating of Muslim women who wear scarves. This prejudice is a form of Islamophobia that has unfortunately been propagated by fundamentalist extremists and in the media, which fails to seek out the truth.

Undeniably, there are a number of common misunderstandings about the acceptability of certain practices in Judaism, Christianity, and Islam. However, there are also guidelines for correcting these misunderstandings. Each faith tradition encourages its followers to self-actualize in virtues by avoiding vices that have a deleterious impact on personality and behavior.

7 Virtues

The Concept of Virtue

Throughout the course of history, secular and religious scholars have posited theories about how to identify and define virtues. Judaism, Christianity, and Islam have articulated the concept of virtues via the Old Testament, New Testament, and the Qur'an. A universal thread among these religions is that virtues function interdependently. For example, courage, bravery, valor, and fortitude depend on discernment, judgment, temperance, and restraint.

Aristotle's theory of moral virtue contends that our ultimate goal in life should be to attain the highest level of good (e.g., happiness). By using both intellectual understanding and moral virtue, we learn to make decisions that are right and just. Our intellectual understanding of virtue allows us to perceive what is right, while our moral virtue helps us carry out what we know to be the correct and just course of action. This interconnectivity of intellectual understanding and moral virtue is what Aristotle calls the "moral theory of virtue," or achieving the highest level of happiness by finding the middle ground in one's life and achieving a balance (Smith 2011).

There is virtue in taking responsibility for oneself. Yet along with this comes the idea that one should strive for balance. Balance is key to virtue. No one should do anything in the extreme. A sensible nature is attached to individual choice, but the choice is always to seek a balance. Good and evil are concepts that coexist in modern society. Both are linked together. They form a balance, and one cannot exist without the other.

Morality is comprised of virtues, values, and ethics. These actions help us to distinguish between right and wrong. Virtues are moral, and vices are immoral. For example, honesty is morally right while dishonesty is morally wrong. A person's attitude and behavior are connected with one's value system. Judaism, Christianity, and Islam specify values that must be followed and practiced. Values such as tolerance, freedom, kindness, and empathy should be adhered to. Ethics are sets of rules that help strengthen one's character by differentiating right from wrong. The Ten Commandments comprise a set of mandated and actionable ethics or moral limitations.

To obtain an understanding of the concept of virtues as it relates to values and ethics, table 17 shows examples of deficiency, moderation, and excess within each of the four powers of the human soul:

Table 17
Four Powers of the Human Soul

Source of Power	Deficiency	Moderation (Patience)	Excess
• Intellect	• Ignorance	• Wisdom	• Slyness
• Anger	• Cowardice	• Courage	• Recklessness
• Passion	• Laziness	• Chastity	• Voraciousness
• Imagination	• Prejudice	• Justice	• Tyranny

Source: Tallal Alie Turfe, *Patience in Islam: Sabr*, 1996.

It is in the arena of the power elements that we now focus our attention. We need a prescription or remedy to turn our virtues from weakness to strength. Weaknesses occur when we are not in control of the powers of our human soul, specifically 1) power of intellect, 2) power of anger, 3) power of passion, and 4) power of imagination. The remedy for turning weaknesses into strengths is patience.

Power of Intellect

How the power of intellect is utilized determines its weakness or strength. For example, the absence of mind, logic, and reason is the source of ignorance, while their presence is the source of knowledge. Patience turns the weakness of ignorance into the strength of knowledge. Patience is the origin of the intellect, which is the origin of the human mind. The more intellectual one becomes, the wiser and stronger that person becomes, and the better equipped that person is to overcome any adverse emotion. Bad emotion results in a loss of realistic thought, which lessens one's intellect. This bad emotion can emanate from a deficiency in the power of intellect (ignorance) or from an excessive use of the power of intellect (slyness). The end result is that the person succumbs to ignorance or slyness by becoming emotionally unstable (i.e., the person passes the limit of reasonable thinking).

People face problems, particularly, in times of sickness and adversity, from various standpoints. The losers are those who are ignorant and sly and do not know how to deal with those problems, while the winners are those who are patient and know how to deal with the problems wisely.

Powers of Anger, Passion, and Imagination

Cowardice can be overcome with courage (the power of anger); laziness can be overcome with chastity (the power of passion); and prejudice can be overcome with justice (the power of imagination). Cowardice and impatience are vices of deficiency. The relevant vices of excess are a reckless bravado and a sort of witless passivity in the midst of avoidable suffering and hardship. We think of courage as the paramount virtue of self-restraint. Indeed we are more than a little tempted to speak of it as the only virtue of self-restraint. This grossly underestimates the importance of patience.

The moral failures of war may be caused by those without the patience to survive great anger as well as those without the courage to resist great fear. Consider the affinity between patience and devoting one's life to doing good. If we allow emotions such as despair or anger to engage our thoughts and actions, we cease to give ourselves to the good. The more we assume that the hardships or evils we experience can be set right with justice or courage, the less room there is for the reasonableness of a moral posture that counsels acceptance of the limits of our capacity to make the good we crave our own.

Courage derives from steadfastness. To be steadfast against every personal passion or calamity—and not run away—is true courage. Thus, there is a great difference between human courage and the courage of a wild beast. A wild animal moves in only one direction when it is roused, but a man who possesses true courage chooses confrontation or nonresistance, whichever is appropriate for the occasion.

There are many examples of how patience can purify the four powers of the human soul. People lose control of their inner selves because they lack the quality of patience. It is very important to purify ourselves with patience so that our souls will be cleansed of evil and corruption, and we will be guided by ethical and moral virtues. For example, moderation of the power of passion is chastity, because it overcomes the deficiency of laziness and the excess of voraciousness. Only in this way can we prepare ourselves to receive the unlimited devotion of God. Our struggle is for perpetual purification.

With justice, we reach the highest level of the power of imagination. Justice is the origin of all ethical virtues. It illuminates all four powers of the human soul and guides us as individuals or a society. Justice is the means by which each person receives his due.

Justice represents the individual's metaphysical relationship with God. Our actions in this world determine our reward or punishment in the hereafter. Individual justice means that we should refrain from committing sins. When we reach this level of purification through patience, we have become just.

Social justice honors the rights of others within a society or community. We should not trespass upon the rights of others, and we should establish justice and goodness in society. The prophets endeavored to establish piety in the lives of individuals so that truth and justice would prevail in every society.

Finally, there is the justice that requires us to remember our loved ones who had passed away. We remember our dead by practicing ethical virtues such as kindness and charity. And it is patience that helps us achieve this end.

In addition to justice and patience, other virtues appear in the scriptures of all three Abrahamic faiths. Table 18 is a list of selected virtues (optimistic) and vices (pessimistic) and the estimated number of times they appear in the Old Testament, New Testament and other Christian texts, and the Qur'an:

Table 18
Virtues/Vices in Biblical Scriptures
Estimated Number of Occurrences

Virtues/Vices	Old Testament	New Testament	Other Christian Texts*	Qur'an
Optimistic				
Blessing	353	101	366	113
Charity /Gift	179	109	64	269
Faith/Trust	153	300	407	426
Justice	80	35	163	252
Mercy/Forgiveness	268	65	131	246
Righteous/Good	892	378	544	520
Truth	117	109	158	333
Wisdom/Understanding	383	117	275	251
Pessimistic				
Anger/Wrath	393	54	188	94
Envy/Greed	66	76	35	50
Hatred	131	30	46	88
Pride/Vanity	133	9	70	38

*Book of Mormon; Doctrine and Covenants; and Pearl of Great Price.

Sources: Old Testament; New Testament; Old Testament database (www.lds.org /scriptures/ot); Yassarnal Qur'an database (yassarnalquran.wordpress.com).

Virtues and vices are mentioned in the scriptures of Judaism, Christianity, and Islam. The number of occurrences for each virtue and vice is an estimate, as they were generated from databases. Nonetheless, the figures do underscore that there is commonality among the three

Abrahamic religions about the existence and practice of virtues and vices. Let us examine a few of these in more detail: justice, mercy, hatred, and envy.

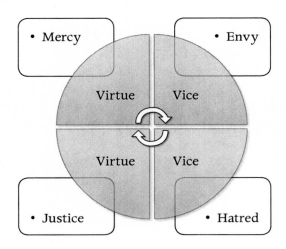

Justice

Each of the Abrahamic religions conveys the same message about the virtue of justice (i.e., the protection of the rights of everyone). Justice demands equality, impartiality, and fairness. To emphasize the justice of God, we observe the existence of this world, which is the most intelligent, well-thought-out, and perfect system.

As man has free will, he alone engages in good or bad deeds. Humans have the freedom and right to choose as they wish. This, then, is followed logically by the concept of reward and punishment in the hereafter, which is based on justice for all. However, justice is heightened and brought to a greater meaning when the righteous person performs a good deed, such as treating an enemy with kindness.

Because justice is the connection between peace and prosperity, it is the basis of the structure within society. Justice has no preference for color, creed, race, ethnicity, tribalism, nationalism, or biases. All people are created equally in this regard. Humanity must enjoy the fruits of justice, despite our differences and disputes. We need to seek moral significance and ethical consequences, which broaden and expand the concept of justice in society.

The Torah reveals that Abraham became the father of the Jewish people when he heeded God's call to adopt a sacred purpose, spreading righteousness and justice in the world:

> For I have chosen him, so that he will direct his children and his household after him to keep the way of the Lord by doing what is right and just, so that the Lord will bring about for Abraham what He has promised him. (Genesis 18:19)

> But let justice roll down like waters and righteousness like an ever-flowing stream. (Amos 5:24)

> Appoint judges and officials for each of your tribes in every town the Lord your God is giving you, and they shall judge the people fairly. Do not pervert justice or show partiality. Do not accept a bribe, for a bribe blinds the eyes of the wise and twists the words of the innocent. Follow justice and justice alone, so that you may live and possess the land the Lord your God is giving you. (Deuteronomy 16:18–20)

In Christianity, the central focus is to work for justice and live peacefully among all people. The pursuit of justice is an essential part of the Christian call to holiness. Pursuing social justice is one of the highest moral responsibilities of the church and of individual Christians:

> Woe to you Pharisees, because you give God a tenth of your mint, rue and all other kinds of garden herbs, but you neglect justice and the love of God. You should have practiced the latter without leaving the former undone. (Luke 11:42)

> Here is my servant whom I have chosen, the one I love, in whom I delight; I will put my Spirit on him, and he will proclaim justice to the nations. (Matthew 12:18)

In the past God overlooked such ignorance, but now He commands all people everywhere to repent. For He has set a day when He will judge the world with justice by the man He has appointed. He has given proof of this to all men by raising him from the dead. (Acts 17:30–31)

In Islam, justice is considered a supreme virtue and an obligation:

O you who believe! Stand out firmly for justice, as witnesses to God, even as against yourselves, or your parents, or your kin, and whether it be (against) rich or poor ... (Qur'an 4:135)

O you who believe! Stand out firmly for God, as witnesses to fair dealing, and let not the hatred of others to you make you swerve to wrong and depart from justice. Be just: that is next to piety: and fear God. For God is well acquainted with all that you do. (Qur'an 5:8)

God commands justice, the doing of good, and liberality to kith and kin, and He forbids all shameful deeds, and injustice and rebellion ... (Qur'an 16:90)

We sent aforetime Our Messengers with clear signs and sent down with them the Book and the Balance (of right and wrong) that men may stand forth in justice ... (Qur'an 57:25)

The concept of justice was revealed not only in the Qur'an but in all the monotheistic holy scriptures as well as to the prophets before Muhammad. God has demanded justice, irrespective of religion, for all faiths and for mankind. Justice is a test that must be fulfilled.

Mercy

The concept of mercy transcends race, age, color, and religion and affects every facet of life. It is a frequently used word, but it is often forgotten as we go about our daily lives. What vast wisdom it represents. Without mercy's energy, there is a void in the linkage between the soul and the person. Mercy strengthens the soul and fulfills the unity within man's life. We need to fill our hearts with mercy and to render mercy to others when they need it.

Some examples of mercy are to humble ourselves to our parents, tend to the needs of the orphans, and maintain relations with our relatives. It is also incumbent upon us to render mercy to one another, irrespective of which religion one follows. To this end, brotherhood and mercy are inseparable. In our remembrance and love of God, we must be grateful for His benevolence and mercy, which are manifested in His Creation and revelations. Here mercy comes full circle, as it is a universal mercy that embraces everything. It is heightened when people live in peace and harmony with one another and are united in brotherhood and solidarity.

In Judaism, mercy is the lifeblood of human conduct. During the time of Moses, people made a golden calf as an idol of worship. God was angered by this transgression. The intercession of Moses was vital, and he asked God to forgive the people. God revealed to Moses the Thirteen Attributes of Mercy, a way for future generations to achieve atonement and healing:

> And He passed in front of Moses, proclaiming, "The Lord, the Lord, the compassionate and gracious God, slow to anger, abounding in love and faithfulness, maintaining love to thousands, and forgiving wickedness, rebellion and sin. Yet, he does not leave the guilty unpunished; he punishes the children and their children for the sin of the parents to the third and fourth generation." (Exodus 34:6–7)

God informed Moses that when Jewish people sin, they should seek forgiveness by reciting the Thirteen Attributes of Mercy. These attributes are recited as the sinner asks God for His mercy, forgiveness, kindness, compassion, and grace (Eisenberg 2004).

In Christianity, the nature of mercy is the benevolent sorrow that Christians feel when they perceive the suffering or approaching calamities of others, connected to the desire to relieve them. Without a compassionate disposition, one cannot be merciful. Mercy resides in the heart, as it guides the senses. It is a passion that leads to action and the desire to relieve misery. Its manner is tender, and its courageous action is one of liberation. Diligence and self-denial are the cornerstones of mercy (James 1820). Justice and mercy go hand in hand. Justice renders to each his due and calls each to assume responsibility. Mercy goes beyond the issue of who is responsible. Mercy is simply love's response to suffering (D'Ambrosio 2013). Divine mercy is manifest in God's actions toward mankind. His mercy extends everywhere and at all times:

> Blessed are the merciful, for they will be shown mercy. (Matthew 5:7)

> His mercy extends to those who fear Him, from generation to generation. (Luke 1:50)

> Let us then approach God's throne of grace with confidence, so that we may receive mercy and find grace to help us in our time of need. (Hebrews 4:16)

The essence of mercy is to take into account not only that which is strictly due, but also weaknesses, infirmities, and defects of all kinds. The scriptures show that mercy is a characteristic of God, the attribute that extends over all of His Creation. Empathy is the hallmark of mercy, as one comes to the rescue of another by feeling his pain and suffering (Michalenko 2009). Mercy is an important trait because it is always needed to reach forgiveness. As God forgives man for his sins, man must be willing to forgive those who have harmed or displayed hostility to him. In this way, man shows mercy for his fellow man.

In Islam, the human family is one. There is no superiority of white over black or black over white. Islam rejects all notions of racial prejudice and teaches that the only basis of distinction between human beings is individual moral qualities. To complete one's faith in Islam, one must be imbued with mercy for others. Disputes are a sign that one is missing the mercy of God. Those who do not deserve the mercy of God are people who do not protect one another and who do not enjoin good and prohibit evil:

> ... My Mercy extends to all things. That [Mercy] I shall ordain for those who do right, and practice regular charity, and those who believe in Our Signs. (Qur'an 7:156)

> We sent you not, but as a Mercy for all creatures. (Qur'an 21:107)

The spirit of mercy is manifested in two ways. First, the believers will love God, and God will love them. Second, the attitude of the believers will be one of mercy and humility, as they strive for truth and justice. This type of spirit even extends to the family. For example, let us look at the sacrifice and attention that a mother provides for her child. During months of pregnancy, the mother is filled with anxiety, stress, and worry regarding the safety of the child in her womb. The mother puts her trust and reliance on God and knows her child is safe. After birth, the mother raises her child with love and gratitude. As our parents have shown us mercy in their care and sacrifice, we should likewise provide the same kind of mercy for our parents. We should always be grateful to our parents.

Mercy in Islam includes all creatures. It dominates the hearts and minds of people, as it embraces not just Muslims but all humans, regardless of religion. It is extended to both friend and foe with kindness.

Hatred

Hatred is a pervasive emotion and sociopsychological problem. Hatred has many forms—enmity, hostility, antagonism, animosity, rancor, antipathy, and animus. Enmity might be felt for an enemy. Hostility is the clear expression of enmity. Antagonism is hostility that results in active resistance, opposition, or contentiousness. Animosity often triggers bitter resentment or punitive action. Rancor suggests vengeful hatred and resentment. Antipathy is deep-seated aversion or repugnance.

Animus is distinctively personal, often based on one's prejudices or temperament.

How does hatred manifest itself in the human persona? People who are imbued with hatred feel that they have been unfairly treated, unjustly accused, or betrayed. Perhaps their honor was questioned, or their needs were never understood, or they never received recognition. As a result, they begin to hate and harbor the most extreme level of anger against those who have hurt them. They become agitated, antagonistic, inflamed, rude, and belligerent toward others. They may hate others because they feel victimized by lies, cheating, rejection, and condemnation. They may feel used and abused. Because of this enmity, those who hate are never fully content. Rather, they are bitter, hostile, sarcastic, embittered, paranoid, suspicious, and defensive. They are irrational, as they feel there is no hope for tolerance, only despair and distrust. Hatred stems from the power of anger and destroys man's spiritual balance.

Slander is one form of this type of hatred. We witness this devastating type of behavior among each of the three Abrahamic faiths. While they all agree that slander is a major sin, there are many instances of encroachment upon the rights of others. Many gossip without thinking. They are so busy spreading gossip; they do not even stop to consider whether or not it is true. They are unaware that they are only harming themselves. This type of behavior causes hostilities as it sows hatred and discord between each other. Each religion demands that we respect one another, and its followers are held accountable for their attitudes and actions. The capacity of the tongue to obey and disobey is great. However, one must guard the tongue to avoid falling into the trap of slander.

> Do not go about spreading slander among your people.
> Do not do anything that endangers your neighbor's life.
> I am the Lord. (Leviticus 19:16)
>
> Slanderers, God-haters, insolent, arrogant and boastful;
> they invent ways of doing evil; they disobey their
> parents; they have no understanding, no fidelity, no

love, no mercy. Although they know God's righteous decree that those who do such things deserve death, they not only continue to do these very things but also approve of those who practice them. (Romans 1:30–32)

O you would believe! Avoid suspicion as much (as possible): for suspicion in some cases is a sin: And spy not on each other, nor speak ill of each other behind their backs. Would any of you like to eat the flesh of his dead brother? Nay, you would abhor it...But fear God: for God is Oft-Returning, Most Merciful. (Qur'an 49:12)

To overcome slander, those who hate must be able to assess and analyze their own irrational behavior. They must identify how others react to them. Is the cause of their hatred a figment of their imagination, or is it real? Had they been intentionally mistreated or neglected? Or were they just wrapped up in their own egos?

There is much concern about hatred in the world, that people have become disinclined to be intolerant of hatred. Is each culture too myopic and autonomous to look to other cultures for workable insights and solutions? Are we so wrapped up in technology that we are incapable of dealing with hatred? Hatred has no single location, for it permeates all national, ethnic, and religious spheres. And it often erupts into violence and war. Ignorance breeds hatred, as it closes one's eyes to what is actually happening and isolates people from the rest of humanity. Lack of knowledge is the ultimate barrier. Ignorance enslaves and leads to the enslavement of others. As Albert Einstein said, "Condemnation without investigation is the height of ignorance" (Einstein 2010).

Here in America we are confronted with the disease of xenophobia (fear and hatred of strangers or foreigners). It is fear of that which is different. It is fear that leads to hatred and a desire for control over those who are different. Xenophobia is based on ignorance, which breeds fear. Fear brings about intolerance, which gives rise to hatred. In America, we find many people who are ignorant and naïve regarding other cultures and nations, and the foreign policy of the American government at times is representative of this unjust reality. For example, the American government's lack of a genuine even-handed policy in the Middle East has severely tarnished its credo of democracy and justice.

There is a lack of trust, partnership, and shared values among people within the same community. To be sure, reconciliation in resolving religious disputes, ethnic quarrels, and marital problems is indeed a great challenge if brotherhood and solidarity are to be effective. Hatred in all forms offends not only the dignity of man but also is an offense against God. In overcoming hatred, we must seek ways to foster the vitality and moral well-being of society. Each of the Abrahamic faiths offers us the way to enlightenment. When hatred appears, each religion provides the solution to overcome this evil. Each provides the necessary and trustworthy values, norms, motivations, and ideals, all grounded in an ultimate reality. To overcome hatred, we can extend a helping hand to one another by being compassionate and understanding. Above all, we must be forgiving, even of those who hate. We must overlook the mistakes of others as we learn how to forgive.

Envy

Envy is a feeling of discontent about another's advantages, successes, or possessions. It is often referred to as one of the seven deadly sins; the others are pride, gluttony, lust, anger, greed, and sloth. Envy is a common sin and the perpetual tormenter of virtue. It is treacherous because it draws people to its venom. It renders its victims miserable and unhappy. It is associated with hypocrisy, hatred, and discord. It is like a vampire that feeds on others. Envy pollutes the heart.

Envy is a complex and puzzling emotion. Aristotle described envy as pain at the good fortune of others. It is a frustrated desire turned destructive. The impulse to make contact with others becomes the impulse to destroy others. An envious person wants to destroy the morals and ethics of others and works to demoralize them and have an adverse impact on their lives. Envy distorts and then insidiously devours the thoughts and views of others.

Jealousy is directed toward the possession of values; envy is directed toward the destruction of values. Envy works out of fear and resentment toward others. The envious are insatiable, fed by a diet to consume the values of others. Ignorance breeds suspicion, and suspicion breeds envy, all of which are incompatible with the essential attitude of sympathy and love. In addition, greed also breeds envy and hate. Imitation is the result of envy. Many social structures are based on envy and imitation. Envy and the craving for success are two of the main causes of division in society; each person is imitating the one above him. Envy spreads among Jews, Christians, and Muslims, making them hate one another.

The remedy for envy is love. Envy is born in hate and cured in love. It can be overcome by spirituality, cooperation, comfort, and confidence. We can strive for unity among Judaism, Christianity, and Islam if we overcome ignorance, allay our fears and suspicions, and combat envy with love and respect for one another.

Throughout the course of history, there have been vivid examples of envy. Cain envied Abel; Sarah envied Hagar; Joseph's brothers envied him. The Old Testament describes the evil of envy: "A heart at peace gives life to the body, but envy rots the bones" (Proverbs 14:30).

Cain and Abel were the sons of Adam and Eve. Cain was envious of his brother, because he realized that God preferred the pious Abel. Cain was overwhelmed by jealousy and anger and killed Abel. He then realized, via Divine intervention, that he'd erred. Consequently, the ugly head of envy tormented Cain for the rest of his life (Genesis 4:1–16). The story of Cain and Abel shows how envy can permeate everyday life as well as any abstract description, and also suggests that it can motivate extreme behavior (Smith 2008).

Sarah and Hagar were the wives of Abraham. Sarah was the preferred wife, and Hagar was her maid. While married to Sarah, Abraham married Hagar, who gave birth to a son, Ishmael. Because Sarah could not bear a child at that time, she became envious of Hagar. Years later, Sarah gave birth to Isaac. But the envy did not subside, and Sarah had Abraham send Hagar and her son away (Genesis 21:1–14). One can make the distinction between jealousy and envy. For example, jealousy is embedded in the fear of losing what is already ours. Envy emerges from the passion to have what someone else has (Berinstein 2009).

Joseph's older brothers envied him because he was their father's favorite. The jealousy was so intense, Joseph's brothers sold him into slavery, and Joseph was taken to Egypt. Since he was able to interpret dreams, he became well liked and respected for his knowledge and insight. As a result, the pharaoh put Joseph in charge of all the land in Egypt. Grain was in short supply throughout the region, owing to the drought that Joseph's dream had predicted. Joseph's older brothers came to Joseph to buy grain, but did not recognize him. He revealed himself to his brothers and reunited with them and his father (Genesis 41:37–46). Joseph's older brothers were jealous and perceived him as a threat. However, their envy emanated not from the desire of an object but from their father's fervent love for his favorite son.

Judaism condemns envy and jealousy on the grounds that these emotions amount to idolatry. Jealousy is at the root of all human conflict. Feelings of intense jealousy and envy often mark the first freefall in a downward spiral toward anger, a sense of helplessness, and, finally, depression (Strasser 1996).

Christians view envy as one of the seven deadly sins. As a deadly sin, envy is offensive to the human spirit: "For where you have envy and selfish ambition, there you find disorder and every evil practice" (James 3:16). Envy is triggered by immaturity (Genesis 37:3–4), pride (Daniel 6:1–5), leadership insecurity (1 Samuel 18:6–9), low esteem and inferiority (Genesis 30:1), greed for fame and public approval (Matthew 27:18), uncontrolled desire for material gain (Genesis 12:10–13), and frustration (Psalm 73:3). Many committed Christians may unconsciously harbor envy in their hearts. It is a very common, seldom confessed emotion, and yet it is heavy enough to condemn our souls (Perera 2011).

In Islam, envy is called *hasad*, which is the desire for the destruction of something good that belongs to someone else. *Hasad* is the greatest obstacle toward establishing and cementing relationships with others. The envious person is content when he wishes evil for others, and overjoyed when misfortune befalls them. Envy is a disease of the heart that leads to vulgar behavior, hatred, deceit, and the abandonment of others. God commands believers to protect themselves from the evil of the envious person: "And from the evil of the envious one as he practices envy" (Qur'an 113:5).

There are two types of envy. The first is when someone hopes to acquire another person's blessings—his wealth, his knowledge, his status, his power, etc. The second type of envy is when he hopes the person loses his blessings, and he does not desire them for himself (Jabir al-Jaza'iry 2012).

Summary

While it is the nature of man to seek happiness and satisfaction, there are those who fall victim to the vices of the world. Hatred and envy are just two of the vices that erode into the powers of the human soul. These deficiencies lead man astray. Man-made laws and systems are manifestations of human ideas, which are unable to penetrate the human soul. They cannot be as effective in curing the ills of the human persona as spirituality. They cannot bring genuine happiness and satisfaction to mankind. It is the prophets or messengers of Judaism, Christianity, and Islam that have given us the criteria by which to avoid these vices. People can do this by evaluating the level of their beliefs in order to attain the purity of their values and virtues. Each of the Abrahamic faiths prohibits people from sacrificing their morals for the sake of lust and cravings. Each tradition is immersed in justice and mercy, qualities that play a crucial role in seeking happiness and satisfaction as well as the resolution of conflicts. Justice and mercy are the bases upon which the unity of the family is preserved.

The virtues of justice and mercy and the vices of hatred and envy are part and parcel of life itself. The mechanism by which we uphold justice and mercy—by preventing hatred and envy—is struggle. However, vices are having a devastating impact on the behavior of Americans, and we are witnessing a continuing decline in morality.

Part Two
Children of Abraham: Divided We Fail

"The reason why the world lacks unity, and lies broken and in heaps, is because man is disunited with himself."—Ralph Waldo Emerson

Source: *Nature*, by Ralph Waldo Emerson, CreateSpace Independent Publishing Platform (December 12, 2012), 58 pages.

Threats to the Abrahamic Faiths

There has been a steady decline in moral values in the United States. We have witnessed a gradual and continuous degradation of national morality, which threatens the very fabric of American society. While Christianity is the predominant religion in America, the country is experiencing an unparalleled decline in spirituality. As the principles and commandments that God has bestowed on mankind are gradually challenged, modified, or abandoned, our nation will continue to experience even greater moral decay. Americans who hold steadfast to the precepts of Judaism, Christianity, and Islam must work together to restore the moral consciousness that has made America great. We must thwart this violent storm of immorality and decadence in our society.

Can we turn on the television without finding a program that has sexual undertones? Can we surf the Internet without finding sexual predators? Can our children turn on the television, watch a movie, or open a magazine without being bombarded with an array of sexual messages? Shouldn't our educational institutions teach about the immorality of having premarital sex rather than about methods of having safe sex? Can society stop sexualizing our youth? Can we rewind and instill in our minds the moral and ethical standards that allow us to differentiate between right and wrong? Can we, as Americans, be cleansed from the unrestrained immorality around us?

Morality in America

During the last half century, moral integrity in America has been on a constant decline. During the 1960s, America struggled with a number of issues—poverty, racism, women's rights, gender equality, and the Vietnam War. Young people were rebellious and sought to define their own identity and place in American society. They paid a heavy price for that search and began to experiment with drugs and sex. During this time, gays and lesbians also became more vocal. Undeniably, the turbulent times of the 1960s had an adverse affect on culture, moral standards, and religion in America. Dysfunctional behavior became the norm. One cannot blame government for all of society's problems. Nonetheless, economic and social legislation over the past fifty years has had a negative impact on the moral virtues we consider sacred.

Who is to blame for this moral decadence in American society? Blame can be directed toward parents, schools, and religious institutions. Parents need to go beyond teaching morality to actually living morality. For example, some teenage girls dress solely to entice teenage boys to have premarital sex. And how do their parents respond? They just sit back and say, "That is the trend today." It takes initiative, commitment, and a willingness to go against the trend to bring our children back to what is morally and religiously right. Jews, Christians, and Muslims are all faced with the challenge to restore our God-given rights of moral beliefs and faith to our communities. Moral values need to be taught and practiced very early in life.

In July 2012, psychologists at Knox College in Galesburg, Illinois, conducted a study of elementary school students in the Midwest region of the United States. The study revealed that girls as young as six already think of themselves as sex objects. The psychologists used paper dolls to assess self-sexualization in six- to nine-year-old girls. Sixty girls were shown two dolls; one was dressed in tight and revealing "sexy" clothes, and the other wore a trendy but covered-up, loose outfit. Using a different set of dolls for each question, the researchers then asked each girl to choose the doll that "looked like herself, looked how she wanted to look, was the popular girl in school, she wanted to play with." Across-the-board, girls chose the "sexy" doll most often. The results were significant in two categories: 68 percent of the girls said they wanted to look like the sexy doll, and 72 percent said the sexy doll was more popular than the non-sexy doll (Abbasi 2012). No doubt, these young girls were heavily influenced by the revealing sexual themes on television and other media. Therefore, moral values are being challenged very early in life, and this continues as they become teenagers and adults.

According to a study conducted by researchers at the University of Texas School of Public Health, middle-school students are engaging in sexual intercourse as early as age twelve. The researchers examined sexual risk behaviors among middle-school students in a large southeastern US urban public school district. The study disclosed that by the age of twelve, 12 percent of students had already engaged in vaginal sex, 7.9 percent in oral sex, 6.5 percent in anal sex, and 4 percent in all three types of intercourse. Students who have sex at this young age are "more likely to have multiple lifetime sexual partners, use alcohol or drugs before sex and have unprotected sex, all of which puts them at greater risk for getting a sexually transmitted disease or becoming pregnant" (Markham 2009).

However, according to the Centers for Disease Control and Prevention, the proportion of high-school students who had ever had sexual intercourse declined from 54 percent in 1991 to 46 percent in 2001 and has stabilized since that time to 47 percent in 2011. There was a significant decline in sexual intercourse among black students, from 82 percent in 1991 to 60 percent in 2011. During the same time period, there was a decline among Hispanic students (from 53 percent to 49 percent), and among white students (from 50 percent to 44 percent) (CDC 2012). Even so, the numbers are still very high and alarming.

Peer pressure among teenagers, the media, and popular culture endorse permissiveness and casual sex. Alarmingly, the US government indirectly funds programs that promote contraception and safe sex. In 2008, the Department of Health and Human Services spent $610 million on such programs targeting teens, at least four times what it spent on abstinence education. Unfortunately, eventually the government eliminated all federal funding for abstinence education, increasing instead funding for comprehensive sex education (Kim 2010).

Sexual intercourse among students presents a moral dilemma. Some argue that we are no longer a moral society. America has reached a point where almost anything is tolerated and nothing is deemed intolerable. Morality points to a code of conduct or a set of beliefs that distinguish right from wrong. Discipline is a hallmark of sustaining our moral ethic. Children who are not disciplined become self-centered and irrational and undermine authority. How bad has America become? Turn on the television or the computer, or watch a movie, and the answers will be right before your eyes. There has been an increase in violence, crime, and sex in the media. It isn't pretty or godlike. Even cartoons have more and more grotesque themes.

The media have a major influence on our cultural values, and Americans know it. Most assuredly, we should be concerned because they present various social, cultural, and political views that are not compatible with Judaism, Christianity, and Islam. For example, television is becoming the main vehicle by which viewers find viewpoints that reflect their lifestyles and ways of life. Television is no longer just competing for our attention and dollars but for our very souls. As it rapidly becomes the dominant role of expression, it is having a deleterious impact on the minds of its viewers, who seem to glue themselves to their programs. Television is becoming a kind of religion, shaping the faith and values of many people. These values are in many ways opposed to and in conflict with the values of monotheistic principles and ideals. This means that we must take a new and completely different view of the profound role television has assumed in our culture, unless we are prepared to surrender our own role as the place where people search to find meaning, faith, and value for their lives.

America needs a transformation. It needs to get back to the basic principles that made our country great. Liberty and justice, based on the moral and ethical demands of faith, were the hallmarks of what our Founding Fathers so arduously worked for and believed in. Religious freedom for all citizens was mandated, as the Founding Fathers knew that morality springs from religious faith. We have a moral and spiritual crisis in America that has been brewing for some time. It is a crisis of character that has produced a crisis of behavior. It is a poverty of values caused by a poverty of faith. We remove all value judgments from society and then wonder why we have a generation that is morally confused.

Our society has continually and increasingly dismissed the relevance of religion and, as a consequence, has diminished its importance. If religion is ignored or banned, then its components, such as the Ten Commandments and the teachings of Moses, Jesus, and Muhammad, are likewise made irrelevant. The end result is that "If there is no God, then anything is permissible" (Ream 1993).

Mankind's moral sense is not a strong beacon light, radiating outward to illuminate all that it touches in a sharp outline. It is, rather, a small candle flame, casting vague and multiple shadows, flickering and sputtering in the strong winds of power and passion, greed, and ideology. But brought close to the heart and cupped in one's hands, it dispels the darkness and warms the soul (Athal 2012).

From May 3 to May 6, 2012, Gallup conducted a poll on values and beliefs in the United States. The results were based on telephone interviews conducted with a random sample of 1,024 adults, ages eighteen and older, living in all fifty US states and the District of Columbia. According to the survey, Americans remain largely pessimistic about the direction in which the nation's morals are headed.

Table 19
Moral Values in America, 2002–12

Year	% Getting Worse	% Getting Better	% Same
2002	67	24	7
2003	67	24	7
2004	77	16	5
2005	77	16	5
2006	81	11	6
2007	82	11	4
2008	81	11	6
2009	71	21	6
2010	76	14	7
2011	69	22	6
2012	73	19	5

Source: Gallup, May 2012.

Seventy-three percent of Americans say moral values in the country as a whole are getting worse, up from 69 percent last year. While there was a resurgence of those saying that moral values were getting better in 2011, it dipped to 19 percent in 2012. Five percent state that moral values are staying the same.

In response to the Gallup question, "In your view, what is the most important problem with the state of moral values in the country today," some of the most frequent answers included:

•	Consideration of others/compassion/caring/tolerance/respect	18%
•	Lack of family structure/divorce/kid's upbringing	10%
•	Lack of faith/religion	10%
•	Lack of morals	7%
•	Sense of entitlement/government dependency	5%
•	Greed/selfishness	5%
•	Poor leadership/poor guidance	4%
•	TV/media/Internet	4%
	Subtotal	63%

Americans are most likely to cite a lack of respect or tolerance for other people as the most important problem related to moral values. Other frequent responses include the decline of family structure, lack of religion and faith, and lack of morals in general. These deficiencies are construed as societal weaknesses that impinge upon and erode the very sanctity of morality.

Societal Weaknesses

Social problems have a negative impact on moral values and the human persona. Some of these problems include crime and juvenile delinquency, teenage pregnancy and abortion, and unemployment and divorce. Today, it is common to lose one's virginity by the age of sixteen. Bombarded with messages of sex, our youth try to look sexy, because sex sells!

As Jews, Christians, and Muslims, we strive toward perfecting our personalities by overcoming these social problems that affect both our youth and adults. The personality is self-actualized when we make it our duty to reach out into society and struggle against all forms of immorality, evil, and corruption. The personality must be instilled with the determination to fight against the immoral evils, injustice, tyranny, oppression, pessimism, hatred, and envy that plague our society. American society should be morally and ethically sound.

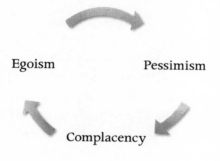

Egoism   Pessimism

Complacency

Egoism and Egotism

Dictionaries include many meanings associated with the word *ego*. Ego is the conscious mind and the consciousness of one's own identity. *Egoism* is the doctrine that the supreme end of human conduct is the happiness of the ego, or self, and that it is virtuous, moral, and just to operate in pursuit of self-interest. It is the excessive preoccupation with one's own well-being and interests, usually accompanied by an inflated sense of self-importance. It is the tendency to evaluate everything in relation to one's own interests (i.e., self-centeredness).

Egotism is the habit or practice of thinking and talking too much about oneself, or the spirit that leads to this practice (i.e., self-exaltation). It is the tendency to consider oneself to be better and more important than other people. It is an exaggerated opinion of one's own importance and an inflated feeling of pride in one's superiority to others. It is the concept in which a person is so possessed by the ego that he becomes convinced that he is the center of the universe.

Whether one is egoistic or egotistic, he is morally depraved and suffers from false impressions of himself. This self-centeredness and self-absorption immensely diminishes his chances of ever reaching moral fulfillment and having self-respect. Occupied with thoughts and actions of materialism, greed, center of attention, and conceit, he continues to fall deeper and deeper into a pit from which he cannot escape. This obedience to himself further erodes his soul, as he commits every act of transgression, deception, and sedition in order to achieve his superiority or authority over others. In a nutshell, he begins to worship himself, thereby becoming totally impervious to spirituality and the common good.

The person who continually boasts about himself is someone whose self-worth is meaningless, and he feels the necessity to tap other avenues or sources to restore his self-esteem. This need for replenishment is vital since the ego functions out of fear. The ego operates in such a way to give the egotist a sense of loneliness and separation from the world. The egotist feels he is obliged to act the way he does since no one really cares about him. This leads him to constantly seek approval in any way he can get it. His addiction to his inner self makes him even more anxious, so he starts to demand approval from others as well. The end result is that the egotist finds himself rejected. Still he revitalizes himself and seeks other means for acceptance, even if it means engaging in corruption and immoral acts.

One fulfills his needs by devoting himself to spirituality, not to vanity. Spirituality helps mold one's personality and sets the individual on the right track. Vanity severely limits a person's self-worth, leading to humiliation and disgrace. With humility and self-sacrifice, a person can recover his sense of worth and his spirituality, free of pride and complacency. There is no room for selfish ambition, conceit, or self-delusion associated with those who have the superior attitude that they are always right. They confront others to prove their point, and they must have the final say in all matters. Rather than recognizing their mistakes, they keep on pressing forward against those who support truth. Egotists believe that those who oppose them are rivals. But their real rival is within them.

Ego is the cause of disarray in Judaism, Christianity, and Islam. Even though the same God revealed the scriptures of the Old Testament, New Testament, and Qur'an to the prophets, beginning with Abraham, much confusion and discord still exists. Clerics and scholars have disillusioned their constituents and readers with false information and untruths that have resulted in confrontation, violence, and war as well.

Because of a lack of unity within, the egotist becomes weak, suffers from low morale, and consumes his energy focusing on trivial issues and problems. This in turn leads to personality clashes and hostility. The egotist is ignorant about his obligation to strive for unity within himself and within others. His love of this life and the propensity to control others are reasons for discord. To combat egotism, we must have a strong sense of solidarity and brotherhood, which will help us better understand one another and work toward the common good.

Pessimism

Pessimism is the tendency to emphasize or think about the bad part of a situation rather than the good part, or the feeling that bad things are more likely to happen than good things. Pessimists look at the worst side of a situation and take the opposing view in any positive conversation. They turn conversations into griping and complaining. They ridicule attempts to rectify a dysfunctional situation.

Pessimists are moral skeptics, who deny the existence of an external spiritual realm or any other unchanging source of moral values. They believe that morality is either the invention of individuals or of different societies and cultures. Because moral values differ from person to person and from society to society, they do not apply universally to all people at all times. All that truly exists is the physical world, so there is no transcendent guarantee for moral beliefs (Fieser 2000).

The optimist, however, believes that moral values are objective in the sense that they are based on some spiritual component of the universe, which is independent of human activity in the physical world. The optimist believes that moral values are absolute, or external, in that they do not change, and universal in that they apply to all people (Fieser 2000).

Pessimism is a dangerous spiritual illness. It is the cause of many losses, defects, and disappointments. It is a painful calamity that torments the human soul and leaves irreparable defects on man's personality that cannot be expunged. Pessimists are resentful because they believe they have been isolated, abandoned, or deceived, or were not invited. Pessimists lack friendly interaction with others, because they are adamant and one-sided in their views. They may have had tragic events in their lives, such as the loss of a family member or a permanent disability. They may be ashamed at having done something wrong but are unable to seek atonement and forgiveness. When pessimists are continually reminded about their shortcomings, they become very resentful and seek revenge. When in pain or annoyed, they become overly responsive, exhibiting adverse emotional outbursts, as they revolt against those they consider to be enemies.

Pessimism inflicts anxiety and pain on its victims, and ultimately denies them hope and optimism. It harms the body and corrodes the soul. Pessimists experience seclusion and distrust when interacting with others. How do people overcome pessimism? They need to reassess their lives and their actions toward others. This requires recognition and identification of deficient behavior and attitude and an understanding of the negative impact this has on them as well as others. They must rejuvenate their spirituality and reconnect with faith. The Old Testament, New Testament, and Qur'an clearly count pessimism among sins and evil deeds and caution that we should not think negatively about each other. Social order and unity are the benefits of optimism, while decay and the disintegration of society are the consequences of pessimism.

Complacency

Complacency is self-satisfaction accompanied by unawareness of actual dangers or deficiencies. It is a lack of care or interest. It is a feeling of contentment. Complacency can interfere with taking action when it is needed. It can lead to the death of a community. An example of complacency is when a person says he will never need to see a physician because he will never get sick. Sometimes we are shaken out of complacency, particularly when we are faced with adversity or hardship. At that time, we reexamine our lives and our faith. The menace in our lives is complacency, which generates ignorance.

How can American society be motivated to move away from the drowning depths of complacency, when it is what most seem to desire? Does irresponsibility make Americans complacent? Actually, apathy and laziness are causes of complacency. The more we cling to apathy, the less we can do with our lives, because our minds are too full of inactivity to do anything else. We are not depressed; we are simply complacent. We are stubborn in our complacency. In essence, complacency lessens the self and corrodes the soul. As such, it degrades our moral values.

Complacency is one of the problems that Jews, Christians, and Muslims confront in the life of faith. Some people don't respond to God because they are comfortable in their routines. They are not mindful of God because other things occupy their thoughts. They don't pray because other things occupy their time. They do not put their trust in God because they put their trust in other things.

Self-righteousness is a weakness of the human soul. If we feel that we are what we ought to be, then we will remain what we are. We will not seek to make any changes or improvements in our lives. This will quite naturally lead us to judge everyone by what we are. This is the judgment of which we must be careful. Self-righteousness leads to complacency, a great sin. Some people have the attitude that if they are satisfied with their spiritual condition they need not concern themselves with helping others, and that God will be pleased with them and grant them Paradise. These people are just fooling themselves. It really boils down to self-deception.

Complacency in a community may lead to the erosion of moral values and the eventual destruction of spiritual endeavors. Wherever there is complacency, there are the seeds of corruption, chaos, confusion, and ultimate destruction. Complacency is not outside us, but inside us. This mentality leads both individuals and institutions to become estranged and disconnected from the realities of life. In this condition, one has no vision and can only produce ineffective solutions. When people move in the mental atmosphere of complacency, they are essentially cut off from their real selves and fall into a monotonous routine—the same old thing, day in and day out. Complacency is self-destructive, and a family, institution, or community can be destroyed by it.

America is the most affluent nation in the world. We are accustomed to a lifestyle that is viewed as extravagant by much of the rest of the world. We pursue riches and material things, as if they will last forever. Some people seldom stop to think about their relationship to God, as they place more emphasis and time on pursuing wealth and power.

Is there a cure for complacency? Yes! The first step is to recapture faith. We must contemplate the value of eternity, that is, we must begin to live for eternity rather than for now. We must pray and seek God's help. The solution is to bring the mind and self into harmony with one another. When a person enters a synagogue, church, or mosque, he feels peaceful and tranquil. The self experiences this, and the mind is no longer in confusion or turmoil. We need synergy by working together. So let's kick down the door of complacency and restore our moral virtue.

Good deeds and charity are not confined just to monetary help or to providing relief from physical suffering and hardship. Rather, spiritual assistance, moral guidance, and correction of moral conduct and qualities have a higher and greater value than material charity. The most valuable act of charity is to help the deviant and those bogged down in the mire of complacency, corruption, and wretchedness.

When a person becomes ill, he consults a physician, who diagnoses his sickness and often writes a prescription for the patient. The patient takes that prescription to a pharmacy so it can be filled. Once the medicine is taken, the patient begins to feel relief, and his pain is eased. Likewise, the human soul has an ailment, such as complacency, and needs cleansing. But where can the soul go to for help? The best avenue and cure for the human soul is achieved by way of prayer. In prayer, the person says that he loves and remembers God and asks God to purify his soul.

Together, we can make a difference in our communities. We can rid ourselves of complacency. We can seek peace, harmony, and justice. In the end, we will have become self-actualized in spirit; our families will be well cemented; our institutions will be unified; our community will be enriched; the Abrahamic faiths will seek common ground and common principles; and God will be pleased.

Egoism, pessimism, and complacency are primary reasons why people have deviated from God's commandments and scriptures.

Deviation from Scriptures

Throughout history man has deviated from the straight path. In the past, this deviant behavior had been relegated to a small minority among the followers of the Abrahamic faiths. Today, we find evidence that a growing trend of Americans is pursuing a path of deception and deviation in order to distort the teachings of Moses, Jesus, and Muhammad. There are those who believe that the perfection of thought can be attained by combining Aristotle's philosophy with religious beliefs.

Theologians of the three Abrahamic faiths view the philosophy of Aristotle with both appreciation and resentment. On the one hand, they generally approve of Aristotle's view of a disciplined order of nature in which natural processes were directed toward the fulfillment of particular ends. On the other hand, Aristotle's philosophy rejects the belief that God is the ultimate cause of the existence of the universe. Similarly, an increasingly number of the followers of the Abrahamic faiths have invented their own orders and set their own criteria relative to monotheistic laws, while still maintaining that God is the Creator of the universe. Essentially, this has led to fragmentation within the religions. These individuals have a blatant disregard for God's commandments. In America, the government has passed laws that erode into the very soul of these faiths. This has caused consternation and grave concern among those who wish to maintain the practice of the doctrines and principles within the faiths. Let us examine some of the types of deviant behavior and the implications for the three Abrahamic traditions.

Homosexuality, Same-Sex Marriage, and Adultery

A Gallup poll survey of more than 121,000 people was conducted between June 2012 and September 2012 to determine how many American adults identify as lesbian, gay, bisexual, or transgender (LGBT). The results were shocking. An estimated 3.4 percent of American adults fall within the LGBT category. Younger adults, ages eighteen to twenty-nine, are more likely than their elders to identify as LGBT; of this group, 8.3 percent are women and 4.6 percent are men. Twenty percent of LGBT individuals said they are married and an additional 18 percent are living with a partner. The survey also disclosed that 44 percent of LGBT adults identified as Democratic, 43 percent as Independent, and 13 percent as Republican. The survey findings did not account for people who did not want to acknowledge their sexual orientation (Crary 2012).

According to LifeWay Research, a survey conducted among a random sampling of 2,144 adult Americans in September 2011, 44 percent of

Americans believe that homosexuality is a sin. But a 2011 Gallup poll revealed that 56 percent of Americans consider gay and lesbian relations morally acceptable (Weber 2012). The Gallup survey also indicated that 53 percent of Americans believe same-sex marriage should be recognized by law, with the same rights as traditional marriages. This is double the number of Americans who approved of same-sex marriage in 1996 (27 percent) and an increase of nine percentage points over the 2010 level (44 percent) (Newport 2011). The same survey revealed that about 25 percent of Americans are gay or lesbian. More specifically, more than half of the population (52 percent) estimates that at least one in five Americans are gay or lesbian, including 35 percent who estimate that more than one in four are (Morales 2011). If 25 percent of the American population are estimated to be gay or lesbian, that means that there are many who hide their homosexuality when asked about their sexual preference. Undeniably, these surveys underscore the challenge the Abrahamic faiths have in addressing issues associated with LGBT.

All three Abrahamic faiths agree that the scriptures set the standard of morality and sexual behavior. The religions abhor and forbid any deviation from the decorum of sexual behavior, which include immoral indulgence in heterosexual activity outside of marriage, homosexuality, same-sex marriage, adultery, etc.

The Old Testament, New Testament, and Qur'an are very clear in the condemnation of immoral behavior:

> If a man has sexual relations with a man as one does with a woman, both of them have done what is detestable. They are to be put to death; their blood will be on their own heads. (Leviticus 20:13)

> If a man commits adultery with another man's wife—with the wife of his neighbor—both the adulterer and the adulteress are to be put to death. (Leviticus 20:10)

> Or do you not know that wrongdoers will not inherit the kingdom of God? Do not be deceived: neither the sexually immoral nor idolaters nor adulterers nor men

who have sex with men nor thieves nor the greedy nor drunkards nor slanderers nor swindlers will inherit the kingdom of God. (1 Corinthians 6:9)

For you practice your lusts on men in preference to women: you are indeed a people transgressing beyond bounds. (Qur'an 7:81)

Of all the creatures in the world, will you approach males, and leave those whom God has created for you to be your mates? Nay, you are a people transgressing [all limits]! (Qur'an 26:165–66)

We also sent Lot: He said to his people: "Do you commit lewdness such as no people in Creation ever committed before you? For you practice your lusts on men in preference to women: you are indeed a people transgressing beyond bounds." And his people gave no answer but this: they said, "Drive them out of your city: these are indeed men who want to be clean and pure!" (Qur'an 7:80–82)

The woman and the man guilty of adultery or fornication—flog each of them with a hundred stripes: let not compassion move you in their case, in a matter prescribed by God, if you believe in God and the Last Day: and let a party of the believers witness their punishment. (Qur'an 24:2)

The verses above clearly show that homosexuality and adultery are deviant behaviors that are forbidden by the scriptures. Thus, same-sex marriage also is not allowed. Regarding Lot's dilemma in Sodom and Gomorrah, only the Qur'an clearly identifies the lewd behavior as homosexuality. However, Jewish and Christian scriptures mention that Lot offered his two virgin daughters to the men of Sodom, who went to Lot's home to "know" his two male visitors. Here, the word "know" means that the men of Sodom wanted to engage in homosexual activity with the two men; otherwise, why would Lot offer to let his daughters have sex with the men instead? However, the Qur'an states that Lot only offered his daughters in marriage.

While scriptures from the three Abrahamic religions adamantly state that homosexuality is a sin, practices regarding homosexuality may vary. Traditional Judaism and Liberal Judaism are at odds about homosexuality. Traditional Judaism holds that homosexual acts are a violation of Jewish law. According to the Torah, homosexual acts are an abomination and wrong. Liberal Judaism does not condemn homosexual people; rather, it condemns only the act itself. Christians have become divided on the issue, even though the Bible clearly states that homosexuality is a sin. Some Christians condemn homosexual acts as sinful, while others regard it as a natural, acceptable alternative. Undeniably, homosexuality is forbidden in Islam. Some Muslim nations still impose the death penalty on those that commit homosexual acts. From an Islamic perspective, men are men and women are women and there should never be same-sex interaction. Homosexuality deprives a man of his manhood and a woman of her womanhood. Islam holds firm to its condemnation of homosexual acts. However, we find many new movements and liberal denominations in Judaism and Christianity that encourage people to be more tolerant of homosexuals. Truly, it is a sad commentary.

Adultery is a sin and is viewed as such not only in the scriptures of the three faiths but also in practice. All the Abrahamic religions agree that if a married man sleeps with another man's wife, it is considered adultery. According to the Old Testament, "If a man is found sleeping with another man's wife, both the man who slept with her and the woman must die. You must purge the evil from Israel" (Deuteronomy 22:22). However, an affair between a married man and a single woman is not considered adultery. Adultery is any illicit sexual intercourse involving a married woman. The wife is considered to be the husband's possession, and adultery constitutes a violation of the husband's exclusive right to her. When a man, married or single, sleeps with another man's wife, it is considered as adultery.

As the Gospel of Matthew tells us, Jesus said:

> You have heard that it was said, "You shall not commit adultery." But I tell you that anyone who looks at a woman lustfully has already committed adultery with her in his heart. (Matthew 5:27–28)

This passage from the New Testament clearly states that even if a man gazes at a woman with lust, it is construed as adultery. In Christianity, lewd thoughts may be just as harmful to the soul as actual adultery and carry the same weight or guilt.

The Islamic definition of adultery is the involvement of a married man or a married woman in an extramarital affair. It differs from Judaism and Christianity in that Islam not only says that adultery should not be committed but also that one should not even approach or contemplate adultery. In addition, Islam never considers any woman to be the possession of any man.

Misconceptions

There are a great number of misconceptions and untruths about Judaism, Christianity, and Islam. Some of these misconceptions are listed in table 20.

Table 20
Misconceptions about Judaism, Christianity, and Islam

Judaism
- Only Chosen People
- Non-Jews cannot convert to Judaism
- All Jews are Zionists
- Jews don't believe in the Messiah
- Jews reject Jesus
- Jews crucified Jesus

Christianity
- Three Gods
- One can enter Heaven only via baptism
- Only Christians enter Heaven

- All sins are forgiven
- If you are American, you are Christian

Islam
- Spread by sword
- Intolerant of other religions
- Racist
- Terroristic
- Muhammad is worshipped; the founder of Islam; a pedophile
- Muslims worship a different God
- Muslim men can have four wives at the same time
- Muslims reject Jesus as Messiah
- Muslims hate Americans
- Muslim women are oppressed, inferior, degraded, without rights, confined
- Jihad means to kill non-Muslims

Sources: Various literature; Internet.

These misconceptions are merely the fabrications and illusions of misguided people. Jews don't really believe they are the only chosen people of God. Conversion to Judaism is not only accepted but also encouraged. Not all Jews are Zionists. Jews believe in the coming of a Messiah. They did not reject Jesus as a person but as a prophet. Furthermore, Jews did not crucify Jesus; the Romans did.

Christians do not believe in three Gods but in one God within the concept of the Trinity. In addition, Christians do not believe that Heaven is the domain of only those who are baptized, or that they will be the only ones to enter the Kingdom of Heaven. They do not believe they will be forgiven for all their sins, irrespective of the transgression. Moreover, being American does not necessarily mean one is Christian.

The religion of Islam did not spread by the sword. As there is no coercion in Islam, converts join of their own free will. Islam is tolerant of other religions, and the Qur'an mentions the Torah, Psalms, and the Gospel as holy books of Islam. Islam is not racist or terroristic. Muhammad is not worshipped; only God is. The religion of Islam came into existence long before Muhammad was born (e.g., Abraham considered himself a Muslim). Muhammad was neither a pedophile nor did he marry Aisha until she was of mature age.

Muslims worship the same God that is worshipped in Judaism and Christianity, albeit a different name. God has many attributes in all three Abrahamic religions. Therefore, He is Jehovah in Judaism, God in Christianity, and Allah in Islam. The Qur'an is the only Abrahamic religion to specify that man can marry up to four women at the same time, provided he can give simultaneous satisfaction and equality to all, which is not possible. Therefore, marriage in Islam is monogamous. Muslims do not hate Jesus as the Messiah but respect him as one of the five great prophets; the others are Noah, Abraham, Moses, and Muhammad. Muslims do not hate Americans but love and respect them; they especially love the pluralism that is protected by the US Constitution, which grants tolerance to all religions, races, and ethnic groups.

Women are not oppressed, inferior, or degraded in Islam but highly respected. The Qur'an stipulates that husbands and wives are the garments of each other and that women have their rights, and are not confined to their homes. Jihad is a struggle against oppression, exploitation, tyranny, fear, corruption, and denying the masses basic human rights (Qur'an 4:75–76). It is ordained to establish peace and justice, freedom of religion and security, compassion and equity (Qur'an 2:193). "The essential condition for jihad is to struggle in the way of God; meaning that all actions undertaken must be done for the benefit of mankind, purely for the sake of pleasing God and not for selfish motives" (Al-Qazwini 2004). Jihad is when one controls his own desires and self-actualizes himself in the virtues of tolerance, empathy, reconciliation, and forgiveness.

Religious Extremism

A tide is sweeping America's shores. It is called religious extremism and threatens the very sanctity of our great country. While the US Constitution grants freedom to all US citizens, interpretation of these precepts has led people to twist and defame the very soul of its intent. As a result, religious extremists have taken this freedom for granted without any consideration of the injurious defamation and security threats they are imposing on those they wish to harm and destroy.

Religious extremists have targeted Jews, Christians, and Muslims as well as the nation itself in the infamous attack on America on September 11, 2001. They have no mercy. They consider every faith other than their own as fair bait for their dastardly deeds. They believe that their religion is the only true faith and, therefore, must take immediate action to destroy anything that disagrees with their philosophy. Religious extremism has its roots in militant theology.

Religious extremism and terrorism are linked. Religious extremists are willing to murder because they embrace theologies that sanction violence in the service of God. They have no sympathy for their victims, because they view those victims as enemies of God. Traditional academic theories of religion have no way to explain the persistence of extremist groups, except to view their adherents as victims of ignorance, coercion, deception, or psychopathology (Iannaccone 2006).

While Islamic extremism may be foremost in the minds of Americans, Christian and Jewish extremism are also on the rise. Religious extremists take the position that damnation will strike those who do not follow their views. The weakness of these religious fanatics is their gross misunderstanding of their own faiths and their lack of genuine spirituality. Religious extremism does not come from the doctrines of Judaism, Christianity, or Islam. Rather, it comes from their alleged followers, who distort the true meaning of what the religions convey. They misinterpret biblical scriptures to cause hatred and violence. Moreover, they use religion as a shield to hurt and even kill, as long as it is performed in the name of faith. These religious fanatics preach intolerance against all who disagree with them.

Interfaith dialogue can be a vehicle for addressing the issue of religious extremism. Despite the differences between Judaism, Christianity, and Islam, there are common values among these religions, including human dignity, human rights, peace, and reconciliation. We know that Osama bin Laden was a religious extremist, but how did he become one? The American government engaged his services, terrorist or otherwise, to fight against the Russians in Afghanistan. Saddam Hussein had weapons of mass destruction, which he used during Iraq's war against Iran and against his own people, but who gave him those weapons?

President George W. Bush was steadfast in his belief that Saddam Hussein had weapons of mass destruction. While we brought Saddam Hussein to justice, we did not bring to justice those who supplied him with these weapons. We did not even pursue that issue or the issue of state-sponsored terrorism. We know that it was not Islam that drove Osama bin Laden or Saddam Hussein to commit their violent and inhumane acts, but the men themselves. In short, it is not the religion that promotes terrorism but the followers of that faith, who claim to be religious when, in fact, they are not. Islam is a religion of justice, and that concept is mentioned more than 250 times in the Qur'an. Likewise, justice is mentioned many times in the Old Testament and the New Testament.

Summary

Today, the atmosphere in America is reeking with immorality, and we are suffering from moral decay and cultural decadence. The trend of immorality will only get worse. Americans have betrayed the values that made us a great nation. How will future generations behave in a climate of uninhibited sex, deviation from biblical scriptures, and complacency? Can we truly restore the greatness that made our nation a symbol of morality, democracy, and brotherhood? Will we head back to the lifestyles of Sodom and Gomorrah? Or can we regain the roots upon which our nation was founded? Can we truly take back what has been stolen from us by the immoral principles that have drenched our minds and eroded our souls? Or is it just too late?

There is no question that America can outdo any nation when it comes to technology, architecture, agriculture, drilling for oil, and increasing the speed of travel. But when it comes to morality, we have a hard time staying above water, as we are sinking and sinking fast. Sadly, we are viewed by the outside world as arrogant, shameful, rich, extravagant, self-centered, and sinful. If we are to avoid the snake pit that other empires have fallen into, then the moral decline in America must come to an immediate halt! How? We have to work together in cooperation. We need to bring together faith leaders, government officials, educators, and all who want to revive the morality in our nation. We need to discuss the ways to restore our nation back to its moral greatness. This is going to take a great deal of time and effort, but it has to be done for the sake of our nation, our children, and the future of America.

Implications of
Losing the Faith

America is a pluralistic nation made up of many ethnic, racial, and religious groups. However, the predominant religion in America is Christianity.

Table 21
Major Religious Traditions in America
2012 versus 2007

Religion	Among All Adults (%)		
	2012	2007	Point Change
Christianity	73.0	78.0	(5.0)
Protestant	48.0	53.0	(5.0)
Catholic	22.0	23.0	(1.0)
Mormon	2.0	2.0	—
Orthodox	1.0	1.0	—
Other Faiths	6.0	4.0	2.0
Unaffiliated	19.6	15.3	4.3
Atheist	2.4	1.6	0.8
Agnostic	3.3	2.1	1.2
Nothing in particular	13.9	11.6	2.3
Don't Know	2.0	2.0	—
TOTAL	100.0	100.0	

Note: Due to rounding, figures may not add to 100.

Source: Landscape Survey, Pew Research Center, 2012.

According to the Landscape Survey, 73 percent of adults are Christians; the largest denominations are Protestants (48 percent) and Catholics (22 percent). Other faiths, including Jews, Muslims, and other religions, comprise 6 percent. Those who consider themselves unaffiliated constitute 19.6 percent, of which agnostics and atheists comprise 5.7 percent. Interestingly, the unaffiliated group has increased by 4.3 percentage points since 2007, mostly at the expense of a 5-percent drop from the Christianity category.

This was the first time the number of US adults identifying themselves as Protestant dipped below 50 percent. About 20 percent of Americans say they have no religious affiliation, an increase from the 15-percent level of five years ago. This unaffiliated group also includes people who say they believe in God as well as those who pray daily or consider themselves "spiritual" but not "religious." Most of them are not actively seeking a religion, and indicate that their ties with organized religion have been permanently broken. Interestingly, one-third of adults under thirty have no religious affiliation, compared to 9 percent of people sixty-five and older. The Pew researchers wrote that, "Young adults today are much more likely to be unaffiliated than previous generations were at a similar stage in their lives," and they are not expected to become more religiously active as they age (Zoll 2012).

The General Social Surveys (GSS) of the National Opinion Research Center at the University of Chicago conducted a survey between 1972 and 2010. In that survey, 7.7 percent of the public indicated that they were not affiliated with any religion in 1990. However, by 2010, the GSS disclosed that 18 percent of American adults had no religious affiliation. Therefore, the number of unaffiliated had more than doubled in the last two decades. Moreover, from 1990 to 2010, the number of those under thirty who disclosed they were unaffiliated increased from 10.5 percent to 25.3 percent. While the American population self-identifies as predominantly Christian, the trend is that it is becoming less Christian.

The above findings are substantiated by other surveys as well. Among the key findings in the 2008 survey conducted by the American Religious Identification Survey, many Americans (15 percent) claim to have no religion at all, up from 8 percent in 1990 (Grossman 2009). According to another poll, religion is on the decline in the United States, and atheism is on the rise. The worldwide poll, called the Global Index of Religiosity and Atheism, found that the number of Americans who said they were "religious" dropped from 73 percent in 2005 to 60 percent in 2012. At the same time, the number of Americans who said they were atheists rose from 1 percent to 5 percent. The poll was conducted by WIN-Gallup International and is based on interviews with fifty thousand people from fifty-seven countries and five continents. China has the most "convinced atheists," at 47 percent, followed by Japan with 31 percent, Czech Republic with 30 percent, and France with 29 percent (Winston 2012).

Religion in America is on the decline and has been dropping since the turn of the century. That is the conclusion of researchers of Faith Communities Today (FACT), the multiyear study of American religions supported by the Hartford Institute for Religion Research. The Cooperative Congregational Studies Partnership conducted the FACT 2010 survey, and analyzed responses from 11,077 randomly sampled congregations of all faith traditions in the United States. The results indicated that fewer congregations report high spiritual vitality—down from 42.8 percent in 2000 to 28.4 percent in 2010. This decline in spiritual vitality is true across the board—denominational family, race and ethnicity, and region and size. Among the trends that have a negative impact on spiritual vitality are decreasing financial health, shrinking worship attendance, aging membership, and high levels of conflict. The number of congregations with excellent financial health declined from 31 percent in 2000 to 14 percent in 2010. About 14 percent of the congregations surveyed in 2010 indicated they had shared worship across faith traditions (i.e., other religions) in the past year, up from about 7 percent of those surveyed in 2000.

The *National Catholic Reporter* states that Christianity is in decline in the West. A March 2009 *Newsweek* cover story reported that 86 percent of the US population self-identified as Christians in 1990. By 2009, the percentage had dropped to 76 percent, while the number who claimed "no religion" doubled to 16 percent. Among those under the age of thirty, the figure declaring "no religion" was close to 30 percent. If the trend continues, the "no religion" plus the "non-Christian" categories will outnumber Christians by the year 2042 (Mann 2012).

All of these surveys affirm that more and more believers are turning away from religion altogether. We need to examine why such a movement continues to take place. Some of these believers have a tendency to abandon their faith and to seek a faith outside the Abrahamic tradition. Seemingly, although youth do care about religion, they have nonetheless become disenchanted and uninterested in the theology of their own faith. Having a passion for one's religion requires one to study, understand, and personally experience its precepts. If a believer doesn't understand his faith, then he is more likely either to find another faith or abandon religion entirely.

Over the centuries, we have witnessed wars and conflicts between the Abrahamic religions (interfaith) and within the denominations of each one (intrafaith). There has been infighting within each religion (e.g., Orthodox Jews versus Conservative Jews, Catholics versus Protestants, and Sunnis versus Shi'as). As a result, some of their followers have abandoned the religion altogether by joining a non-monotheistic religion or becoming atheists.

The number of Americans with no religious affiliation has more than doubled in the past twenty years, primarily in the under-thirty population. The polling data shows that a dramatic exit is taking place from American Christian churches. Why? According to the Barna Group, churches are no longer intellectually challenging. More and more young people are college-educated thinkers who are expanding the limits of their curiosity and knowledge. These young adults are no longer stimulated by the sermons of clerics. They are not willing to accept the church's rigid catechism, an educational method that teaches the religious questions and the correct answers. Because young adults are eager to question and discuss, they feel that catechism is outdated and provides no challenge. Furthermore, churches are no longer leaders in moral and ethical discussions. Young adults have grown weary of churches that cannot get past issues such as homosexuality and abortion (Barna Research Group 2010). While Christianity constitutes the largest population of Abrahamic faiths in America, they have borne the brunt of this exodus of young adults. However, Judaism and Islam are also experiencing the disenchantment of their youth.

In America, many Christians believe that since Jesus died for their sins, they have an automatic passage to Heaven. They live shallow and baseless lives, "of petty emotions and jealousies, of distraction and escape, of ego and pride, and sometimes of gross corruption and treachery" (Kupelian 2002). However, there are sincere Christians who grieve over their sins by reawakening and living a good and religious life. In between these two groups are Christians who try to be good but are duped by the evils of society, such as Internet porn. For millions of people, Christianity has become a "bumper-sticker religion" (Kupelian 2002). While the Internet has become a viable source of information for Jews, Christians, and Muslims who want to know about their faith and the faith of others, it also has its drawbacks.

Social Media Sites

Technology has advanced considerably in the past few decades and has transformed how we receive information. The consumer public is becoming and more and more attuned to using the Internet for learning and entertainment. While social media is a good vehicle for communicating various aspects of religion to people, it is also a channel for funneling images and texts that counter the precepts of the Abrahamic traditions. Social networking may take on various meanings depending on the form that is used. For example, social networking sites are different than social sharing sites, and each has an approach that may be targeted to a different audience.

While some religious leaders express a growing concern about putting their faith in social media networks, others are finding these forms of media useful. Those who are concerned state that spirituality (i.e., the experiential aspect of religious practice) is diminished and even lost online. Those who encourage social media state that since Internet users are online more often than they are at religious facilities, it is a way for them to be continuously connected to religion and a way for organizations to attract new followers. Sermons, theological seminars, and religious classes can be conducted and viewed online. Moreover, religious organizations and clerics have met with great success in maintaining pages on social media networks and by creating their own online networks (e.g., ChristianNetwork, GodTube, MyChurch. org, JewTube, and Muslimsocial.com). Social media sites can also give users the opportunity to be more aware about and understanding of their faith, share ideas about religion, and engage in healthy interfaith dialogue.

While social media transmits useful information on various religions, the material on the Internet also conveys erroneous information that may have an adverse impact. Viewers may be confused, especially if they have limited knowledge and understanding of their own or other faiths. As false information creeps online, users may not know fact from fiction and accept whatever they see or hear as true. People can upload anything they want on the Internet, such as antireligious texts, false publications, and distorting religious scriptures that confuse their readers. The danger evolves, as social media networking may become its own religion.

A 2011 survey by Pew Internet and American Life Project disclosed that 65 percent of all adult Internet users said they used social networking sites like MySpace, Facebook, or LinkedIn, up from 61 percent in 2010 and more than double the 29 percent who did so in 2008. This is a remarkable surge in the use of social networking sites, as the number of users in 2005 was only 8 percent. Among Internet users, social networking sites are most popular with women, young adults under thirty, and parents. Young adult women ages eighteen to twenty-nine are the power users of social networking; 89 percent of this group who are online use the sites and 69 percent do so on an average day. The bottom line is that as more and more people are accessing the social networking sites, they will be exposed to various forms of religious texts and messages.

What can we expect from the social networking sites relative to religion? According to Prof. Scott C. Alexander, transmitting information via social network sites means sharing knowledge in the context of personal exchanges. Communication of information between the producer and the user is both an exchange of data and a form of sharing. Toward this end, communication is seen as dialogue, exchange, solidarity, and the creation of positive relations. Nevertheless, this should be compared with the limits of digital communication: the one-sidedness of the interaction, the tendency to communicate only parts of one's interior world, and the risk of constructing a false image of oneself, which can become a form of self-indulgence (Alexander 2011).

Undeniably, social media sites have transformed the way people interact by providing instant access irrespective of time and location. They have their advantages and drawbacks. Users should be very cautious about what information they seek and how it is shared. The advantage is that since their fees are free or minimal, anyone can access the sites. Another advantage is that the sites are actually useful and can provide information that is urgently needed and readily accessible. However, the drawback is that users may become vulnerable to stalkers or scams, identity theft, and safety threats. Some users become obsessed with the sites, a form of addiction that can impair relationships with family and friends.

Social media sites are here to stay. The challenge for the Abrahamic faiths is to use these tools cautiously and effectively. There needs to be continuity between social media sites and the synagogue, church, and mosque. Clerics and religious leaders from all three faiths must come to grips with the positive and negative aspects of these sites. Interfaith dialogue can address the issues and challenges of social media networking as a tool for enhancing the knowledge of and enlightening religious believers while at the same time instituting safeguards for its use.

Ignorance

If it is vital for the children of Abraham to unite in the spirit of collaboration, then why is this kind of collaboration not a reality? The answer is deep and complex. There are many reasons, and some of these are the result of hatred, suspicion, intolerance, and deficiencies in control and collaboration. The underlying root cause of these deficiencies is ignorance.

Ignorance thrives on the absence of education. Those who are ignorant evidently lack proper theological instruction and training. One example of ignorance is not being tolerant and understanding about the differences among various religious philosophies. This example unfolds into a major aspect of ignorance, which is the reluctance to engage in diversity. Although ignorance continues to spread throughout the world, there are scholars who will emerge to rectify misunderstandings in the minds of others. They will educate others about what Moses, Jesus, and Muhammad preached, and will caution against those who breach the laws of the Abrahamic faiths. The challenge is to remove ignorance from all of the different denominations within Judaism, Christianity, and Islam.

However, in bringing the followers of these religions to the table for effective dialogue, we must recognize that ignorance by any party can be an impediment to success. We must understand that ignorance exists primarily at two levels: simple ignorance and compound ignorance. A person who is candid and admits that he simply does not know the answer to a question falls under the category of simple ignorance. This is a fundamental unawareness that can be easily resolved and replaced with knowledge. A far more complex and real problem is that of compound ignorance. Here the person will say that he knows the answer to a question when he really does not know it. This person is not only ignorant; he is ignorant about his ignorance. People who fall into this category frequently possess insufficient knowledge. Such ignorance is considered an affliction on the human soul, as it impedes learning and understanding. The danger is that those afflicted with this disease will render views and analyses even though they lack the knowledge to do so. The tragedy is that they think they have knowledge when, in reality, it is only their invention of what they think they know. In addition, they think that they can reform others without first reforming themselves.

There is the issue of whether or not the children of Abraham can unite for the common cause of peace and tolerance. The axis at which a myriad of obstacles converge is that of ignorance (fig. 1). Conversely, the axis at which a myriad of solutions converge is that of knowledge (fig. 2). Through knowledge we gain wisdom. And it is education that is the vehicle for increasing our knowledge and nurturing our wisdom as we overcome ignorance.

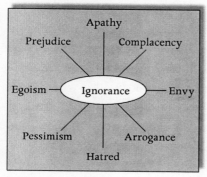

Fig. 1
Obstacles to Unity

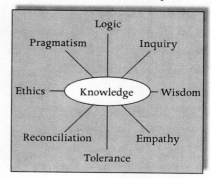

Fig. 2
Solutions to Unity

The impediment to uniting for the common cause is discord, which runs rampant among the followers of the three Abrahamic religions. It is ignorance about their obligation to achieve and maintain unity within diversity. Some of the obstacles related to ignorance are apathy, complacency, envy, arrogance, hatred, pessimism, egoism, and prejudice. Some of the solutions related to knowledge are logic, inquiry, wisdom, empathy, tolerance, reconciliation, ethics, and pragmatism. Compound ignorance naturally dampens any sense or desire to broaden a viewpoint or opinion. How we overcome ignorance with knowledge will determine the outcome of unity.

To understand the consequences of ignorance, it is vital to separate simple ignorance from compound ignorance; the latter is also labeled closed-mindedness. Everyone is ignorant about something. Ignorance, by itself, is no reason for embarrassment. When one is ignorant about something, he may be willing to listen and learn. A closed mind, however, is not willing to listen and learn. The fundamental difference is that a mind that is simply ignorant does not defend its ignorance. As it is open-minded, it will accept guidance and new knowledge. By contrast, a mind in the clutch of compound ignorance employs a range of strategies to prevent new knowledge. It has obtained a particular set of beliefs and obstinately refuses to change them. What we should remember about compound ignorance, or closed-mindedness, is that it is a defensive position. We must be cognizant of the fact that compound ignorance is not only a spiritual disease but is also detrimental to one's life. Because compound ignorance is an illness, it is dangerous to one's well-being. It is also a cause of discord and fragmentation within society.

Knowledge is the panacea for overcoming ignorance. When we seek knowledge, we are enlightened. Knowledge is not only a cure for ignorance, it also guides us. Those who have knowledge are conscious of the truth and have a favorable influence on those with whom they come in contact. In contrast, those who are ignorant muddle through their lives, unsuccessfully trying to gratify their desires. In short, the ignorant fail to gain consciousness of their purpose and duty in life.

Knowledge is a means to an end. When God created us from the wombs of our mothers, we were ignorant. God gave us the senses of hearing, sight, touch, smell, and taste. Through these senses, we are able to acquire knowledge. Whether we acquire knowledge from reading or hearing the scriptures or whether we witness the marvels of Creation, it is through these senses that we are able to function. God has provided us with the sources of knowledge, two of which are His Creation and His revelations.

Seeking knowledge is part of our faith, as it helps us get a clear perception about our origin, our purpose, and our way of life. Knowledge becomes the lamp that illuminates the soul and brings about happiness. There is a great difference between those who seek knowledge and those who wish to remain ignorant. Those who seek knowledge learn the truth and obtain insight, while the ignorant remain blind, traveling the path of Satan.

Knowledge is vital to understanding where we came from and to where we are going. How we conduct our daily lives is based on knowledge. As we increase our knowledge, we must also put it to practice. Faith and knowledge without practice is insignificant. We must find the means in which knowledge can be the vehicle for driving home the unity among the faiths of the children of Abraham.

There is a great deal of truth in the adage that knowledge is freedom and ignorance is slavery. Human freedom cannot and does not rely on ignorance and randomness. Human freedom is the capacity to make choices based on reason, and this expands with knowledge. The best way to combat ignorance is to heighten the struggle against the ego, the major barrier to clear thinking. The struggle against ignorance requires that we continue to escalate our understanding of each other, which is the prescription for dealing with social issues, including ethnic conflicts, religious and cultural differences, poverty, and ethical and moral failings. The struggle against ignorance is the most important struggle we will ever fight. It is a struggle that we ultimately must win in order for the religions of Judaism, Christianity, and Islam to survive, as the covenant of Abraham envisaged.

The issues facing us today are far more difficult and complex than they ever have been, and the stakes are getting progressively higher. The survival of the Abrahamic faiths depends on our abilities to participate in the quest for unity. Yet participation requires that we understand the relevant issues before us. Knowledge is indeed power. The less we know, the less we can contribute. We have a major job ahead of us to ensure that education becomes our number one priority and that we ultimately are victorious in the struggle against ignorance.

Summary

Division among the three Abrahamic religions is a horrid evil. How can they work for unity without compromising the truth? How can they maintain their own views without sacrificing their desire for unity? Some may say that their insistence on truth is a prerequisite for unity, and that they cannot and will not compromise the truth.

To become united requires the humility to rethink some things that have been very important to us. While we need to deal with the unavoidable conflict between our desire for unity and our commitment to truth, we need to reflect on those things that bring about unity.

We are going to have to revive a passion for the principle of unity among all believers. Having the commitment to abide by God's commands is the avenue toward brotherhood and solidarity. We must be cognizant of the fact that our passion to reject each other over issues of politics, theology, and provinciality are not virtues. They are indications that we are too often controlled by our ego and not by God's commandments. We need a passion for unity. Unity is not something we invent; it is God's gift. Let us make every concerted effort to be unified. Let us exhaust every possibility and leave no stone unturned in the quest for unity. Let our efforts be the result of an earnest desire and willingness to succeed as we celebrate our differences as windows of opportunities. Let us uproot ignorance with knowledge, as we learn to cooperate with one another. As God has already given us that passion for unity, we must move forward to fulfill His command.

In order to unify, we need to allow for diversity. Without diversity of opinion, our hope for unity will be severely weakened. Unity must prevail over disunity. We can no longer preach unity and practice division. This requires us to find the means by which to have a sound and workable dialogue. Our pledge to unity must begin within ourselves, within our families, within our communities, and with each other. With an open mind and open heart, we can have effective dialogue with each other. As we engage in dialogue, let us seek to understand before we seek to be understood.

Yet, in the quest for unity in diversity in America, at both the interfaith and intrafaith levels, the major threat to monotheism does not come from non-Abrahamic faiths but, rather, from the followers of the traditions themselves. The challenge is how to win the unity *within* our own religions as well as *with* other Abrahamic faiths.

PART THREE
Children of Abraham: Prescription for Unity

"Kindness is the language which the deaf can hear and the blind can see. The universal brotherhood of man is our most precious possession."—Mark Twain

Source: *The Wit and Wisdom of Mark Twain: A Book of Quotations (Dover Thrift Editions)* by Mark Twain. Dover Publications (December 23, 1998), 64 pages.

Winning the Unity

While convergence of brotherhood has met with some success, much more needs to be done. To be sure, Jews, Christians, and Muslims have made inroads into cooperation and collaboration with one another. They have been engaged in faith-based initiatives and dialogue with each other, although it has been minimal. There are a number of Jewish and Christian initiatives in America that exclude Muslims, for example, the Judeo-Christian dialogue among Jews and Christians.

What is needed is a mechanism to effectively win the unity. That mechanism is knowledge. To promote unity is to promote knowledge, which is an inescapable duty for all Jews, Christians, and Muslims. Knowledge and ignorance are always at war with each other. To oppose knowledge is ignorant. Knowledge is the light and the means of reaching the threshold of unity. Knowledge is parallel to guidance, while ignorance is akin to torment. Knowledge gives rise to wisdom.

As with King Solomon, wisdom consists of judgment, perception, insight, and all the branches of mind that come under the area of knowledge. Spiritual judgment constantly positions wisdom above the other faculties of mind and reveals that knowledge and intelligence are supplementary to understanding. As experience results in knowledge, knowledge results in change. Knowledge is the forerunner of wisdom; the more we know, the more we become. Where there is wisdom, there is neither fear nor ignorance.

To dispel fear is to lift the veil of uncertainty to help advance unity—not essentially the unity of accord, but of mutual respect and understanding. For example, to promote and win the unity between Jews, Christians, and Muslims means that we must overcome our prejudices. Prejudice is a sign of ignorance and the lack of ethical sensitivity. We promote unity by rebelling against the ignorance of intolerance and fanaticism. It is through the spirit of detachment that we experience the meaning of freedom to help influence change for the sake of unity.

Distrust and hatred that has rankled the lives of Jews, Christians, and Muslims through the centuries has caused much confusion and discord between their communities. While interfaith initiatives speak of unity and make attempts to unify, the end result has been dismal. The reason is that over the course of history this enmity and hatred among each other has been inculcated and imbedded within people's minds. Their offspring continue the dissension and, at times, even magnify the distance between the groups to even greater heights of animosity.

While it is one's right to believe that his religion is the best one, it is not the right to ridicule and debase the followers of other religions. We should not put a wedge or barrier between the followers of different religions. Rather, we should meet with each other to determine how to work with each other. Having pride in one's religion is encouraged; however, that sense of pride should not translate into belittling other religions. Those who want to attack and destroy another's religion feed upon this erosion, as they insidiously plot their evil doings. As this erosion widens, the Jewish, Christian, and Muslim communities weaken, and their followers may become victimized and oppressed by wicked leaders who usurp their rights. Instead of coming together in unity to receive God's blessings, this erosion leads the communities into the realm of darkness and ignorance.

Intention

To resolve this erosion, Jews, Christians, and Muslims must work together. Before this can happen, each group has to decide to do so. That intention will stimulate emotional intelligence, which will awaken creative energy.

What people think and feel underscore the essence of intention, which requires energy to bring it into concentration. The energy is emotion. The intensity of emotional energy elevates our spirituality. The strength of our emotion brings about a strong intention. Our thoughts and feelings are affected by emotional energy. The more strongly we think and feel about something, the more energy we give to it.

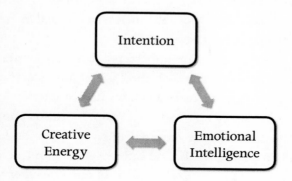

Our intention sets the direction in which we are headed. In deciding to work together, we must be absolute in stating our intention. It is not sufficient to simply make our intention and then forget about it. Our intention energy field is integrated and includes both our thoughts and feelings. To express a thought in the form of a desire, without accompanying it with deep and sincere feelings, will not result in a clear intention. In addition, there must be consistency between the desire we set in our intention energy field and the physical actions we take. Bringing discipline into our intention requires a shift in our awareness (Hornecker 1996). Intentions are conscious mental states, if one is aware of having them.

When Jews, Christians, and Muslims meet in an atmosphere of interfaith dialogue, they should first and foremost be guided by their internal intentions and free will to do so. While external intentions are important, it is easy for the external world to influence and distort our true inner feelings. We are often caught up in worldly functions and lose sight of what is most important. We fail to grasp the inner meaning of what life is really about. When we allow the external world to overtake our internal intention, the higher self will be overtaken by the basic self. Daily, external forces and activities take up much of our time, because we allow them to. We just have a very difficult time in letting them go. Unless an external influence has a bearing on our true intention and path in life, we should let it go. We need to contain the ego. For example, donating to a charitable cause because a charitable organization had a fundraiser is fine. It is of a higher order to make one's internal intention to help those in need rather than just oblige those who are throwing the fundraising event. Similarly, participating in an interfaith dialogue should be based on those who make their true internal intention to meet rather than just satisfying external forces.

Yet external intentions are important. Assume the intention of the participants to meet in interfaith dialogue is an elicited act, entirely internal. Each participant carries out his or her internal intention by collecting and preparing information relevant for the meeting. Exchange of information becomes the external intention. The juxtaposition of internal and external intentions is influenced by the free will of each participant. Our lives gain a greater sense of purpose when we cultivate internal and external intentions.

Each pulse of intention is an electrical spark, a powerful life current, and a signal transmitted from us, outwardly, to seek the blessings of God. Our faiths are formed and shaped from a positive, powerful, and active intention. We have intention not just of the mind but also of the heart that commands the truth. Rather than searching for our intention, we simply become that intention. Since the cells in our bodies march to the tune of consciousness, let intention be our guide. The manifestation of this guidance is heightened by our emotional intelligence and creative energy.

Emotional Intelligence

Emotional intelligence can be defined in terms of self-awareness, altruism, personal motivation, empathy, and the ability to love and be loved by friends, partners, and family members (Goleman 1995). It is a type of social intelligence that involves the ability to monitor each other's emotions, to discriminate among them, and to use that information to guide our thinking and actions. People with highly emotional intelligence skills get along better and don't let anxieties and frustrations get in the way of efficiently solving problems. Emotional intelligence increases understanding between people, which minimizes time wasted arguing and being defensive. It is the ability to sense, understand, and effectively apply the power of emotions and appropriately channel them as sources of human energy, creativity, and influence.

Emotions are the primary source of human energy, aspiration, authenticity, and drive; they activate our innermost feelings and purpose in life and transform them from things we think about to values we live. The heart is the place of courage and spirit, integrity and commitment— the source of energy and deep feelings that call us to create, learn, cooperate, lead, and serve. When we have painful feelings, the heart is telling us that we have unmet needs or that we are interpreting reality through some kind of distorting filter. When we have positive feelings, the heart is telling us that we are pointing in the right direction, toward fulfillment of our needs and toward truth. Emotions stimulate energy and bring things into motion or manifestation. The force behind what we feel is what allows us to create. First, we have our thought or perception. But the emotional energy is the fuel that allows something to get created (Shepherd, n.d.).

Creative Energy

Creative energy transforms our thoughts and feelings by empowering and inspiring us to make positive changes in our lives. As such, creative energy is internally released from within us and channeled to the external environment as an expression of who we are or what we want to do. The dynamic nature of creative energy demands release; it must be expressed. For example, as the artist paints a picture, he channels his creative energy by releasing his thoughts and feelings. This release is a form of emotional expression as well as a representation of how he feels his viewers will interpret it. The viewers, in turn, channel their creative energy in the form of their actual emotional response and interpretation of the artwork.

Creative energy fosters a sense of inner security and confidence that allows one to experiment with new ideas. These experiences are realized, once our emotions are motivated and ready to act. Like a stream of consciousness, expression can release creative energy and free the person to be more lively, vibrant, and spontaneous. To become directly aware of creative energy, however, we must steer our perception outside consciousness itself. To think creatively, one must break through repressed energy barriers and begin to experience a larger energy field.

Once the interrelationship of intention, emotional intelligence, and creative energy comes full circle, we are better able to cope with the myriad of problems that are barriers toward achieving a genuine and lasting unity among the three traditions. We will resolve these problems by having a much deeper insight into the solutions that enable us to collaborate with each other. One such solution is conflict resolution.

Conflict Resolution

Judaism, Christianity, and Islam have all had periods of conflict, due to political upheavals, social disputes, or cultural biases. We often lack the confidence or vision of what is appropriate. Many of us are under the assumption that conflict is something to be avoided. Many people view conflict as an experience of failure.

Understanding similarities and differences, in an atmosphere free of bias, will enable scholars and religious leaders of the three faiths to meet together to further the goals of equality and justice. Attitudes, behaviors, and environmental pressures can work toward positive tolerance or negative intolerance. It all depends on the mind-sets of the participants and their willingness to work toward unity.

For conflict resolution to be effective, the parties must adhere to the following:

- an atmosphere of mutual respect and trust
- reciprocal communication
- promoting self-worth
- a free expression of ideas and thoughts
- advancing scholarly questioning and methodical decision-making
- promoting open-mindedness and a regard for different points of view
- deciding on an outcome after carefully considering alternatives
- differentiating between rational behavior and emotional behavior

Conflict resolution is more than just focusing on ethics or morality. It has to do with a myriad of issues that are very complicated and difficult to resolve. The following are at the center of many conflicts:

- preconception and narrow-mindedness
- opposition and antagonism
- absence of constructive criticism
- disrespect for others

Ignorance leads to preconceived notions, which may be obstacles to creating alternative solutions. Frequently, people do not get the chance to learn how to find alternative solutions or develop constructive ways of resolving conflicts. Learning to manage conflict without hostility can move people toward healthy communication. Conflict resolution rescues us from ignorance, and it is an important way of helping people understand each other. It encourages people to be proactive and face their problems, rather than avoid them. The objective is to reach a win-win situation with a remedy that is satisfactory to everyone involved. The fundamental themes of conflict resolution include collaboration, communication, and confirmation.

Effective communication and social skills—arbitration, conciliation, problem-solving, and critical-thinking skills—are the basis of conflict resolution. Generally, the process is to a) define the problem, b) obtain a joint solution, c) implement the solution, and d) test the solution. Interfaith groups can conduct workshops to show people how to employ this process.

Conflict resolution ascertains the causes and outcomes of behavior. In addition, it takes into account the feelings and emotions of all the people involved. Certain methods are used to identify and understand the situation that caused the disagreement. One method is to recognize and confirm the frustration of the participants. Another is to encourage the exchange of ideas and thoughts. Successful conflict resolutions are the result of teamwork, interaction, and tolerance.

Conflict resolution generates empathy, reconciliation, candidness, and forgiveness. Interfaith leaders who have the fortitude to seek social justice and peace must lead reconciliation initiatives. These leaders will move in the direction of unity, even if it means that ridicule will be visited upon them. People's attitudes and behaviors reflect, in part, their family values and state of mind. They need to transform their inner selves in order to resolve deep-rooted conflicts. Empathy and advocacy are critical parts of the process.

We need to move from the traditional mode of conflict resolution to a higher level called "incremental conflict resolution," which goes a step further by addressing long-term methods for how interfaith groups can collaborate with each other. The best way to characterize the work of religion, peace-building, and conflict resolution is to see it in terms of a complex social network of peace (Gopin 2011).

For incremental conflict resolution to be effective, interfaith brothers and sisters must build relationships by exercising empathy and tolerance and generating a common bond between the parties. For example, dialogue between Jews, Christians, and Muslims could focus on the concept of empathy as a vehicle for understanding the needs and concerns of others. Walking in the shoes of another and seeing the perspective from the other's vantage point can help people understand the feelings of the other party. Tolerance is the vehicle by which empathy can manifest itself in conflict resolution.

Tolerance

Tolerance is one of the greatest strengths of interfaith, because it is the attitude of truth. In Judaism, Christianity, and Islam, tolerance is a religious moral duty. Tolerance means to put up with the convictions of other people and not to impose one's will upon others. In all three Abrahamic religions, tolerance acknowledges the self-respect, equality, and freedom of all people. The Abrahamic faiths are made up of diverse cultures. To be tolerant is to have respect and understanding of these diverse cultures. Each culture has its distinct form of expression. We need to find ways to communicate and to be open, compassionate, and tolerant with each other.

Reconciliation

The word *reconciliation* has taken on many different meanings and interpretations. When reconciliation is mentioned, what does it really mean? Does it mean the same from a cultural or a political perspective as it does from a religious perspective? What are the sociopsychological aspects of reconciliation? Who is responsible for bringing about reconciliation? How do different parties in a conflict respond to the concepts of justice and reconciliation? What major theoretical principles and lessons can be drawn from the experience of working on reconciliation? How do varying perceptions of justice contribute to or prevent reconciliation?

Reconciliation can be defined as the act of bringing people together for the purpose of settling their differences. It is the act of bringing people together for the purpose of agreement, concord, or harmony. Another definition looks at reconciliation as one of accountability, that is to render one account consistent with another by balancing apparent discrepancies. One can also reconcile different versions of the truth or different statements of fact. Even if the end result is not perfect, the two sides have been brought into some kind of accord.

We can look at the concept of reconciliation from a business standpoint. For example, balancing debits and credits in an account statement is the same as reconciling that account. Still another definition of reconciliation may be to inspire a person to return to his faith. In any of these situations, truth, as painful as it may be, is essential. When we recognize concealed and agonizing truths, we take a major step toward the elimination of disagreements.

Building Cultures of Reconciliation

Recognizing the origin of conflicts is a major first step in the process of reconciliation. This requires an understanding of the structure of conflicts and how to deal with them. Conflicts lie just beyond the horizon of our own interests. To attain mutual cooperation, we need to learn how to cope with practices and attitudes that contribute to conflicts. Social conflict is innate in human relations and internal to the involved parties. While the outcome of the dispute may be negative, all efforts should be made to achieve reconciliation and mutual happiness. This does not mean that the parties in the dispute should forgo their differences. Instead, these differences should lead to enrichment rather than provocation. Building cultures of reconciliation means developing proactive attitudes and practices that make cooperation possible.

Reconciliation advances as the parties in dispute begin to shape their lives in positive relation to one another. Reconciliation is a journey as well as an encounter. We need to understand the culture and emotions of the people who are in conflict. When they realize what separates them, they will bridge the gap between their differences, which will enable them to live in peace with one another.

While reconciliation is difficult to achieve, it can be attained. This, of course, does require moving into realms that have not yet been considered or revealed and counting on the emergence of new possibilities. It necessitates an understanding that all parties in a conflict have been hurt and that their wounds are deep. We heal the wounds by having a compassionate understanding about the conflict, which requires all parties to be nonjudgmental and non-adversarial. Good listeners do not defend themselves in reconciliation, but, rather, try to understand each other's perceptions. By listening, they validate each other's right to those perceptions. This listening is not physical in nature but spiritual. The listener does not decide in advance who is right and who is wrong and then seek to rectify it.

Criteria for Reconciliation

What leads to genuine reconciliation is the following sequence: specific facts, integrity, conflict resolution. These decisive factors are both ethical and moral. Promoting reconciliation is an arduous task, since we must be cautious about the pessimists and cynics who will say it is not possible. These skeptics believe that reconciliation is dreadfully culture bound, unattainable, and unrealistic. Pessimists say it is better to strive for a practical compromise than for reconciliation.

Reconciliation signifies not merely a renewal of old relations, but also an intensification and reciprocal acknowledgment and admission of wrongdoings. In addition, there must be accountability, and each party must continue to pursue the relationship long after reconciliation is done. The reason is that even though parties may come together and may forgive one another, this may not be a genuine reconciliation. Rather, it is a step in the right direction. Reconciliation is desirable but not essential to forgiveness. For example, if an offender has serious character flaws, then the victim may feel that it is not in his best interest to reconcile. Reconciliation used in the sense that the offense is forgiven and forgotten, as if it never happened, is a theoretical concept and not practical. Forgiveness can be one-sided, while reconciliation must be reciprocal. We must unconditionally declare our willingness to forgive and reconcile.

We do not agree with skeptics who view forgiveness as ineffective. Rather, we must find a way to build a bridge of compassion between the dissenting parties. We deal with anguish and pain in different ways, and forgiveness requires emotional and moral resources that many people are unable to assemble. Reconciliation does not mean giving up one's individuality or sacrificing one's principles, but it does mean doing whatever is reasonable to normalize relationships. Soothing relationships between parties occurs at any level of conflict, whether it is political, international, institutional, familial, or communal.

There needs to be education and discipline in order for reconciliation to be effective. This means we need to educate people about integrity and cooperation, whether at the political or cultural level, in order to achieve a lasting reconciliation. And that is the work that faith-based initiative groups have to be about first and foremost.

Reconciliation is very difficult because it requires the recommencement of broken relationships and the coming together in harmony of those who have been separated. Attempts must be made to adjust to new responses and to new situations in a climate where aggression is fruitless and pointless.

In a conflict, there are always issues of injustice. Justice is not the direct result of peace; rather, peace is based on justice. Peace is a vehicle in which Jews, Christians, and Muslims can work together for the sake of justice, which must be achieved at the same time as a harmonious coexistence—the element that sustains peace. The role of Judaism, Christianity, and Islam is essential to the process as well. Each of these religions helps the reconciliation process, which must be inclusive.

Everyone has something to bring to the party, and all concerned must be willing to have an open mind and open heart, particularly to those with whom there is disagreement. We must realize that both sides are hurt, and their injuries are in need of treatment. What goes a long way toward treatment is for all parties to be good listeners, which requires them to be noncritical and focused during the discussion. By listening, they corroborate each other's insights. In effect, listening becomes a form of spirituality as each person listens to all sides of the conflict. Effective listening requires that there is no predetermination of who is right or wrong.

Diversity

Diversity is an effective tool for bridging the gap between those in a dispute. It is the awareness that divergent issues do exist among Judaism, Christianity, and Islam, and these issues are fomented by distinctly different and significant views. The first issue that comes to mind is the nature of unity. Barriers toward achieving this unity have made meaningful dialogue more difficult.

All of the Abrahamic faiths demand unity, and an unwillingness to accept this is a sin against that unity. If our mission is to confront the moral, political, and social influences of each of the religions, then surely there is sufficient basis for a common cause. Yet, these religious communities have been marked more by discord than by collaboration, more by hostility than by mercy, more by doubt than by trust, more by misinformation and lack of knowledge than by respect for the truth.

We do not take the time to comprehend the issues, but are simply satisfied to rudely pass along unnecessary insults in the place of frank and insightful reflection. In many instances, we are motivated by pride and prejudice. It is not that disparities between these religions matter. The issue is whether these disparities should be allowed to restrain religious groups from dealing with a greater common enemy: disunity.

We must support each other, irrespective of how profound our differences are. Unity necessitates awareness, patience, and concentration in order to work. Diversity must be respected; diversity must be valued; and diversity must be managed. We respect diversity by promoting tolerance, mercy, and flexibility among faith leaders. We value diversity by understanding and appreciating each other's heritage. We manage diversity by being goal oriented in order to achieve that unity. We respect diversity by being willing to listen to the points of view of others. We value diversity by promoting a qualitative sense of well-being that is based on ethics and ideals. We manage diversity by being strategically driven, pragmatic, and synergistic.

Diversity must ensure peace and stability. However, there are difficulties in achieving it. For example, all parties must be convinced that unity is needed. If unity and diversity are going to be promoted, then the costs associated with them must be paid. Of course, bitterness and cynicism will arise from those who feel they have been excluded.

With a change in the current state of affairs, religious leaders may feel their leadership is threatened and decide to polarize the community. The challenge is to convince all parties that mutual exchange is mandatory and beneficial. For diversity to work, the process must be continuously evaluated for accountability and improvement. Perceptions and points of view will change when individual prejudices and moral attitudes are recognized and preconceptions and stereotypes are confronted.

Diversity focuses on distinctions among people with respect to ethnicity, religion, and other human differences. Pluralism incorporates mutual respect, acceptance, and teamwork. Pluralism allows people to hold to their faith and, at the same time, engage other faiths to learn more about their paths and how they want to be understood. Pluralism and dialogue are the means for building bridges and relationships that create harmony and peace in society. Pluralism does not mean just tolerating religious differences but, rather, accepting the other's point of view, despite cultural, political, psychological, sociological, or philosophical disparities. Pluralism is unity plus diversity.

Brotherhood and Solidarity

Unity in diversity is the cornerstone of brotherhood and solidarity. Communities are infected by ignorance, envy, egotism, and ambition, which are threats to achieving unity among the believers. In striving for unity in the community, we must be cautious and cognizant of these threats. We must deflect these threats and make the community a safe haven.

Believers must address each other in the best possible manner in order to cement solidarity. In many societies, there are people who want to obtain supremacy over others and establish themselves as leaders with a higher status. These people try to use coercive means to attain their supremacy and as a result their faith and trust is weakened in that community. People must guard against such aggressive ambition and strive for reassurance within themselves as true believers unaffected by irrational behavior.

Competition that breeds distrust, suspicion, and disunity will severely harm brotherhood, damage the soul, and lead to moral decay. Rather than competition in a community, believers should seek cooperation with one another. Believers must be compassionate toward one another.

The enforcement of brotherhood is the greatest social ideal of each of the Abrahamic faiths. We must search to discover our creative intelligence and rid ourselves of indifference and ignorance, as we strive for brotherhood and solidarity. This must be done and it can be done, if we have effective leadership.

Leadership

Leadership is a word on everyone's lips. Discussions on the topic are often as majestically useless as they are pretentious. It is like the abominable snowman, whose footprint is everywhere, but he is nowhere to be seen. Leadership is the process of moving a group in some direction through mostly noncoercive means. Effective leadership produces movement in the long-term best interests of the group. While this definition of leadership is appropriate for those who manage companies or businesses, interfaith partners need to link themselves to another kind, spiritual leadership. Here, leadership demands results and provides the courage to overcome ignorance, fear, and denial. Ignorance holds back far more leaders than does either a lack of talent or skill.

Ethics of Leadership

Ethical practices are always a crucial factor, particularly, when integrity is compromised. Ethical standards are a direct reflection of one's values. Trust, care, and excellence are characteristics of sound, ethical leadership. When these core values are instilled in leadership, it is more likely that consistent ethical decisions will be made.

Leaders often base their decisions on whether there will be an associated personal benefit and satisfaction. But being a successful leader is predicated on one's ability to becoming efficient and effective. A leader succeeds in his endeavors by getting the job done.

An ethical dilemma may occur when the leader becomes overzealous and achieves his goals using suspicious and unprincipled means. If a leader's personal priority is to attain power or wealth, then his decisions will be based on that priority and will interfere with the completion of his task. A leader seeking power or wealth wants to make it known that he is in charge. He wants to be respected by everyone, to the point where it is felt that his very presence is needed for the viability and sustainability of an organization. This gives the leader a sense of supremacy.

A leader who wants to control everything does not have the time to address minor problems. But if he does not delegate authority to his subordinates, he will be placed in a problematic state in which overlooked minor problems catapult into uncontrollable major ones. These types of leaders believe that if they cede authority, they will lose control. When money controls the decision-making process, that will have a severe impact on morale, and the organization will suffer immensely. An effective leader focuses on the organization by delegating authority to his subordinates.

Judaism, Christianity, and Islam teach us a code of ethics. Religious leaders from these faiths must espouse admirable traits in life, by being friendly, sociable, and kind. Other important traits are to be just and to defend the rights of others. Leaders must exhibit qualities of respect, equality, self-restraint, self-sacrifice, and self-denial.

Leadership and Motivation

Leadership style is related to motivation intensity. During a person's lifetime, his motivation will be intensified by the leadership style that he develops. Empowerment augments these aspirations. As he strives for empowerment, the leadership of domination and authority wear off. Empowerment is team motivated.

A motivated leader is focused on achievement and change. Unfortunately, domination- and authority-style leadership are common in our society, because most people resist and dislike change. For example, the affairs of a synagogue, church, or mosque are run by tradition, and the members of the congregation prefer the status quo. This is a reason why many Jewish, Christian, and Muslim institutions may find it difficult to cope with contemporary issues.

It is a challenge to promote leadership unity in an interfaith arena.

Jewish, Christian, and Muslim communities should become proactive about the treatment of potential conflict as well about understanding the inclinations of others. By working in faith groups toward common principles, conflict becomes avoidable. Rather than being competitive, it is better to cooperate with each other. This requires a commitment to develop more profound friendships with and respect for other leaders. Encouragement of a fellow leader can go a long way in building sound relationships.

This interfaith leadership can unfold in the following way. Religious leaders must demonstrate a genuine passion for each other to elicit the acceptance of others. One of the main attributes of good leaders is that they have vision and can see beyond the big picture. Effective communication is vital if each interfaith leader is to embrace the religious and cultural values of others. Creating an atmosphere of trust and truth is vital to success.

Leadership and Character

Character has a great deal to do with leadership. To build character, one needs to strengthen relationships and associations. Leadership also leads to power, and power leads to relationships. Therefore, character and leadership are complementary. One cannot be an effective leader without genuine character. Throughout our lives, we deal with both significant and insignificant situations. It doesn't matter how large or small an item is or how wealthy or poor a person is, but how we conduct ourselves with each item or each person. This conduct brings out the best in character and shapes us into effective leaders.

The requirements for building excellent character are integrity, accountability, ethics, humility, patience, and courage. And courage equips leaders to be confident as they try to drastically alter the course of events. Courage builds character and gives the person enough stamina to lead the way. If one doesn't stand up for his own convictions or tries to hide his faith, then that person is not a leader and severely tarnishes his character.

Jews, Christians, and Muslims who do not stand up for their faith when religious and political antagonists are attacking them considerably demean their character and leadership qualities. Courageous leaders stand up for justice and truth, even if they stand alone. They uphold their religious values at all costs. However, there are those who do not take a stand at all; they remain neutral. These people are opportunists who wait until the final outcome to see who to side with, even at the expense of their own faith and morality.

Leadership must be earned. Leadership is both an art and a science. On the one hand, a leader must be adroit and understanding, while on the other hand he must be skillful in strategic thinking and organizational wisdom. Leaders fail when they drastically make a shift in their focus and lose sight of what is important. They become deterred by affluence and fame. Rather than delegate responsibility and authority, they micromanage and pay too much attention to trivial matters and details. Leaders succeed when they instill character into their decisions, establish open channels of communication, take risks, and stay the course in an ethical manner.

Character is comprised of different qualities. The strengths are elements of a person's basic personality and the way he portrays himself across circumstances and occasions. These individual strengths grow with the person through various occurrences and over time. The environment plays a major part in defining one's character. Wisdom, courage, compassion, justice, self-control, and spirituality are other qualities. We begin with wisdom, which deals with creativity and social intelligence, and we end with spirituality, which deals with forgiveness and gratitude.

Summary

Achieving unity among the Abrahamic faiths requires finding the common denominator that binds them together. Perhaps, imagination is that bond. Imagine that in a forum of interfaith dialogue all participants are wondering how to come together and seek God's love and blessing.

As Judaism, Christianity, and Islam were established by Divine inspiration, they are obligated to enjoy harmony and stability and to move toward an understanding of their relationship with the Creator. Toward this end, they must acknowledge that they are partners and work in collaboration with each other through a coordinated effort.

The three Abrahamic faiths are revealed religions that share the same God. Prayer is the cornerstone of the three faiths; each person prays in the words that God has revealed. It is a covenant that binds each pious Jew, Christian, or Muslim to the Divine. Religion and morality are inseparable in all three faiths.

As the covenant was one of obedience and faithfulness, we must also be obedient and faithful to God and His commandments. Abraham needed to be obedient and faithful to the covenant to obtain the promise; we must also do the same. That promise is conditioned upon our righteous behavior. Abraham is a focal point in our history, as we seek to follow his example of righteousness. He steadfastly committed himself to obey God, and therefore was privileged to enter into a covenant with Him.

As the children of Abraham, we should follow his example. It is imperative that we find the roadmap to working together for the sake of peace and consciousness. We can peacefully resolve our differences through mutual understanding and cooperation. We can escape the destructive spiral of hatred and prejudice. It can be done, and it has been done time and time again because of the idea of brotherhood. Let us build upon that idea by engaging in interfaith dialogue.

Today, there is great demand for eyes that see, ears that hear, minds that think, and hearts that feel. As religious leaders and scholars, we can no longer be too content in our own respectability, or too complex and too difficult to please because of our own self-importance. As the black and bloody pages of the turmoil throughout the world unfold in our presence, we must open our eyes to the tale of mankind's suffering, open our ears to the call for brotherhood, broaden our minds by being tolerant, and soften our hearts by self-restraint. We must live lives that are compassionate and self-denying.

As we meet in interfaith dialogue, we must not surrender to social pressure. Leaders of vision, will, and courage must stand against the multitude, follow their own lights, and withstand the ridicule visited upon them. Leaders must not be indifferent to the moral darkness and misery that feeds on the poor and innocent in each of our faiths. Leaders must take an active part in the quest for tolerance and cooperation, not just to get something out of it but, more importantly, to put something into it. Leaders need to make it easier for people to remain good and wrestle hand to hand with all their power, so that peace, truth, brotherhood, and freedom shall no longer be the rhetoric of the platform but dominant, sovereign facts of life.

Here is an optimism that can be attained by all. It is founded not so much on thought as on action. Leaders must be nurtured in the ideals of true brotherhood, must be trained to estimate rightly the trend of events, and must be animated with the noble purpose of brotherhood for the sake of brotherhood. Real love for one's faith, not violence; universal knowledge, not ignorance; pride of right, not might; respect for man, not envy—these are the virtues of truth and the true standards of equality and justice. They spell the end of jealousy, bring in the day of promise, and usher in the brotherhood of man, the birth of peace. The dream of yesterday becomes the confident hope of today and the realized fact of tomorrow.

As religious leaders and scholars, we are obliged to win the peace. It will not be won without great sacrifices. If we have good sense, if we have courage, if we have integrity, and if we work a little smarter, we will succeed in our quest for peace. The challenge for us is to join together—Jews, Christians, and Muslims—hand to hand, heart to heart, in peace. Let us begin right now!

The hour of our generation may be the dusk and sunset of peace. Let it be our prayer, whether in Judaism, Christianity, or Islam, that through the cooperative efforts of all freedom-loving people, our generation will see the dawn and sunrise of permanent peace. Today is a sunrise of hope, a unique and wonderful opportunity for us to work together toward a better world.

The traits of leadership and character can be the conduits by which religious scholars, academicians, organizations, and others can bridge the gap between the three Abrahamic faith traditions. Toward this end, interfaith trialogue can be the vehicle by which the faiths come together in peace, solidarity, and brotherhood.

11 A Call for Interfaith Trialogue

Throughout history, relatively few religious leaders and scholars have endorsed a trialogue of Abrahamic interfaith partners, who would learn about each other's religion in an atmosphere of openness and fairness. It is of vital importance that Jewish, Christian, and Muslim religious leaders and scholars work toward peace and reconciliation by overcoming bigotry and ignorance. In America, the Judeo-Christian dialogue must step up to the challenge of turning itself into a Judeo-Christian-Islamic trialogue, not for the purpose of conversion but in reverence of each other's faiths and traditions.

Some of the groups that promoted the Judeo-Christian dialogue later evolved into the National Conference for Christians and Jews and then the National Conference for Community and Justice (I was a previous chairman of the Michigan chapter). Supporters affirm that Jews and Christians have many sacred texts and ethical standards in common and worship the same God. They conduct dialogue sessions in an atmosphere of respect, tolerance, and compassion. Although a trialogue among Judaism, Christianity, and Islam has occurred, it has thus far been at a minimal level.

The three faiths share elements of a common theology. All three worship the same God and affirm that He is One. All concur that God rewards virtue, punishes sin, and governs the fate of all humanity. All believe that God sent prophets to mankind. All three are based on books revealed by God—the Torah, the Bible, and the Qur'an. All three share a common heritage of narrative contained in scriptures, lessons told through stories. Moses is a prophet in Judaism, Christianity, and Islam.

Abraham and Sarah are parents of a lineage that gave us Moses and Jesus, while Abraham and Hagar are the ancestors of Muhammad.

As Islam has reemerged as a principal force in world affairs, there is an urgent need to bring it into interfaith discussions. In such an effort, the three Abrahamic faiths would not confer legitimacy on or stand in judgment of each other. Rather, each would explore the path of peace and cooperate with the others to worship and honor the one God. The challenge is not to find an answer to pluralism but to appreciate why people from other faiths believe what they do. Increasing knowledge of each tradition will allow Jews, Christians, and Muslims to understand that all three traditions are authentic expressions of truth and are parallel paths to the same God. In a world where religion is increasingly used to justify violence, this is a much-needed perspective. If the resources of these faith traditions are to be used constructively as a basis for conflict resolution, it is necessary to have a tripartite encounter so that the mistrust and fear generated by ignorance or prejudice can be dispelled (Neusner 2009).

There have been successful interfaith trialogues in America. Religious leaders, scholars, and other concerned citizens have established discussions on all three Abrahamic traditions—Judaism, Christianity, and Islam. One of the early pioneers in this work was the Kennedy Institute of Ethics at Georgetown University in Washington, DC. Sargent Shriver, brother-in law to President John F. Kennedy, initiated the program in 1978, and it continued until the mid-1980s. Following are some other initiatives that have followed the path of trialogue.

The Oklahoma Center for Community and Justice, Tulsa, Oklahoma

This diverse group meets monthly to discuss a wide range of topics related to the three Abrahamic faiths. Established in 1991, the objective is to progress far beyond tolerance and cultivate understanding about how Jews, Christians, and Muslims think, act, and live. Its Jewish, Christian, Muslim Trialogue Study Group has adopted a set of guidelines and requirements for discussion that emphasize personal perspectives based on core beliefs. Group members pay close attention to one another, avoid arguments, and stress understanding. They leave each meeting having learned valuable historical facts, fundamental beliefs, and personal opinions of the participants.

Dialogue Institute, Temple University, Philadelphia, Pennsylvania

Since 1978, the Dialogue Institute has sponsored the International Scholars' Abrahamic Trialogue (ISA). These conferences bring together leading scholars from each of the Abrahamic faiths in regions where interreligious understanding is crucial to promoting stability and peace. Through intensive dialogue, academic scholars and regional leaders use diplomacy to address communities in crisis. For more than thirty years, Jewish, Christian, and Muslim scholars have met for "Trialogue" in various countries around the globe. These scholars have gathered with regional leaders in varied fields to exchange ideas, establish principles for dialogue, and advance interreligious understanding and cooperation.

Abrahamic Trialogue Online

Professor Solomon Schimmel, Hebrew College, Newton Centre, Massachusetts, has proposed conducting a Jewish, Christian, and Muslim trialogue on interreligious understanding and reconciliation over the Internet. This would make it feasible for teachers and students in different countries to communicate with one another both "live" and asynchronously. In addition, websites make the Hebrew Bible, the New Testament, the Qur'an, and other religious literature—both traditional and critical-academic—easily accessible. This can be done in a synoptic format, for study, contrast, and comparison.

The Internet provides a forum for bringing Jewish, Christian, and Muslim voices under a single "virtual roof" and enabling students and scholars to interact with their counterparts around the world. A goal is to provide participants with access to multiple interreligious voices and multiple intrareligious voices as well, such as Conservative Jews and Reform Jews, Catholics and Protestants, and Sunnis and Shi'as. The educational goals of the trialogue are to

- give participants a better understanding of some of the ideological and theological sources of conflicts, animosities, and hatreds that have so often characterized the relationships of the three faiths toward each other; and

- study concepts within each religion that explicitly or implicitly teach prosocial attitudes and behaviors toward others.

Bridges for a Just Community, Cincinnati, Ohio

Formed in 1944, Bridges for a Just Community has a mission to achieve inclusion, equity, and justice for all and is governed by a group of prominent civic leaders. Its interfaith trialogue program was established to learn about Judaism, Christianity, and Islam, develop a shared respect, and exercise interfaith leadership in the community by speaking on issues with a "mutual voice."

Gaston Interfaith Center, North Carolina

The Gaston Interfaith Center is a place where people can explore their religious and spiritual paths with people of other religions. By promoting an understanding of other religions, the Center helps build harmony among and appreciation for many religious communities. The Trialogue, a discussion and prayer group made up of Jews, Christians, and Muslims was formed in 2002. It seeks to be a space where people can learn more about each other and help create better peace and understanding.

Boston Interfaith Dialogue, Boston, Massachusetts

This small, intimate Jewish-Christian-Muslim trialogue has a membership that has remained fairly constant since it was founded in 2002. Members are committed to education, social action, and relationship building in small group settings and also network with other interfaith organizations in the area to help publicize larger, public interfaith events. Participants are drawn from three Boston-area faith organizations: Temple Israel, Trinity Episcopal Church, and the Muslim Student Association at the Massachusetts Institute of Technology.

Christian-Jewish-Moslem "Trialogue" Series, Boston College, Newton Centre, Massachusetts

Organized by the Theology Department of Boston College, the Jewish-Christian-Muslim series hold conferences to increase mutual understanding between scholars of the three faiths. The Trialogue was formed in 1989 and, by design, remains slow and deliberate. Early meetings focused on explanations of the different faiths and each tradition's perspective on major theological topics, such as Creation. The Trialogue also developed an interreligious panel to visit schools and explain the different faith traditions to students.

The Institute of Interfaith Dialog, Houston, Texas

The Institute of Interfaith Dialog grew out of the need to address the question, "How can citizens of the world live in peace and harmony?" The Institute was established in 2002 to eliminate or reduce false stereotypes, prejudices, and unjustified fears through direct human communication. To achieve these goals, the Institute organizes academic and grass roots activities, such as conferences, panels, symposia, interfaith family dinners, and cultural exchange trips. In addition to its headquarters in Houston, it has branch offices in five states and representatives throughout the south-central United States.

The Institute promotes the study of world religions and spiritual faiths to help people gain wisdom and knowledge so that they will have a renewed sense of gratitude and respect for the spiritual beliefs they hold closest to their hearts.

United States Institute of Peace, Washington, DC

The United States Institute of Peace is an independent, nonpartisan institution established and funded by Congress. Its goals are to help prevent and resolve violent conflicts, promote post-conflict peace building, provide conflict-management tools, and increase capacity and intellectual capital around the world. The Institute does this by empowering others with knowledge, skills, and resources as well as by its direct involvement in conflict zones around the globe.

The Institute convened a number of scholars in October 2008 to address the topic, "Abrahamic Alternatives to War: Jewish, Christian, and Muslim Perspectives on Just Peacemaking." A summary of their conclusions follows.

- Jewish, Christian, and Muslim sacred texts all contain sections that support violence and justify warfare as a means to achieve certain goals. In particular historical circumstances, these texts have served as the basis of legitimate violent campaigns, oftentimes against other faith communities.

- Many of the passages from the sacred texts that are misused in contemporary situations to support violence and war have been taken out of context, interpreted in historically inaccurate ways, or can be better translated. Finally, all of these passages need to be understood within (and constrained by) the primary spiritual aims of the individual faith.

- There are also a great many teachings and ethical imperatives within Jewish, Christian, and Muslim scriptures that promote peace and present the means to achieve it. These include mandates to strive for political, social, and economic justice; tolerant, intercommunal coexistence; and nonviolent conflict resolution.

- The three religious delegations that participated in the conference presented slightly different and yet overlapping methods for peacemaking articulated by their sacred scriptures. The considerable overlap led the scholars to affirm the existence of a coherent "Abrahamic Just Peacemaking" paradigm, which began to take focus through their rigorous interfaith debates.

- Further work is needed to articulate fully this "Abrahamic Just Peacemaking" paradigm. The conference scholars committed themselves to continued development of this model in pursuit of a rigorous and effective faith-based program to promote alternatives to war. (Thistlethwaite 2008)

Summary

All of the above organizations have made considerable strides toward cementing an interfaith relationship among the religions of Judaism, Christianity, and Islam. Interfaith is an ongoing endeavor, and each organization continues to draw the three Abrahamic faiths to a closer understanding of each other. As such, each must remain open to learning about the other's faith. Our challenge is not to find solutions to pluralism but, rather, to appreciate each tradition's point of view. We all have a path to the same Creator, and that should be the theme that permeates all discussions and endeavors. We can take a unified stand against ignorance, prejudice, bigotry, and their violent manifestations by issuing a declaration from the three faith traditions.

God gave mankind spiritual consciousness so that people could understand each other. As stewards of the natural world, humans must be in control at all times and act with moderation and reason so we do not disrupt the pattern of Creation or cause corruption on Earth. We are guardians of the Earth, trustees with duties and responsibilities to safeguard and maintain the balance that exists within the environment. As such, we will be held accountable for our actions.

Judaism maintains that God has dominion over the Earth and people act as God's stewards to conserve and cultivate the environment (Genesis 2:15) and not destroy it (Deuteronomy 20:19–20).

Christians consider themselves to be caretakers and caregivers of each other (Luke 10:29).

Islam states that God is sovereign over all Creation (Qur'an 2:106), and that people are tested on how well they use what God has provided.

Whichever of the three Abrahamic faiths one follows, the message is the same. As the children of Abraham, we must pursue equality, brotherhood, justice, and a compassion for each other to protect the environment and our families. The legacy we inherited will be passed on to our children.

We live in a tumultuous and volatile world, beset by violence of endemic proportions. Many institutions have worked steadfastly to bring about peace, making progress only to lose it, because of a lack of consistency and sustained efforts. The interfaith trialogue of Judaism, Christianity, and Islam is a roadmap to a genuine and sustained peace that can be embraced by all.

The question is, are we up to the task? Are we clear about where we want to go and how to get there? Do we understand our responsibilities? It is not right to pull children in different directions in the hope that they will sort out things for themselves. Interfaith trialogue can bring our children into focus because it instills and nurtures the elements of knowledge, empathy, tolerance, and collaboration. It paves the way for reaching a consensus on norms and values and bridges the gap between religions and cultures by encouraging dialogue and respecting diversity. Global peace and global justice are the outcomes of interfaith trialogue.

The children of today will be the future leaders and advocates of a vision of peace. We can teach our children that though we may be of different faiths or races or speak different languages, our hearts are the same. Our hearts are passionate and compassionate.

If we hope to raise peaceful children, we must develop a better understanding of how children grow and learn. Children will become moral individuals if we cultivate their minds and hearts, and give them opportunities to actually see family values being put into practice.

Children need social and emotional competence and resilience to face the problems in society. Children need to be taught intrapersonal and interpersonal skills to ensure they develop positive relationships, to be encouraged to achieve and aspire, to feel cared for, valued, and supported. Children need to form positive habits early, so they will not depend on aggression and violence to settle their disputes.

Adults need to learn how to manage their own anger and hostility, to express feelings without hurting others, to communicate in ways that do not lead to conflict, to set limits, to comprehend what is negotiable, and to establish problem-solving routines.

Violence makes our children feel frightened and insecure. Children often have to cope with violence before they are ready to comprehend all aspects of complicated situations. We need to control our own behavior and develop open communication with children: monitor the media, tone down the effects of violent messages, recognize children's fears and reassure them of their safety, hold family meetings, express strict rules about weapons, open dialogue with other parents, and get educators involved.

Can we create a future in which we live peacefully and in harmony with each other? We need to understand who we are, where we come from, and where we are going as well as the repressed pain we carry that has been handed down from previous generations or from our childhood experiences.

We need to commit ourselves to resolving and transforming conflicts, to understand from where our own unresolved childhood feelings of frustration and despair arise, and to relive and resolve them.

We need to be able to cultivate peace in the home where children grow intellectually, spiritually, and socially. We need to channel our children's energy into peacemaking activities, as they learn to understand and deal with emotions and conflicts. We must teach our children the evils of terrorism and the benefits of peace, to uphold democratic principles and maintain moral and ethical standards.

Children solidify their personality characteristics long before they become adults. The problem is that we have not been great models for our children. Much of our sophisticated adult social behavior is incomprehensible to them. We have a hard time entering the world of our children, even though it may seem similar to the one in which we grew up. Each generation must learn to adapt to the world they live in rather than the one their parents live in. We may not be in control or even the determinant of our children's character, but we have influence.

As we spend time with children and truly open our hearts, we will find that they have something to give and to teach us—their innocence, their trust. Children come into the world carrying the light of peace with them. As we open ourselves to their teaching, they can show us how to be peaceful, how to be absorbed in the present. While children can help us rediscover peace, they also need to see us working for peace, peace for us, peace for everyone, and peace for the world.

Interfaith trialogue is the vehicle by which we can work together for a more peaceful world and, particularly, our children. Collective responsibility is a test that requires strong cooperation and the willingness to succeed. Together we can shape the world our children will inherit so they in turn can shape the future of peace. There must be security for all or no one will be secure. As children of Abraham, let us embrace the covenant.

Epilogue

Judaism, Christianity, and Islam share Prophet Abraham in their lineages, and more than half the people in the world identify themselves as members of the Abrahamic faiths. The Abrahamic faiths are monotheistic, believe in one God, and have Semitic origins. Abraham made a covenant with God, and his descendants are known as the children of Abraham.

I examined the scriptures of Judaism, Christianity, and Islam to document the commonalities among them and to understand what has caused dissention, hatred, animosity, and violence between the followers of these faiths. History is replete with myriad examples of confrontation, belligerency, and war that have caused the loss of many lives. Power and ego eroded the true meaning and significance of the religions. Abraham was the cornerstone in the evolvement of the three faiths and the binding tie that links them together.

My study did not focus on differences in ideology, but only discussed them to render explanations when necessary. This research was based on the notion that Jews, Christians, and Muslims have a great deal in common regarding philosophy, traditions, biblical stories, personages, and family values as well as a shared legacy. The most important connection—our monotheism, which is that we all believe in and worship the same God.

The major threats facing Judaism, Christianity, and Islam are primarily from adherents within these faiths and less frequently from believers from other religions. Unfortunately, religion is on trial rather than those who distort the scriptures. Among these threats are a lack of understanding of one's own faith, complacency, ignorance, intolerance, impatience, immorality, and altering the meaning and intent of the

Divine revelations. We witness religious zealots attack the religious beliefs of others. These extremists either do not understand what they read in their own scriptures, or they just want to attack someone else because they are of another faith. They are indeed ignorant about their own ignorance.

To bring the followers of the three Abrahamic faiths together, we need to promote peace and tolerance for each other's point of view. This requires a mutual understanding of the similarities that bind us together, as we build bridges across religious and cultural differences to foster a deeper sense of unity. We can strengthen our relationships by listening and empathizing with each other, rather than assuming we understand other people's lives.

The challenge we face is coming to grips with the current confusion and disarray in society, which makes it hard to respect the Abrahamic faiths. The Golden Rule, an ethical code that states one should treat others as one would like to be treated, applies to all three faiths:

> Do not seek revenge or bear a grudge against anyone among your people, but love your neighbor as yourself. I am the Lord. (Leviticus 19:18)

> Do to others as you would have them do to you. (Luke 6:31)

> Those who believe (in the Qur'an) and those who follow the Jewish (scriptures), and the Christians and the Sabians, and who believe in God and the Last Day, and work righteousness, shall have their reward with their Lord: on them shall be no fear, nor shall they grieve. (Qur'an 2:62)

> Do unto others as you wish others to do unto you. Whatever you like for yourself, like for others, and whatever you dislike to happen to you, spare others from such happenings. Do not oppress and tyrannize anybody because you surely do not like to be oppressed

and tyrannized. Be kind and sympathetic to others, as you certainly desire others to treat you kindly and sympathetically. If you find objectionable and loathsome habits in others, abstain from developing those traits of character in yourself. If you are satisfied or feel happy in receiving a certain kind of behavior from others, you may behave with others in exactly the same way. Do not speak about them in the same way that you do not like others to speak about you. (Imam Ali, *Nahjul Balaghah*, Letter 31)

While the Golden Rule applies to Judaism, Christianity, and Islam, ignorance prevents many from practicing it. Knowledge will uproot ignorance. People should take the time to comprehend the scriptures and follow its doctrines and principles. It is vital to engage in interfaith trialogue across America and throughout the world so that Jews, Christians, and Muslims can share, collaborate, and understand one another. Equality among the faiths is the driving force behind reconciliation and diversity. The Qur'an zeroes in on the essence of equality: "O mankind! We created you from a single [pair] of a male and a female, and made you into nations and tribes, that you may know each other [not that you may despise each other] ..." (Qur'an 49:13).

Islam is the anchor of the three Abrahamic faiths, and it brings us full circle into a Judeo-Christian-Islamic tradition. Islam upholds the equality that Abraham embraced, and his legacy was passed on to Moses, Jesus, and Muhammad. As the children of Abraham, let us carry the banner of equality so we can begin to know one another.

Shalom! Peace! Salaam!

References

Abbasi, Jennifer. 2012. "Girls as Young as 6 Want to Be 'Sexy,' Study Says." *Today Moms*, July 16.

Adler, Richard B., Lan Jen Chu, and Robert M. Fano. 1968. *Electromagnetic Energy Transformation and Radiation*. Cambridge: The MIT Press.

Ajrouch, Kristine J. 2004. "Gender, Race, and Symbolic Boundaries: Contested Spaces of Identity among Arab American Adolescents." *Sociological Perspectives* 47: 371–91.

Al-Baghdadi, Allamah Murtada. 1999. *Tahrim Halq Al-Lihyah (Unlawfulness of the Shaving of the Beard)*. Translated by Shaykh Mubashir Ali. Birmingham, UK: Al-Mahdi Institute of Islamic Studies.

Alexander, Scott C. 2011. "The Spiritual Union of Form and Function: The Challenges of Using Social Media in Interreligious Dialogue." Ninth Doha Conference of Inter-Faith Dialogue, Doha, Qatar, October.

Ali, Abdullah Yusuf. 1978. *The Holy Qur'an: Text, Translation and Commentary*. Washington, DC: The Islamic Center.

Ali, S. V. Mir Ahmed. 1995. *The Holy Qur'an*. Elmhurst, NY: Tahrike Tarsile Qur'an, Inc.

Alkassimi, Sherif. 2008. "The Qur'an on the Expanding Universe and the Big Bang Theory." *The Religion of Islam*, July 1. www.IslamReligion.com/articles /1560.

Al-Qazwini, Imam Sayed Moustafa. 2004. "'A Just War or Just a War?' Iraq a Year Later." *Nexus: A Journal of Opinions* 9 (Chapman University School of Law).

Arabic Language Institute. Katy, Texas, 2007.

Ashraf, Faheem. 2003. "Islamic Concept of Creation of the Universe, Big Bang and Science-Religion Interaction." *Science-Religion Dialogue* (Mansehra, Pakistan: Hazara Society for Science Religion Dialogue), Spring.

Athal, Krishna. 2012. "The Decline of Morality in Our Society." Seventh International Youth Peace Fest.

Atkins, Peter. 2007. *Four Laws That Drive the Universe*. London: Oxford University Press.

Augustine of Hippo. 2012. *Expositions on the Psalms*. Amazon Digital Services, Inc., August 4.

Ault, Michael K. 2012. "Straight Is the Gate: An Ethnographic Study of the Centennial Park Polygamist Community." Master's thesis, Southern Utah University, May.

Axelrod, Alan, and Charles L. Phillips, eds. 2001. *Encyclopedia of Historical Treaties and Alliances, Vol. 1*. New York: Zenda, Inc.

Barber, R. *Pilgrimages*. 1993. London: Boydell Press.

Barna Research Group. 2010. Ventura, CA, November 28.

Berinstein, Judith. 2009. *Fountainhead of Emotions—Jealousy: A Collection of Thoughts on the Emotions from a Jewish Perspective*. The American Jewish Joint Distribution Committee.

Bible Illuminated: The Book New Testament. 2008. Stockholm: Illuminated World.

"Big Bang Theory Busted by 33 Top Scientists." 2004. *New Scientist*, May 22–28, p. 20.

Browne, Sylvia. 2003. *Book of Angels*. New York: Hay House, Inc. Publishers.

Bullock, C. Hassell. 2007. *An Introduction to the Old Testament Prophetic Books*. Rev. ed. Chicago: Moody Publishers.

Burg, David F. 2003. *A World History of Tax Rebellions: An Encyclopedia of Tax Rebels, Revolts, and Riots from Antiquity to the Present*. New York: Routledge.

Burkett, Larry. 1998. *Giving & Tithing.* Chicago: Moody Publishers.

Caner, Emir. 2007. "First-Person: Are God & Allah The Same?" Baptist Press, Nashville, TN, August 23.

CDC. 2012. "Trends in HIV-Related Risk Behaviors among High School Students— United States." *Morbidity and Mortality Weekly Report* (Centers for Disease Control and Prevention, US Department of Health and Human Services, Atlanta, Georgia), July 24.

Cline, Eric, H. 2004. *Jerusalem Besieged: From Ancient Canaan to Modern Israel.* Ann Arbor: University of Michigan Press.

Cohen, Abraham. 1995. *Everyman's Talmud: The Major Teachings of the Rabbinic Sages.* New York: Schocken.

Collins-Kreiner, N. 2010. *Researching Pilgrimage: Continuity and Transformations.* Pergamon: Annals of Tourism Research 37, no. 2, pp. 440–56.

Columbia Electronic Encyclopedia. 2004. New York: Columbia University Press.

Comerford, Patrick. 2009. "Should Priests Shave? Should Priests Have Beards?" http://revpatrickcomerford.blogspot.com/2009/05/should-priests-shave -should-priests.html, May 29.

Crary, David. 2012. "Gallup Study: 3.4 Percent of US Adults Are LGBT." Minnesota Public Radio, October 19.

D'Ambrosio, Dr. Marcellino. 2013. *The Meaning of Mercy.* Flower Mound, TX: A Ministry of Crossroads Productions, Inc., February 25.

Dirks, Jerald F. 2007. "Did Islam Just Copy from Judaism & Christianity?" *The Cross & the Crescent.* Beltsville, MD: Amana Publications.

Disney, Kate. 2007. "Pilgrimage Destinations for Christians." *Helium: Where Knowledge Rules,* December 13. http://www.helium.com/items/746927 -pilgrimage-destinations-for-christians.

Domb, Cyril. 1982. *Maaser Kesafim: On Giving a Tenth to Charity.* 2nd ed. Nanuet, New York: Philipp Feldheim Publisher.

Doumani, Beshara. 1995. "The Meanings of Autonomy: The City of Nablus." In *Rediscovering Palestine: Merchants and Peasants in Jabal Nablus, 1700–1900.* Berkeley: University of California Press.

Durham, A. S. 1998. "Why Do Orthodox Priests Wear Beards, When Until Recently Catholic Priests Were Actually Forbidden to Wear Beards? And Why Did Catholic Monks Have Tonsures, But Not Orthodox?" *Orthodox England on the Net* 2, no. 2 (December 1). http://orthodoxengland.org.uk/v02i2.htm.

Einstein, Albert. 2010. *Relativity: The Special and the General Theory.* Mansfield Centre, CT: Martino Fine Books Publisher, December 1.

Eisenberg, Ronald L. 2004. "The 13 Attributes of Mercy: Asking God for Forgiveness." *The JPS Guide to Jewish Traditions.* Philadelphia: Jewish Publication Society.

Esposito, John L. 1992. *Islam the Straight Path.* Oxford: Oxford University Press.

Etshalom, Rabbi Yitzchak. 1998. "Parashat Vayyikra: The Korban Minchah." Educational Coordinator of the Jewish Studies Institute of the Yeshiva of Los Angeles.

Faigin, D. P. 2009. *Frequently Asked Questions and Answers.* Soc. Culture Jewish Newsgroups, October 10. http://www.shamash.org/lists/scj-faq/HTML/faq /intro.html.

Fairchild, Mary. n.d. "Day of Atonement." *About.com Guide.* http://christianity .about.com/od/biblefeastsandholidays/p/dayofatonement.htm.

Fernflores, Francisco. 2012. "The Equivalence of Mass and Energy," *The Stanford Encyclopedia of Philosophy.* Edited by Edward N. Zalta. http://plato.stanford .edu/archives/spr2012/entries/equivME.

Fieser, James. 2000. "Are Moral Values Objective?" *Moral Philosophy through the Ages.* Mountain View, CA: McGraw-Hill.

Frank, Julia Bess. 1981. "Moses Maimonides: Rabbi or Medicine." *The Yale Journal of Biology and Medicine* 54, no. 1, pp. 79–88.

Freeman, Ken, and Geoff McNamara. 2006. *In Search of Dark Matter.* New York: Springer.

Fry, Ian Rex. 2012. "Dialogue between Christians, Jews, and Muslims: The Concept of Covenant as Basis." Thesis, MCD University of Divinity, Melbourne, March 14.

"George Smoot Wins Nobel Prize in Physics." 2006. Berkeley Labs press release, University of California at Berkeley, October. http://www.lbl.gov /Publications/Nobel/.

Goleman, Dr. Daniel. 1995. *Emotional Intelligence*. New York: Bantam Books.

Gopin, Rabbi Marc. 2011. "Social Networks and Intervention for Global Change." Ninth Doha Conference of Inter-Faith Dialogue, Doha, Qatar, October.

Grimes, B. F. 1996. *Ethnologue: Languages of the World*. 13th ed. Dallas: Summer Institute of Linguistics.

Grossman, Cathy Lynn. 2009. "Most Religious Groups in USA Have Lost Ground, Survey Finds." *USA Today*, March 17.

Haddad, Yvonne Yazbeck. 2007. "The Post-9/11 Hijab as Icon." Sociology of Religion (Georgetown University) 68, no. 3: 253–67.

Haeri, Shaykh Fadhlalla. "The Origin of Islam and Its Universal Truth." http:// www.nuradeen.com/archives/Reflections/OriginOfIslam1.htm.

Harden, J. M. 1926. *An Introduction to Ethiopic Christian Literature*. Maidstone, Kent, UK: The Oriental Orthodox Library.

Harrigan, Neil Patrick. 2010. *The Spirituality of Pilgrims: A Study of an Australian Experience of El Camino de Santiago de Compostela*. Fitzroy, Victoria: School of Theology, Australian Catholic University, December 1.

Hartono, W. 1996. "Canon of the Old Testament." Nanyang Technological University, Singapore, September 19.

Hassan, Riffat. 2000. *Trialogue among the Abrahamic Faiths*. Global Dialogue 2, no. 1 (Winter).

Hetzron, Robert. 2006. *The Semitic Languages*. London: Routledge.

The Holy Bible: New International Version. 2011. London: Hodder & Stoughton.

The Holy Bible: New King James Version. 1982. Nashville, TN: Thomas Nelson.

The Holy Bible: New Revised Standard Version. 1989. London: Oxford University Press.

Hornecker, John. 1996. *Cosmic Insights into Human Consciousness.* Internet.

Hubble, Edwin. 1929. "A Relation between Distance and Radial Velocity among Extra-Galactic Nebulae." *Astrophysical Journal* 15: 168–73.

Huehnergard, John. 2011. "Proto-Semitic Language and Culture." *The American Heritage Dictionary of the English Language.* 5th ed. Boston, New York: Houghton Mifflin Harcourt, pp. 2066–78.

Huffpost Politics. 2009. *Religion in America in Decline,* September 11.

Iannaccone, Laurence R. 2006. "The Market for Martyrs." *Interdisciplinary Journal of Research on Religion* 2.

Ibn Abi Talib, Imam Ali. 1999. *Nahjul Balagha (Peak of Eloquence): Sermons and Letters of Imam Ali Ibn Abi Talib.* 12th ed. Islamic Seminary Publications.

The International Standard Bible Encyclopedia Online. 1939 [2011]. Wm. B. Eerdmans Publishing Co., 1939. http://www.internationalstandardbible.com.

Isles, Greg. 2004. *Dark Matter.* Philadelphia: Coronet.

Jabir al-Jaza'iry, Abu Bakr. 2012. "Bad Characteristics: Envy." Islamic Network. http://www.islaam.net/main/display.php?id=1226&category=141.

Jacobs, Rabbi Louis. 1995. *The Jewish Religion: A Companion.* New York: Oxford University Press.

James, John Angell. 1820. "Christian Mercy Explained and Enforced. A sermon preached on Sunday evening, May 21st, 1820."

*The Jewish Bible: Tanakh: The Holy Scriptures – The New JPS Translation According to the Traditional Hebrew Text: Torah *Nevi'im *Kethuvim.* 1985. Philadelphia: Jewish Publication Society, First Edition.

Jewish Encyclopedia. 1906. 2002–2011, JewishEncyclopedia.com.

Kanipe, Jeff. 2007. *Chasing Hubble's Shadows: The Search for Galaxies at the Edge of Time*. New York: Hill and Wang Publishers.

Kardec, Allan. 1865 [2008]. *Heaven and Hell (Divine Justice Explained by the Spiritist Doctrine)*. International Spiritist Council.

Khan, Dr. Muhammad Muhsin. 1994. Sahih Al-Bukhari. Islamic University, Al-Medina Al-Munauwara. Vols. 1–9.

Kim, Christine, and Robert Rector. 2010. "Evidence on the Effectiveness of Abstinence Education: An Update." Washington, DC: Heritage Foundation.

Kohler, Jon. 2010. Rabbinical Judaism, Rabbinical Judaism Slides, April 8.

Kupelian, David. 2002. "Why Are Christians Losing America?" *WND Commentary*, August 9.

Lari, Sayyid Mujtaba Musavi. 1996. *Imamate and Leadership: Lessons on Islamic Doctrine (Book Four)*. 1st ed. Translated by Hamid Algar. Tehran, Iran: Foundation of Islamic Cultural Propagation in the World.

Lowe, B. 1985. "Islam and the Media in New South Wales." *Islam in Australia*. Sydney, Australia: New South Wales Anti-Discrimination Board.

MacDonald, Kevin. 1998. *The Culture of Critique*. Westport: Praeger Publishers.

Maddison, David S. *Talmud Expose*. Accessed February 12, 2007.

Magee, Dr. M.D. 2007. "Truth: The Big Bang and the Christian Scientists." ASKWHY, March 12.

Mahmood, Mahmood. 2008. "Al-Andalusia … Decline of a Plural Culture." Islamic Research Foundation International, Inc., January 1.

Majilsi, M.B. 1983. *Bihar al-Anwar (Ocean of Lights)*. Beirut: Dar Ihya al-Turath al-Arabi Publications.

Mamre, Mechon. 2013. *Torah 101*. http://www.mechon-mamre.org/index.htm.

Mann, Brian. 2012. "Survey Finds Massive Decline in Religion in US, World." North Country Public Radio, St. Lawrence University, Canton, New York, August 9.

Marcus, David. 1978. *A Manual of Akkadian*. Lanham, MD: University Press of America.

Markham, Christine. 2009. "Middle School Youth as Young as 12 Engaging in Risky Sexual Activity." *Science Daily*, April 10.

Martens, John W. 2011. "Purgatory: Feel the Burn." *America: The National Catholic Weekly*, January 14.

McCutcheon, Mark. 2004. *The Final Theory: Rethinking Our Scientific Legacy*. 2nd ed. Boca Raton, Florida: Universal Publishers.

McElwain, Thomas. 2002. *Islam in the Bible*. London: Minerva Press.

McGill International Colloquium on Judaism and Human Rights. 1974. "Declaration on Judaism and Human Rights." Jacob Blaustein Institute for the Advancement of Human Rights of the American Jewish Committee; Canadian Jewish Congress; and the Consultative Council of Jewish Organizations, Montreal, April 23.

Mernissi, Fatima. 1987. *Women & Islam: An Historical and Theological Enquiry*. Oxford, UK: Blackwell.

Metzger, B. M., and M. D. Coogan. 1993. *The Oxford Companion to the Bible*. New York: Oxford University Press.

Michalenko, Fr. Seraphim. 2009. *Look It Up: How the Bible Defines Mercy*. Marian Fathers of the Immaculate Conception, June 2.

Modi, Dr. Bhupendra Kumar. 2000. *One God*. New Delhi: Modi Foundation.

Morales, Lymari. 2011. "US Adults Estimate that 25% of Americans Are Gay or Lesbian." *Gallup Politics*, May 27.

Muller, Hans-Peter. 1995. "Ergative Construction in Early Semitic Languages." *Journal of Near Eastern Studies* 54: 261–71.

Mullins, Christopher. 2005. "On the Origin and Inherent Meaning of the L-Stem." *IULC Working Papers Online* 05-07 (Indiana University, June 14), https://www.indiana.edu/~iulcwp/pdfs/05-mullins.pdf.

Neusner, Jacob. 2009. "Time for Islam: From Dialogue to Trialogue in Interfaith Relations." *Journal of Interreligious Dialogue,* June 23. http://irdialogue.org /articles/time-for-islam-from-dialogue-to-trialogue-in-interfaith-relations-by -jacob-neusner/.

The New England Bible. 1970. London: Oxford University Press.

Newport, Frank. 2011. "For First Time, Majority of Americans Favor Legal Gay Marriage." *Gallup Politics,* May 20.

Nicholson, Iain. 2007. *Dark Side of the Universe: Dark Matter, Dark Energy, and the Fate of the Cosmos.* Baltimore: The Johns Hopkins University Press.

Orsi, Rev. Michael P. 2012. "The Mormon People: The Making of an American Faith." *Crisis Magazine,* May 8.

Parsons, John J. n.d. "Jewish Tzomot: Fast Days of the Jewish Year." *Hebrew for Christians.* http://www.hebrew4christians.com/Holidays/Fast_Days/fast _days.html.

Peedin, Philip. 2011. "Conversation of the Week XI: The Muslim American Experience." *USA on Race,* January 24. http://www.usaonrace.com/national -collegiate-dialogue/conversation-week-xi-muslim-american-experience.

Perera, Yohan. 2011. "Sermon Notes: What Does the Bible Say About Envy— How Do I Overcome It?" *The Virtual Preacher,* February 23. http://www .virtualpreacher.org/sermon-notes/sermon-notes-bible-envy-overcome-it/.

Posner, Menachem. 2012. "On Which Days Is It Forbidden to Shave?" *Chabad.org,* November 4. http://www.chabad.org/library/article_cdo/aid/931778/jewish /On-which-days-is-it-forbidden-to-shave.htm.

Post, P., J. Pieper, and M. van Uden. 1999. *The Modern Pilgrim: Multidisciplinary Explorations of Christian Pilgrimage.* Leuven, Belgium: Peeters Publishers.

Read, Jen'nan Ghazal, and John P. Bartkowski. 2000. "To Veil or Not to Veil? A Case Study of Identity Negotiation among Muslim Women in Austin, Texas." *Gender and Society* 14: 395–417.

Ream, Dr. Norman S. 1993. "Morality in America." *The Freeman: Ideas on Liberty* 43, no. 7 (July).

Reed, Pastor Robert W. 2008. "The Riches of Grace." Victory Baptist Church, Coden, Alabama, September.

Rizvi, Sayyid Muhammad. 1993. *Khums: The Islamic Tax.* Qom: Ansariyan Publications.

———. 2000. *Shi'ism: Imamate and Wilayat.* Richmond Hill, Ontario: Al-Ma'arif Books.

Robinson, B. A. 2007. "The Christian Concept of Atonement." *Religious Tolerance* (Ontario Consultants on Religious Tolerance), August 26. http://www .religioustolerance.org/chr_atone7.htm

Rosen, Rabbi Yisrael. 2002. "Shiur #11: Electric Shavers." The Israel Koschitzky Virtual Beit Midrash. Lecture delivered at the Yeshivat Har Etzion in Shevat.

Sainz de Aja, Sofia. 2011. "The Importance of Jerusalem for the Three Monotheistic Religions." Centro de Estudios de Oriente Medio Fundacion Promocion Social de la Cultura. Working Paper, MA in Islamic and Middle Eastern Studies, the Hebrew University of Jerusalem, July 6.

Sasson, Jack M. 1995. *Civilizations of the Ancient Near East: Volume IV.* New York: Charles Scribner's Sons.

Sawad, Ahmed Ali. 2008. "Reservations to Human Rights Treaties and the Diversity Paradigm: Examining Islamic Reservations." PhD diss., University of Otago, Dunedin, New Zealand, July 7.

Schimmel, Solomon. 2006. "Developing an Internet-Based Trialogue on Peace and Reconciliation in Judaic, Christian, and Islamic Thought." *Journal of the Interdisciplinary Study of Monotheistic Religions*, February, pp. 40–60.

Schwartz, Gary E. R., and Linda G. S. Russek. 1999. *The Living Energy Universe.* Charlottesville, VA: Hampton Roads Publishing Company, Inc.

Seikaly, May. 1998. *Islam, Gender, and Social Change.* New York: Oxford University Press.

Shakeri, Esmail. 1998. *Muslim Women in Canada: Their Role and Status as Revealed in the Hijab Controversy.* New York: Oxford University Press.

Shamsi, Rashid. 1999. "Why Islam Forbids Pork?" *The Muslim World League Journal*, October.

Shepherd, Peter. n.d. "Emotional Intelligence." http://www.trans4mind.com/heart/.

Simeone-Sinelle, Marie-Claude. 1997. "The Modern South Arabian Languages." In *The Semitic Languages*. Edited by Robert Hetzron. London: Routledge, pp. 378–423.

Simmons, Rabbi Shraga. n.d. "Ask Rabbi Simmons: Interest on Loans." *About .com Judaism*. http://judaism.about.com/library/3_askrabbi_o/bl_simmons _interestloans.htm.

Smith, Huston. 1992. *The World's Religions: Our Great Wisdom Traditions*. San Francisco: Harper.

Smith, Nicole. 2011. "Summary of the Meaning of the Theory of Moral Virtue by Aristotle." *Article Myriad*, December 7. http://www.articlemyriad.com /summary-theory-moral-virtue-aristotle/.

Smith, Richard. 2008. *Envy: Theory and Research*. New York: Oxford University Press.

Sparks, H. F. D. 1985. *The Apocryphal Old Testament*. London: Oxford University Press.

Stanton, Joshua M. Z. 2011. "Jews and Muslims in America: More in Common Than We Think." *Common Ground News Service*, August 14. http://www .commongroundnews.org/article.php?id=30175&lan=en&sp=0.

Steinhardt, Paul J. 2002. "The Endless Universe: Introduction to the Cyclic Universe." Princeton: Department of Physics and Astrophysical Sciences at Princeton University, actionbiosciences.org, May.

Strasser, Teresa. 1996. "Jealousy and the Jews: What Does the Torah Teach?" *JWeekly.com*, August 23.

Tabataba'i, Sayyid Muhammad Husayn. 1979. *Shi'ite Islam*. 2nd ed. Translated by Sayyid Husayn Nasr. New York: State University of New York Press.

Telushkin, Joseph. 1991. *Jewish Literacy: The Most Important Things to Know about the Jewish Religion, Its People and Its History*. New York: William Morrow and Co.

The Torah: A New Translation of the Holy Scriptures According to the Masoretic Text. 1963. Philadelphia: Jewish Publication Society.

The World Forum for Proximity of Islamic Schools of Thought. 2003. Tehran, Iran.

Thistlethwaite, Susan, and Glen Stassen. 2008. *Abrahamic Alternatives to War: Jewish, Christian, and Muslim Perspectives on Just Peacemaking*. Special Report 214. Washington, DC: United States Institute of Peace, October.

Trubshaw, Bob. 2008. "The Black Stone at Mecca." http://realityresearchresource .worldpress.com, March 1.

Tschanz, David W. 1997. "The Arab Roots of European Medicine." *Aramco World*, May/June, pp. 27–31.

Turfe, Tallal Alie. 2010. *Energy in Islam: A Scientific Approach to Preserving Our Health and the Environment*. Elmhurst, New York: Tahrike Tarsile Qur'an, Inc.

———. 1996. *Patience in Islam: Sabr*. Elmhurst, New York: Tahrike Tarsile Qur'an, Inc.

———. 2004. *Unity in Islam: Reflections and Insights*. Elmhurst, New York: Tahrike Tarsile Qur'an, Inc.

Twersky, Isidore. 1980. *Introduction to the Code of Maimonides (Mishneh Torah)*. Yale Judaica Series, vol. 12. New Haven and London: Yale University Press.

United Nations. 1948. The Universal Declaration of Human Rights. Adopted by the United Nations General Assembly at Palais de Chaillot, Paris, France, December 10.

Villa-Vicencio, Charles. 2004. "Christianity and Human Rights." *Journal of Lutheran Ethics*, March.

Warren, Penny. 1998. "Is the Word Allah Similar to Elohim?" PLIM (Power Latent in Man) Report 7, no. 3. http://www.plim.org/1Allah.html.

Watson, David. 2010. "The Conservation of Energy and the First Law of Thermodynamics." *FT Exploring*. http://www.ftexploring.com/energy/first-law.html.

Weaver, Sam. 2006. "In Search of Noah's Ark." RenewAmerica.com, May 30.

Weber, Katherine. 2012. "44 Percent of Americans Believe Homosexuality is a Sin, New Survey Says." *The Christian Post*, October 20.

Williams, George. n.d. "Relationship of Matter and Energy and the Application to the First Cause." http://www.alchemylab.com/First_Cause.htm.

Williams, Kevin. 2008. *Jewish Afterlife Beliefs*. Near-Death Experiences and the Afterlife. www.near-death.com/experiences/judaism06.html, 1/20/08.

Winston, Kimberly. 2012. "Poll Shows Atheism on the Rise in the US." *The Washington Post*, August 13.

Yildirim, Yetkin. 2005. *Peace and Conflict Resolution Concepts in the Madina Charter*. Athens, Georgia: Interfaith Cultural Organization.

Zaimov, Stoyan. 2012. "PETA Thanks Joel Osteen for Anti-Pork Stance, Offers Easter Message." The Christian Post, Inc., Washington, DC, March 30.

Zeolla, Gary F. 2005. "The Original Language of the New Testament: Part One and Part Two." www.dtl.org/bible/article/language/part_one.htm; www.dtl.org/bible/article/language/part_two.htm, May 2.

Zimmer, Carl. 1996. "Beetle of Burden." *Discover Magazine*, April.

Zoll, Rachel. 2012. "Report: US Protestants Lose Majority Status." *Fox Chicago News*, October 9.

Subject and Name Index

f denotes figure; *t* denotes table

Andalusia Spain, 31
angels, 35, 52, 53–56, 60
angels (fallen), 53, 54
anger, 133, 135*t*
Anglican denomination, 38
animal sacrifices, 98, 99, 100
animus, 141, 142
antagonism, 141
antichrist, 40
apathy, 160, 181*f*
Apostles' Fast, 86
Arabic language, 28, 29, 30
Arabic Language Institute, 28
Aramaic language, 29, 30
archangels, 55
Aristotle, 131, 144, 163
Asaph, 71
Asarah B'Tevet, fast (Judaism), 85
Ash Wednesday, 86
assisted suicide, 67
Assyrians, 29
Atenism, xix
atheism, 173*t*, 174, 175
atonement, 97–100
Augustine of Hippo (saint), 127
Ayoub, Mahmoud, 4, 21
Azrael (archangel), 53, 54, 56

B

Babylonians, 29, 93
Baha'i faith, xix
Baptism (baptismal), 92, 98, 167
Baptist denomination, 38
Barna Group, 176
Barnabas, 85
Barzakh, 37, 52
Basilica (Vatican City), 92
bayit (house), 30
bayt (house), 30
bayt-a' (house), 30
Berber languages, 29
Berman, Howard L., 3, 4–6
Bethlehem, 90, 92

Bible
  commandments and guidelines, 42
  Hebrew Bible, xx
  revealed book of instruction, 49
  sacred text for Christianity, 30
biblical scriptures, 35–37
  See also Scripture Index
big bang theory, 40–42
Bilhah (Jacob's wife), 105
bin Laden, Osama, 170–71
Black Stone, 92–93
blood
  consumption of, 123–24
  offering of, 97, 98
  shedding of, 98, 99, 120
blood sacrifices, 100
Bloomberg, Michael R., 3, 6–8
Boethius, 32
Boston College, 210
Boston Interfaith Dialogue, 210
Brethren denomination, 38
Bridges for a Just Community, 210
British, taking of Jerusalem, xxiii
brotherhood, 93-94, 112, 139, 144,
  159, 171, 183, 187, 199-200, 204-05,
  213
Buddhism, 27*t*, 41, 42
burnt offerings, 98
Bush, George W., 171

C

Cain, 145
Canaan, xxii
Canaanite (Phoenician) language, 29
Canon Law, 31
Canterbury Cathedral (England), 92
Carthage, Punic language, 29
Cathedral of Santiago de Compostela
  (Spain), 92
Catholicism
  afterlife (hereafter), 50
  in America, 2012 versus 2007, 173*t*
  on atonement, 98
  Canon Law, 31

division of Christianity, xix
fasting practices, 87
on head coverings for nuns, 101
infighting with Protestantism, 176
Old Testament followed by, xx
percent of American adults
  affiliated with, 174
on Purgatory, 36
saving of the soul, 50
See also Roman Catholicism
celestial beings, 55
Centers for Disease Control and
  Prevention, 153
Chadic languages, 29
champions, of interfaith trialogue, 3
character, 85, 132, 154, 196, 202-203
charity
  belief that unites, xxi, 88–90
  Job as paradigm of, 71
  not just monetary help, 162
  practice of, 134
  as type of jihad, 119
  as virtue, 135*t*
Charter of Medina, 33
chastity, 132-34
cherubim, 54, 55
China, atheism in, 175
Chinese folk religions, 27*t*
Christianity
  on afterlife (hereafter), 50–51
  on angels, 53–54, 55
  on atonement, 98–99
  on big bang theory, 41, 42
  Canon Law, 31
  Catholicism. *See* Catholicism;
    Roman Catholicism
  charitable requirements, 88–90
  church, xix
  on consumption of swine or pig, 123
  on containment of the ego, 104
  Creator referred to as God, xix
  on David, 71
  day of worship, 81, 82
  in decline in the West, 175
  demographic data, 30, 31

difficulty coping with
  contemporary issues, 201
on envy, 146
on fasting, 85–87
on Heaven, 50–51
holy cities, 90
on homosexual acts, 165
house of worship, xix, 31
on human rights, 110–13
influence of Judaism's concepts in,
  43
on Islam as not mentioned in
  scriptures, 43
on Job, 71
on Jonah, 75–76
on justice, 137–38
Lord's Prayer, 82–83
on mercy, 139–40
misconceptions about, 167–68
monotheism, xix
number of adherents, 27*t*
Orthodox. *See* Orthodox
  (Christianity)
percent of American adults
  affiliated with, 174
on pilgrimage, 91–92
pilgrimage experiences, 93
on polygamy, 106, 107
prayer practices, 81, 83
predominant religion in America,
  151, 173
on prophets, 60
Protestantism. *See* Protestantism
Saint Paul as spreading and
  proliferating, 30
on shaving the beard, 125, 126–27
on Solomon, 77, 78
on struggling/striving, 115–17
threats facing, 217
Trinitarian concept, 35, 37, 38–39,
  43, 168
on usury, 120, 121–22
on veil-wearing in ancient times, 101
on virtues and vices, 135–46
youth disenchantment with, 176

dominions, grouping of celestial beings, 55
Christian-Jewish-Moslem "Trialogue" Series (Boston College), 210
ChristianNetwork, 178
church, 31
  as center of Europe's worldview, post-Western Roman Empire, 32
  as Christian house of worship, xix, 31
  as no longer intellectually challenging, 176
Church of Jesus Christ of Latter-day Saints (Mormons), 107, 173*t*
Church of the Annunciation, 92
Church of the Ascension, 92
Church of the Holy Sepulcher, xxii, 92
Church of the Nativity, 92
church rules, adherence to, 98
coexistence
  case studies of, 31–33
  desire for, 16, 17, 25, 31, 197, 212
collaboration, 179, 187, 197
commandment, defined, 64
common denominator, 203
common ground, common principles
  afterlife (hereafter), 50–52
  angels, 53–56
compassion, 118, 200, 203
complacency, 157, 160–62, 181*f*
compound ignorance, 180, 181–82
concubines, 105, 106
conflict resolution, 49, 192-94, 196
Congregationalist denomination, 38
Conservative Judaism, xix, 31, 37, 125, 176
containment of the ego, 104, 182, 189
conversion, to Judaism, 168
cooperation, 187, 195, 200, 202
Cooperative Congregational Studies Partnership, 175
Coptic language, 29
correction of moral conduct, 162
corruption, 16, 117, 134, 157-58, 161-62, 169, 177, 213

courage, 133, 134, 202–3
covenant, as linked to promise, 64
Covenant of Abraham, 60–64
creative energy, 189, 191–94
Crusades, xxiii
Cumming, Joseph L., 3, 12–13
Cushitic languages, 29
Czech Republic, atheism in, 175

D

Daniel (prophet), 59, 84
daraba (to beat; to ignore; to condemn; etc.), 45, 47
Dark Ages, 32
David (king), 77
David (prophet), 59, 71–72, 84, 85, 106
Day of Atonement (Yom Kippur), 85, 86, 97, 99, 126
Day of Judgment, 37, 56
days of worship, 81, 82
demographic data, 30–31
demons, 53, 54
Deuteronomy, 65
  See also Scripture Index
deviation from scriptures, 162–71
Dialogue Institute, Temple University, 209
discord, 181*f*, 197
distrust, 188, 200
diversity, xviii, 8, 13, 15, 21, 24, 49, 79, 180-81, 184, 198-99, 214, 219
Divine grace, 71
Divine inspiration, 203
Divine intercession, 39
Divine intervention, 145
Divine promise, 115
Divine revelation, 38, 42–43, 60, 64
divorce, 106, 109, 156
Dome of the Rock, xxii, 94
dominions, grouping of celestial beings (Christianity), 55
Dormition Fast, 86

E

Eastern Orthodox Church, 86, 87
ego, containment of, 104, 182, 189
egoism, 157–59, 162, 181*f*
egotism, 157–59, 199
Egypt, Maimonides as head of Jewish communities in, 33
Eid al-Adha (Feast of Sacrifice), 99, 100
Eilberg, Amy, 3, 8–9
Einstein, Albert, 143
El (in Aramaic), similarity to Allah (in Arabic), 30
El (in Christian Bible), 30
El (in Hebrew), similarity to Allah (in Arabic), 30
Elah (in Hebrew), similarity to Allah (in Arabic), 30
Elijah (Elias) (prophet), 59, 84
Elisha (prophet), 59
Ellison, Keith, 4
Elohim (in Hebrew), similarity to Allah (in Arabic), 30
Emerson, Ralph Waldo, 149
emotional intelligence, 188–92
empathy, 74, 75, 76, 119, 132, 140, 181*f*, 190, 193
Encyclopedia (Pliny), 32
energy, law of conservation of, 40
enlightenment, 143–44, 182
enmity, 141, 188
Enoch (prophet), 59, 60
envy, 135*t*, 136, 144–46, 157, 181*f*, 199
Epistles of Paul, 44
equality, 57, 113, 194, 219
equality of the sexes, 45–46
Eritrea, Tigrinya language, 29
Esther, 84
Eternal Garden, 52
eternal redemption, 99
ethical principles, shared belief, 42
ethics
    adhering to highest, xxi
    as component of morality, 132

of leadership, 200–201
    as one solution to unity, 181*f*
    requirement for building excellent character, 202
Ethiopia, Amharic language, 29
Ethiopic language, 29
Europe, loss of intellectual heritage, 32
euthanasia, 67
Eve, 145
Exodus, 65
    See also Scripture Index
external intentions, 189, 190
extremism, 119, 169–71
Ezekiel (prophet), 59
Ezra (prophet), 59

F

Facebook, 178
faith, as virtue, 135*t*
Faith Communities Today (FACT), 175
fasting
    belief that unites, xxi, 84–87
    Christianity, 85–87
    fast-free weeks (Christianity), 86
    historical figures who fasted, 84
    Islam, 85–87
    Judaism, 85–87
    mandatory (Judaism), 85, 86
    nonobligatory (Islam), 86
    nonobligatory (Judaism), 86
    obligatory (Islam), 86
    private fasts, 86
    voluntary (Islam), 86
    voluntary (Judaism), 85
father, similarity of traditions' words for, 30
fear, 117, 187
Feast of Sacrifice (Eid al-Adha), 99, 100
Feast of Tabernacles, 91
Feast of Unleavened Bread, 91
Feast of Weeks, 91
female prophets, 60

moral virtue, theory of, 131
morality, xix, 132, 152–56, 164
Moravian denomination, 38
Mormons (Church of Jesus Christ of
  Latter-day Saints), 107, 173*t*
Mosaic Covenant, 64
Moses
  coming with new laws, 44
  covenant as reformulated with, 64
  descendant of Abraham (Judaism),
    63
  and fasting, 84, 85
  as following in Abraham's
    footsteps, 30
  God's covenant with, xxii, 35
  one of Islam's five great prophets,
    169
  prophet, 59, 207
  receiver of Ten Commandments, 65
  receiver of Thirteen Attributes of
    Mercy, 139
  wives of, 106
mosque, xix, 31
motivation, 190, 201–2
Mount Ararat, 74
Mount Judi, 74
Mount Sinai, 65, 85
Muhammad
  beard, 127, 129
  and Charter of Medina, 33
  coming with new laws, 44
  descendant of Abraham (Islam), 63
  descendant of Ishmael, xx
  on equality of the sexes, 46
  God's covenant with, 35
  on hurting a non-Muslim, 119
  messenger of Islam, 30
  prophet, 59
  on reconciling differences, 119
Munkar (angel in Islam), 56
Musa ibn Maymun (Maimonides), 33
Muslim Student Association
  (Massachusetts Institute of
  Technology), 210

Muslims
  attacks on, 101
  portrayal of, 102
  responsible for bad name given to
    jihad, 118

N

Nablus, 91
Nahum (prophet), 59
Nakeer (angel in Islam), 56
Nathan (prophet), 59
National Catholic Reporter, 175
National Conference for Christians
  and Jews, 207
National Conference for Community
  and Justice, 207
National Opinion Research Center, 174
Nativity, 86
Nazareth, 90, 92
negative stereotyping, 101, 104
Nehemiah, 84
Neo-Aramaic language, 28
Nevi'im, religious text of Judaism, 43
New Testament
  on adultery, 166–67
  on fasting, 85
  on food, 123
  groupings of celestial beings, 55
  holy book for Christianity, xx
  on homosexuality, 165
  on human rights, 111
  on immoral behavior, 164
  influenced by Old Testament, 43
  on justice, 171
  language of, 29
  on Lot, 165
  on polygamy, 107–8
  on shaving the beard, 126
  on struggling/striving, 115–16
  Trinitarian concept as very fabric
    of, 39
  on virtues and vices, 135*t*
  on women's rights, 47
  See also Scripture Index

Progressive Judaism, 38
promise, as linked to covenant, 64
prophets, 35, 43, 57, 59–79
  See also specific prophets
prostration, 82, 83
Protestantism
  in America, 2012 versus 2007, 173*t*
  and Canon Law, 31
  division of Christianity, xix, 38
  on fasting, 86
  infighting with Catholicism, 176
  influenced by Roman Catholicism,
    127
  and Old Testament, xx
  percent of American adults
    affiliated with, 174
  on Purgatory, 36, 51
  on salvation, 44
Psalm number 23, 83
Psalms (of David), 44, 71–72, 83
psalms, defined, 71
Punic language, 29
Purgatory, 36, 50
purification of the soul, 90, 134

Q

Qazwini, Hassan, 4, 23–24
qibla (direction of prayer), xxiii
Qiyamah (Judgment Day), 37
Queen Isabella, 32
quorbanot (sacrifices or offerings), 98
Qur'an
  acknowledging existence of Jewish
    and Christian scriptures, 43
  on afterlife (hereafter), 51–52
  central book of Islam, xx
  commandments and guidelines, 42
  on consumption of pigs or blood,
    123–24
  on Great Flood, 73
  on how husband must treat unruly
    wife, 47–48
  husband and wife the garments of
    each other, 46

on immoral behavior, 164–65
  on justice, 171
  language of, 29
  on Lot, 47, 166
  one of four holy books of Islam, 44
  on Psalms, 72
  revealed book of instruction, 49
  sacred text for Islam, 30, 39
  on shaving the beard, 127, 128–29
  on virtues and vices, 135*t*
  See also Scripture Index

R

Rachel (Jacob's wife), 105
Ramadan, 84, 85, 86
Raphael (archangel), 30, 53, 54, 55, 56
Ravidassia, xix
reconciliation, 5, 10, 12, 18, 22-23,
  47, 49, 97, 118-19, 129, 144, 169-70,
  181*f*, 193, 194–98, 207, 209, 219
redemption, 99
Reform Judaism, xix, 31, 37, 86, 87
Reformation, 31
Reformed denomination, 38
religion(s)
  diminished importance of, 155
  number of adherents among major
    religions, 27*t*
  See also specific religions
religious beliefs, comparison of, 36*t*
religious extremism, 119, 169–71
religious fanatics, 170
religious identity development, 102
religious intolerance, xviii
religious statues, 68
religious tolerance, xviii
religious traditions, in America, 2012
  versus 2007, 173*t*
Renaissance, 32
repentance, 74–76, 99
repentance (of Jonah), 74-76
Resurrection, xxiii
resurrection, to Muslims, 51–52
revered humans, 35

Richard the Lionheart (king), 33
Ridwan (angel in Islam), 56
ritual purification, 81
Roman Catholicism, 36, 38, 86, 127
Romans, 93
Rome (the Vatican), 90, 91
Roosevelt, Franklin D., 109–10
Rosh Hashanah, 126
Ros-Lehtinen, Ileana, 4

S

Sabianism, xix
Sacred Mosque (Mecca), xxii, 64
sacrifices
    Abraham of Isaac, 62–63, 64
    Abraham of Ishmael, 62-63
    animal, 98, 99, 100
    blood of, 98
    blood sacrifices, 100
    human sacrifice, 99
    self-sacrifice, 119
sadaqah (voluntary charity) (Islam),
    89
Sadducees, 50
Safed, 90, 91
Saint Augustine of Hippo, 127
Saint Paul, 30
Saint Peter's Square, 92
saints, 30, 35, 127
salaam (peace), 29
Saladin (sultan), 33
salvation, 51, 98
Salvationist denomination, 38
same-sex marriage/interaction, 164, 166
Samuel (prophet), 59
Sarah (Abraham's wife), 105, 145, 208
Satan, 54, 55, 69, 70, 85
Saul, 84, 85
scarves, 100, 102–3, 129
Schimmel, Solomon, 209
scholarly works
    translation of ancient Greek texts
        into Arabic, 32
    as type of jihad, 119

scriptures
    deviation from, 162–71
    God's books, 42–45
    See also Scripture Index
Sebat Bet Gurage language, 28
Second Vatican Council, 127
self-actualization, 76, 156, 162
self-awareness, 190
self-control, 104, 203
self-denial, 85, 140
self-discipline, 104
self-exaltation, 157
self-respect, 194
self-restraint, 85, 133
self-righteousness, 161
self-sacrifice, 119
self-satisfaction, 160
Semite, 27
Semitic languages, 27–30
separation of church and state, 67
September 11, 2011, 25, 102, 103, 170
seraphim, 54, 55
sex education, 153
sexual behavior, 164
sexual disorientation, 67
sexual morals, lack of (America), 102
sexual risk behaviors, 153–54
sexual themes in media, 153
Shafi'i (Sunni school of thought), 39
shalom (peace), 29
Sharia law, xxi, 31, 108–9
shaving the beard, 125–29
Shavuot, 126
shayatin (angels), 55
Sheba, 29
Shem, 27
Sheol, 50
Shepherd, Glen, 124
Shi'a Muslims
    denomination/sect of Islam, xx, 39
    Imams as Divinely inspired, 35
    infighting with Sunnis, 176
    on shaving the beard, 128
shlama (peace), 29
Shriver, Sargent, 208

rights of in ancient times, 45–49
of Solomon, 106
See also adultery; marriage; wives

women
changing status of, 57
and head coverings, 100–105
misconceptions about in Islam, 169
rights in polygamous marriage, 109
rights of in ancient times, 45–49
role of women in primitive
societies, 45

words, similarity of among Abrahamic
faiths, 29, 30, 34, 42

wrath, 135*t*

wrongdoings, acknowledgment/
admission of, 196

X

xenophobia, 143–44

Y

Yemen, Sabaean language, 29

Yemenite Jews, 107

yom (day), 34, 42

Yom Kippur (Day of Atonement), 85,
86, 97, 99, 126

youth, disenchanted and uninterested
in theology of own faith, 176

Z

Zabur (book of Psalms), 71

Zakat (form of charitable payment)
(Islam), 89

Zilpah (Jacob's wife), 106

Zionists, 168

Zoroastrianism, xix

Scripture Index

CPSIA information can be obtained at www.ICGtesting.com
Printed in the USA
BVOW03s1508090813

328268BV00002B/5/P